SALANG

Gold Scoop
Chasing the Dragon
Don't Worry About the Money Now
Behind Russian Lines: An Afghan Journal
Afghanistan: Agony of a Nation

SANDY GALL

SALANG

THE BODLEY HEAD
LONDON

A CIP catalogue record for this book
is available from the British Library

ISBN: 0 370 31309 7

© Sandy Gall 1989

Typeset by J&L Composition Ltd, Filey, North Yorkshire
Printed in Great Britain for
The Bodley Head Ltd,
31 Bedford Square, London WC1B 3SG
by Mackays of Chatham PLC, Chatham, Kent

First published in 1989

Dedication

To all those Afghans who fought so magnificently for their freedom in the bitter years of the Soviet invasion and occupation of Afghanistan, the brave and resourceful mujahideen with whom I and my colleagues travelled through the mountains and across the plains under a burning sun and without whose encouragement and camaraderie I would never have made it.

To those heroes like Ahmed Shah Masud, Abdul Haq, Deen Mohammed, Mohammad Es'haq, Masud Khalili, Jan Mohammed, Agha Gul, Gul Bas, Abdi the horseman and his magnificent stallion, and a hundred more.

To all the journalistic colleagues: Nigel Ryan, Charles Morgan, Tom Murphy, Paul Carleton, Jon Hunt, Noel Smart, and to Andy Skrzypkowiak, killed alas on assignment in Afghanistan in October 1987.

To all those who have given me the benefit of their knowledge: especially to Major Mike Coldrick, MBE, GM, late RAOC, explosives and intelligence authority; to Jill Black, my very expert and long-suffering editor; to my daughters, Carlotta and Fiona, and to Susie Howman who typed the manuscript; to my wife, Eleanor, my sternest critic; and finally to Afghanistan itself which has been the main inspiration. To all of them, I owe a great debt. The shortcomings in this book are, of course, all mine.

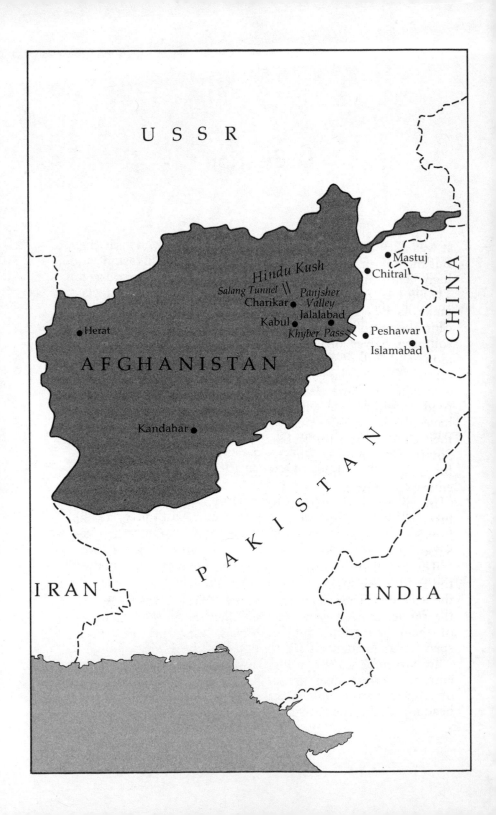

One

It was dark and in the early spring night the wind was cold. But then up in the approaches to the Salang Tunnel, you are high. The tunnel itself, the highest in the world, is over 11,000 feet above sea level. Before it existed, traffic used to make its way laboriously over the pass which crosses this central spur of the Hindu Kush, linking the northern and southern halves of Afghanistan. Then the Russians came along and, full of smiles and bonhomie, offered to build the tunnel. They explained that by drilling through the rock for a distance of more than a mile and a half, and building a road on either side within the tunnel, the Afghans would have the benefit of an all-weather highway, linking Kabul, their capital, with the Russian border. It was only after the Soviet invasion of Afghanistan on Christmas Eve, 1979, that the Afghans realised the Russians' generosity was not entirely altruistic.

In the years that followed the Russian supply columns brought in tens of thousands of troops, and millions of lorryloads of equipment and stores, many of them via the Salang Tunnel.

The bearded men who crouched among the rocks above the road knew how vital a supply line the highway was to the Russians. They knew the convoys toiled up and down to the tunnel almost every day and they had attacked many of them, sometimes inflicting heavy damage. The most spectacular incident of all, though, had been an accident.

In November, 1982, a big Russian convoy arrived at the entrance to the tunnel, going north. At the same time, a line of Afghan petrol tankers was passing through the tunnel, heading south. The Russian commander should have waited until the tankers were through but became impatient – and gave the order to move. The tunnel is not very wide, only twenty-four feet across, with two single lanes giving very little clearance between vehicles. A Russian tank, or tank transporter, probably driving too fast, collided with one of the petrol tankers, tearing a great gash in its side. As the petrol poured out, flooding the floor of the tunnel, it ignited, causing a devastating explosion in that confined space. Soon both vehicles were burning fiercely and choking oil fumes were seeping back down the tunnel. In their panic, and thinking they were under attack by the mujahideen, the Afghan anti-Communist guerrillas, the Russian military police sealed off the entrances. The rest of the convoy was now trapped. There were often stoppages in the tunnel for one reason or another and the rule was to keep your engine running: otherwise you could freeze to death in your cab. This was what happened, and the combination of diesel engine fumes and oily smoke from the blazing tanker proved lethal. Seven hundred people were said to have died of suffocation, half of them Russians.

Panna, the commander of the group of mujahideen among the rocks, raised his night glasses and stared for a long time at the scene below. The road glinted like a black snake in the faint star sheen. The Cyclopean eye of his binoculars moved slowly up the road to a dark mass on the left and hovered there. As his eyes searched the deep shadow, he could just make out the dull gleam of a mirror or a windscreen. He let his breath out slowly. This was a big convoy. Upwards of one hundred vehicles; maybe one hundred and fifty. All neatly drawn up in the lorry park for the night.

Where were the guards? He searched again with the binoculars. The drivers would be asleep in their cabs, but there would be sentries round the perimeter. Panna let the binoculars drop against his chest and turned to the junior commanders who had been waiting until he finished his inspection. He briefed them in a whisper and then dismissed them back to their men, waiting behind rocks on the hillside a hundred yards away. Half an hour later, at three o'clock, when the desire to sleep is almost insuperable, twelve mujahideen started to move slowly from behind their rocks

2

down the hill. Each man carried a small rucksack over his shoulder and an automatic weapon. Another dozen men waited among the rocks. Their job was to give covering fire if anything should go wrong.

The convoy was parked, nose to tail, on an area half the size of a football pitch, right beside the road, and separated from it by a low wall. The first two mujahideen slipped over the wall and disappeared into the darkness. Panna, supervising operations on the far side of the road, waited two or three minutes and then dispatched the second group. They had practised the attack many times, a litter of rocks in a distant valley playing the part of Russian vehicles.

Apart from the faint sound of a distant waterfall the night was absolutely still. Panna and his men had watched the convoy arrive at dusk and had noted that twelve especially large lorries were parked in the centre of the compound. They were carrying bulky cargoes which Panna knew to be bombs: about ten bombs apiece, each weighing 1,000 kilograms. His men had orders to plant their explosives on six of these vehicles, and to ignore the rest. He raised his hand and tapped the shoulders of two mujahideen standing next to him. They moved forward at a crouch, five paces apart. Panna concentrated his attention on the dark mass in front of him, searching for any movement or sound of a Russian sentry. The stillness was complete. He tapped the next two on the shoulder and the team moved soundlessly across the road and disappeared among the shadows.

A few minutes later, with five teams gone, Panna and the last man waiting with him heard the faint crunch of footsteps: slow, deliberate. A torch flashed intermittently, the way it does when a man walks with it swinging in his hand. Crouching against the rocks, they watched the small circle of light come closer. There were two of them, walking between the line of lorries and the road. Panna could hear them talking quietly. When they were almost opposite the sentries stopped and one pointed the torch at the back of a lorry. The white finger of light climbed up the tailboard, found a chink, peered inside briefly and then zigzagged back to earth. One of the sentries said something and the two resumed their pacing. After thirty seconds or so they came

3

to the end of the line and the torch disappeared abruptly from view, making the darkness seem even denser.

Panna waited another couple of minutes and then crossed the road with the last mujahid. Like the others he had tied pieces of cloth round the soles of his black Russian army boots so that his feet made practically no sound on the bare stony ground of the lorry park. They moved slowly, senses keyed up, towards the dark mass of the convoy. As they got close a driver cried out in his sleep, caught in the grip of a nightmare. A huge indistinct shape loomed in front of them: it was one of the bomb lorries. Panna waited for a minute or so, his eyes testing the darkness, his ears straining. But, apart from the beat of the blood in his temples, there was no human sound, only the ghostly cry of an owl, a fellow hunter on the prowl.

Each of the six two-man teams was responsible for one lorry. Panna made for the second last lorry on the left and, after handing his Kalashnikov to the mujahid who would act as a lookout, swung himself up and over the side. He moved forward cautiously and suddenly felt against his outstretched hand the smooth, cold metal skin of a bomb. He ran his fingers over it: it was enormous. Moving with infinite care, he reached farther into the darkness and touched the flank of another bomb. They were only about six inches apart, just what he had hoped for.

He squirmed between the two bombs and, working by feel, pulled a two kilogram half brick of Semtex out of his rucksack and jammed it carefully between the two bombs on the floor of the lorry. It fitted perfectly, making contact with both casings. Then he took a detonator, about the size of a rifle cartridge, out of the rucksack and pushed it into the side of the brick. Finally, his hand closed on a small plastic box, no bigger than a packet of cigarettes, and placed it on top of the Semtex. This was the radio-controlled receiver. From it he unwound a thin black wire, about three feet long, and draped it on top of the casing of the bomb nearest the road. The five other teams had orders to do exactly the same and when all of them had completed their mission and withdrawn across the road, Panna would set off the charges by a radio-operated, remote-control exploder.

4

He made a final check by feel that everything was in place and moved towards the side.

Before he could swing himself down, he saw a glimmer of light to his right. He froze, watching the pinpoint approach. Then he heard the scuffle of boots, and Russian voices. He crouched down in the back of the lorry, keeping absolutely still. The voices came steadily towards him and then seemed to stop beneath him. He saw the light of the torch flicker along the side of the huge lorry and held his breath. He had no gun, having given it to the lookout. If they discovered him he would have to make a run for it.

But after a few seconds the sentries moved on, their voices receding into the darkness. Panna let his breath out slowly and, very carefully, climbed down from the back of the lorry. The lookout emerged from the darkness and handed him his Kalashnikov, but before they could move off a Russian soldier started to snore raucously somewhere above them.

'Enjoy your sleep,' Panna whispered in Farsi. 'We will wake you up in a minute.'

They moved stealthily back across the road and, when all the mujahideen were counted, withdrew to a vantage point about five hundred yards up the hill. Here they settled down to wait, their *pattus* wrapped round them against the chill.

Very slowly, the sky began to lighten and one of Panna's men detected movement below. Cab doors banged. A diesel engine roared into life. Then another. The Russians were getting ready to depart.

Panna moved with great deliberation. The black plastic box lay on the rock in front of him. He pressed a switch and a red light glowed. The mujahideen waited tensely, motionless now. The sound of more engines starting up echoed between the rocks.

Panna reached out slowly and flicked the second switch. It made only a tiny click but every man there heard it, not daring to breathe, tensing themselves for the inevitable.

The blast, travelling at enormous speed, spread up the mountainside like some huge invisible wave. Then, somewhere in the centre of the parking space, there was an enormous burst of red flame. It took a full second for the shock of the explosion to reach them, hitting like a tidal wave. Flashes leapt along the lines of lorries like strobe lights in a discotheque as a string of secondary explosions followed.

For a moment the watching mujahideen were stunned and then they gave a whoop of victory, shouting 'Allahu akbar' – 'God is great' – in their excitement. Bits of debris hurtled past them like bullets and one heavy piece of metal struck a rock with a deep bell-like note.

As a load of anti-missile decoy flares exploded, the lorry park became a demented firework display in a sea of flame and smoke. Flashes lit the scene of carnage in a series of jagged cameos, etching the disembowelling of a vehicle for a split second, the terror of a fleeing soldier for another. The screams of wounded Russians floated up to them, making the watchers' eyes glitter in the lurid light of the burning convoy. Then the ammunition started to explode, crackling crisply like a bush fire and sending tracers high into the sky in slow red arcs.

After half an hour, the noise had died down but the fires still burned fiercely, the diesel fuel and synthetic rubber tyres releasing thick clouds of smoke. By dawn Panna had moved far enough along the mountain to be safe from the helicopters.

They came fifteen minutes later, four big Mi24 gunships, their double rotors making a blur against the pale blue sky. Two stayed high, circling the area with predatory precision, searching for any sign of movement on the mountains while the others landed to pick up the dead and wounded. Panna could imagine the pilots sending back angry reports to their base at Bagram, east of Kabul.

A few minutes later they heard the sinister drone of an Antonov 12 reconnaissance plane. Panna and his men had a healthy respect for its ability to monitor movement on the ground, and as soon as it came anywhere near them they dropped behind a rock and stayed there until it had passed. But the Antonov was there primarily to photograph the still smoking wreckage and when it had done that, it flew off back to base. The helicopters landed and took off all morning. There were a lot of dead and wounded to be brought out.

In Kabul, General Sergei Orlov, head of the KGB in Afghanistan, was summoned urgently to the headquarters of

6

the Commander-in-Chief, General Vassili Ustinov, who had just received the first Antonov pictures. He was tense with rage as he tossed them across the desk to Orlov.

'I want these people caught and exterminated,' he shouted. 'Where did they come from? How the hell were they able to get so close? What's the name of the commander? Come on, General, what have you got to say for yourself?'

They both knew there would be hell to pay when Moscow learned the news. General Ustinov was already under fire for what the Politburo increasingly criticised as his ineffective conduct of the war. They wanted results and they did not seem to be getting them. Not the right ones, anyway. And every time he had hinted at the need for more troops, they saw red. To escalate the number of troops from the current 120,000 to, say, 150,000 or even 200,000, a much more realistic figure in the generals' view, was seen in Moscow as a tacit admission of failure and would be so construed both at home and around the world. After all, they were fighting a mere handful of bandits, albeit aided and abetted by the West, so a 'limited contingent' of Soviet troops, as the army of occupation was always called, should be more than enough to ensure supremacy.

Now the government at home was talking of withdrawing altogether, but until a treaty was signed they wanted the appearance of stability, no suggestion that they were losing their grip.

'We don't have any hard proof yet but I suspect it's one of Durran's gangs.' Durran was the extremely successful guerrilla leader from the Panjsher Valley, and his mobile units operated far afield, including the Salang area.

'It has all the hallmarks of that bastard's work,' Orlov continued. 'He has a young commander called Panna who has been very active recently.'

'I know, I know.' Ustinov's voice was testy. 'I read the bloody sitreps, too. Well, what are you going to do about him?'

'I should get word in a day or two as to who's responsible. If it is Panna, I'll send in a snatch squad.'

Ustinov grunted. 'What about Durran? I want him, dead or alive, before the spring's out. He's getting above himself. And far too well known. These damned Western journalists are always on about him.' He fixed Orlov with a cold stare. 'It's time you mounted a successful operation for a change. Go in there and get the bastard.'

'I'm working on it,' Orlov said. 'A hit team. And I've found the right man to lead it.'

'Who? What's his name?'

'His name is Abdul. He's their man in Kabul, we turned him. I'm sending him in with a handpicked group. Being the man he is he'll be able to get right to Durran and put paid to him.'

Ustinov nodded. 'You're sure he's a hundred per cent ours?'

'Sure as I am of myself.'

Ustinov looked at his watch. 'One o'clock. Have a glass of vodka.' It was more an order than an invitation.

He got up and led the way into his private mess next door. An orderly in a white coat was standing by to pour the drinks. As soon as he saw Ustinov's bulky figure, he took the bottle of vodka and two glasses out of the fridge and poured two full measures.

'Here's to your next operation.' General Ustinov looked hard at Orlov. Then he downed the vodka in one. Orlov did the same. The orderly promptly recharged the glasses.

Ustinov looked out of the window. The mountains that ring Kabul in a huge, jagged circle looked menacing even at a distance. 'Bloody country,' Ustinov said matter-of-factly. 'Be glad to see the last of it. It'll be good to get back to some real soldiering.'

Orlov knew Ustinov was due to take command in East Germany in a year's time. He also knew that he wanted to go back to Moscow with at least one feather in his cap: Durran's scalp. On the wall above the long table hung the battle pennant of the tank in which Ustinov had ridden across Eastern Europe, all the way to Budapest. That had been in 1956 and Ustinov had been the youngest captain in the Red Army.

'If you can get me that bastard Durran, I'll see you get the most glowing commendation I've ever written.' He raised his glass.

March in London can be a foul month, cold, wet and raw with spring still an impossibly remote prospect and summer an indistinct and distant memory. Even in the SIS, the Secret Intelligence Service, which is the eyes and ears of the British government abroad, morale can be low in March, and the men who draw the short straw think longingly of more fortunate colleagues basking on some Caribbean beach or riding the Cresta in St Moritz. So it was for Roger Fulford, the desk man for South West Asia, when the report came in from Pakistan:

'Urgent Pathfinder London from Frontiersman Islamabad. Grade A reports reaching here say between 80 and 100 Soviet ROA vehicles destroyed in raid on parked convoy south of Salang Tunnel. Dead and wounded put at over 300 but unable to confirm. Sources say many Soviet wounded flown to Bagram and Kabul military hospitals. Coffins seen at Kabul airport ready for onward flight to USSR. Grateful any confirmation your end. Acknowledge FM.'

Fulford told his secretary to acknowledge and then he re-read the message. Grade A meant the source was considered highly reliable, someone inside the Communist government in Kabul. Fulford swivelled in his chair to face the computer. He logged in by giving his name and password and two further security codes and was then linked to the central intelligence computer housed in the Ministry of Defence. It had hundreds of different sections, all classified, the most secret being available only to the Prime Minister and the members of the Cabinet Intelligence Committee. Fulford went to 'Afghanistan', then to the 'Resistance' heading and from there to 'Mujahideen Attacks'. From there he selected 'Salang' and within seconds had the answer: nothing.

Fulford lifted his phone and asked the switchboard for the American Embassy. When he was through he gave an extension number which brought him the rich Bostonian tones of William Charleston Stewart, known to his friends inside and outside the CIA as Charlie Stewart.

'Hey there, Roger, what a nice surprise. I'm flattered to be talking to the best-informed man in town. What can I do for you, my good friend?'

The warmth in his voice made Fulford feel that he was the person Stewart most wanted to talk to in the whole of London.

Even though they were on a scrambled line, Fulford was too old a hand to betray his training.

'Something interesting has just arrived from eastern parts. I was wondering if by any chance you happened to be free for a spot of lunch today?'

'So happens I just had a cancellation. Be a pleasure. Where and when?'

'Could you bear my place? I've got some smoked salmon and a fresh brie.'

'Sounds great. About one? See you then.'

Fulford lived in Thames Mansions, one of those blocks of flats near the Houses of Parliament much prized by MPs and tycoons for their discreetness and security. Roger Fulford had acquired the flat through the timely death of an uncle and knew he was lucky to be there.

Stewart greeted the uniformed commissionaire with a genial grin.

'Mr Fulford? Fourth floor, sir.' The lift was small and rose in leisurely fashion. Fulford was waiting at the open door of his flat, a smile of welcome on his face. He had known Stewart a long time and genuinely liked him. He was straight and he was a gent and there weren't too many like that left. Charlie Stewart was something of a connoisseur of wine, and he sipped his Meursault Charmes appreciatively. Fulford gave him copy of the message from Islamabad.

'I wondered if your satellite boys could have a look and give us confirmation or otherwise, as the case may be.'

'I'll certainly try for you.' Stewart squeezed lemon and ground black pepper on to a slice of best Scottish smoked salmon and ate it with relish. 'I'll send this to Washington as soon as I get back to the office and ask for the pictures. How long ago do you think it happened?'

'It's hard to know, but I would guess anything between a week and a fortnight. You know how long it takes to get stuff out of there.' Fulford topped up Stewart's glass.

'You're spoiling me, Roger. This Mersault is damn good. If the news is a fortnight old, the Soviets may have swept up the evidence by now. But we'll have a good try. It may take a couple of days. I'll call you as soon as I hear anything.'

It was in fact three days later that Stewart called Fulford

and asked him to drop by his office, at the top of an elegant house in a cul-de-sac off Curzon Street.

'These just came in by fax.'

He tossed the photographs across his big mahogany desk. Fulford studied them for a few minutes. On one, he could see what looked like long marks, rather like those a Hoover makes on a thick pile carpet. On another, a series of dark dots were spaced at irregular intervals down the middle of the picture. At the bottom of each photograph, the analyst had interpreted the sometimes rather tenuous pictorial evidence. Under the Hoover marks he read: 'Wreckage of vehicles has been bulldozed off the parking lot.'

Below the dots, the text said: 'These are craters from 500 or 1,000 KG bombs, probably detonated while still aboard their transporters.'

In a brief conclusion, the analyst had summed up: 'The evidence points to at least eighty vehicles and possibly one hundred having been towed or bulldozed off the park. Some of the wreckage is scattered along the road. On the craters there is no doubt. The photographs reveal twenty definite big explosions.'

Fulford looked up. 'It looks as if for once the information was spot on. I'm very grateful, Charlie.'

The tall Bostonian uncoiled his long legs and rose to his feet. 'We're grateful you tipped us off. I got some Brownie points for having such good relations with my British colleagues. So just keep it coming.' He grinned and stuck out his hand.

'I might just have something for you, Charlie. I have an idea but it's still very much in the rough draft stage. I'll be in touch.'

Back in the office, Fulford sought a meeting with his department head. Bob Whitehouse was an ex-navy commander with a quiet manner but a very sharp eye. He was responsible to the head of SIS for the whole of South Asia and under his influence, the Afghan war had assumed far greater priority than before.

Fulford slid the photographs across his desk. 'These have just come in from Washington. They seem to confirm beyond doubt what our Grade A sources were reporting from Islamabad.' There was a moment or two of silence while Whitehouse examined the pictures and read the brief text.

'They usually err on the side of caution, these boys, so it's interesting to see them come up with the same conclusions.'

'I checked the records,' Fulford said. 'It is certainly the heaviest Soviet loss of men and material as a result of a single action.'

'Do we know who did it?'

'Durran's people. A young up and coming commander called Panna.'

Whitehouse looked out of his window across St James's Park, as if he were back on the bridge of a ship.

'If we know that, you can bet your life the Russians do too. And they'll be hopping mad.' He took a pipe out of his drawer and filled it. Everything about Whitehouse was calm and precise. There was the rasp of a match, and a whiff of rich Sobranie mixture floated past Fulford's nostrils. He was a non-smoker and disliked the smell of cigarettes, though a pipe or a good cigar he found agreeable.

Whitehouse took the pipe out of his mouth and blew a smoke ring across the desk.

'How do you assess the chances of Durran being snatched or bumped off?' It was a question that concerned them endlessly. They knew Russian policy was to try to eliminate all successful commanders by using hit squads. The Soviets had made great efforts to penetrate the Resistance with agents of KHAD, the Afghan secret police, modelled on the KGB.

'We think his security is as good as anyone's but there's always a chance the KGB will think up a new twist. No marks for guessing that they will try very hard to get their own back. They've already bombed the valley practically flat, so it has to be another effort to take out Durran.'

'Have we any ideas at all, from intercepts or agents, of what they might be up to, so that we can warn Durran?'

Fulford shook his head. 'Nothing at all. But I've asked GCHQ for anything with Durran's name on it.'

'Something else on your mind?' Whitehouse blew another smoke ring towards the window where the tiny breeze shredded it.

'Yes, there is. The success of this particular operation set

12

me thinking. About the tunnel. We sometimes take it too much for granted. Its strategic importance, I mean. We all know it carries a huge amount of the Russian supply traffic: ammunition, petrol, stores of all kinds, from the border to Kabul. And a lot of commercial stuff too. Without it they would be in a jam. Traffic would have to go a very long way round and it would virtually cut off Kabul, from the north at any rate. An air bridge would be very expensive. So, what I'm saying is this: why don't we help someone to take that tunnel out of commission?'

'What do you mean, take it out of commission?'

'Well, ambushes won't do it. The mujahideen can only mount one from time to time, because of the logistics, and there are Red Army convoys going through all the time. So it has to be a more drastic solution. It has to be blocked. Blown up.'

'Who do you propose should do that, and how?'

Fulford smiled his most disarming smile. He usually looked slightly owlish, his dark eyes enlarged by spectacles. But the smile transformed him, made one suddenly realise he was not just an intelligent civil servant but a man of charm and character as well. 'I was hoping you would supply the answers to the first question and that we could research the second.'

There was silence as Whitehouse scraped several matches and finally relit his pipe.

'First of all, we have to see if there is a feasible scheme to block the tunnel. Getting someone to carry it out might not be too difficult. But it would have to be cleared at the highest level, because of possible international repercussions, and I don't mean just in this office.' He took the pipe out of his mouth and squinted down it as if lining up a gun sight.

'I see all that. What I wanted was your reaction to the scheme as an idea.'

Whitehouse took his time. 'Well, as you probably know, the Prime Minister, no less, is personally interested, very interested, in keeping this issue in the foreground. In every way, both nationally and internationally. That means coverage in the media on the one hand, and active help for the Resistance on the other. The latter has to be discreet, of course. Now there is very little doubt in my mind that there would be top-level support for something like this, a, if it's feasible and b, if it can be sanitised. No trace-back. So the personnel would have to be chosen very carefully. That's my general reaction. Specifically, I think your idea is a good one. So go ahead. Consult Plans to see what they can come up with and talk to Personnel about a team. And then you have to sell it. Had any thoughts on that?'

Fulford looked Whitehouse in the eye.

'Well, now that the Russians are saying they might be prepared to withdraw from Afghanistan if an international agreement can be made that involves Pakistan and America, anything that can keep up the pressure and drive the Soviets to the conference table should be welcome. If we can block this hugely strategic tunnel it could prove an enormous boost for the Resistance, as well as a major defeat for the opposition, both in propaganda and morale terms. Not forgetting the amount of bread it would cost them to operate an air bridge until they can reopen the tunnel. Perhaps it's too much to suggest this would be a cross between the Tet Offensive and the Berlin Blockade, but it has elements of both.'

'Don't let your imagination run away with you,' White-house said tersely. 'But go and talk to Plans. As to the team, I think it should be as small as possible. I would favour three, plus local back-up. They would need to be ex-Special Forces, I would think.' He paused and put his pipe down. 'And expendable.'

Fulford spent a long time with Plans after lunch. The head of the department was an enthusiastic pedant called James Frobisher. One of his ancestors had been a naval hero and Frobisher himself had passed through Dartmouth and served in the Caribbean and the Far East before being invalided out with dysentery. This occasionally recurred to lay him low, but here at SIS there was always someone else to man the helm. At sea, on a frigate, it might have been disastrous.

Frobisher listened to Fulford's exposé and then pulled a series of maps and diagrams of the tunnel towards him.

'As you probably know, it's not easy to block a tunnel.

You have to imagine it as a solid great chunk of rock with a small hole bored through it. The hole, that's to say the tunnel, really weakens the whole structure remarkably little. Short of collapsing the whole ruddy mountain, it's very difficult to do a great deal of damage that they can't repair pretty quickly. That's the lesson we've learned over the years and any civil engineer will confirm that.'

Frobisher ran a hand through thinning brown hair and pinned his hornrims more firmly on his nose. 'So we have to work out an effective way to bring about the desired result, if indeed such a result is possible. Have you thought about the Shi'ite technique in Lebanon?'

'You mean the Beirut bombers? The American Embassy and so on?'

'Indeed. I don't imagine SIS is going to call for suicide bombers as volunteers, but the idea of putting a lorryload of explosive into the tunnel isn't a bad one. I'll have a study made to see what the tunnel's weak spots are, if any, and the general possibilities. I'll give you a buzz when we've looked into the thing properly. Say in couple of days or so?'

'I'll go and talk to Personnel,' Fulford said. 'They may take a little longer to come up with the answers.'

Two

In the middle of the day Kabul still gave a reasonable impression of being almost a normal city. The streets were alive with pedestrians and all kinds of wheeled traffic: rickety *gharrys*, ancient cars, broken-down but elaborately decorated lorries. The illusion was spoiled only when some convoy of military vehicles belonging to the Red Army or the Afghan Army thundered through. The shops were better stocked than in Moscow, and busy. And yet, as Orlov knew, come dusk the streets would quickly empty and the few remaining stragglers would be in a hurry to get home. For at night, despite the growing number of roadblocks and patrols, the mujahideen were increasingly active, even in the centre of the city. Rocket attacks, particularly on Soviet and government targets like the Microrayon housing estate, the Russian Embassy and the airport, were an almost daily occurrence: they caused a steady haemorrhage of casualties and made everyone jumpy.

Orlov's car swung down a quiet side street and pulled up outside a dingy-looking wooden-beamed house, one of the many KHAD safe houses that had proliferated in Kabul as more and more families had fled to the penury but comparative safety of the refugee camps in Pakistan.

Orlov's KGB bodyguards were out of the car, automatics at the ready, before it stopped and deposited the General on the broken pavement. He glanced rapidly up and down the street and then in three quick strides was through the doorway and out of sight.

In a courtyard in the middle of the house two of Orlov's aides, both in civilian clothes, and an Afghan sat waiting in the shade. They rose to their feet as the General entered, the

Afghan towering over the three Russians. He was strongly built and had a thick, curly black beard. Orlov waved them to their seats and spoke in Russian to the two KGB colonels.

'Everything arranged? Good. And our friend is ready to leave?' He nodded in the Afghan's direction.

'Yes, Comrade General.' The senior colonel was good-looking and articulate, the new breed of KGB officer. 'We've briefed Abdul thoroughly and the rest of the team are getting ready now. They start first thing tomorrow.'

Orlov turned his cold blue eyes on Abdul and spoke in passable English.

'You are clear about the plan?'

The Afghan cleared his throat and answered slowly, 'Yes. I have chosen two young men. Very good Communists. We take the bus to the end of the road and then we walk until we reach Durran.'

'Do you know where he is?'

'Not exactly, but I find it out very quickly.'

'Suppose he's not in the Panjsher?'

Abdul smiled and shook his head. 'He's in the valley. I know. Do not worry, General Orlov, I will find him quickly and then...'

Orlov studied him in silence for several seconds.

'And how do you intend to rid us of this ... bandit?' Orlov's question was partly pretence. He had approved the plan in outline but he wanted to hear the Afghan expound it.

Abdul reached into his pocket, brought out a fountain pen and unscrewed it. The slim tube was full of blue liquid. Abdul held it up. 'This is ordinary ink. It is also poison.' He nodded towards one of the KGB men.

'Colonel Gradov gave me this poison and instructions how to use it. He says it is very sure. When the time comes I will put some in Durran's food or drink.'

'And if something goes wrong? Suppose they arrest you or you lose the pen?'

The tall Afghan patted his chest under his left arm.

'What does that mean?' Orlov's eyes were expressionless.

Abdul opened his jacket to reveal a shoulder holster, reached in and brought out a small black Makarov pistol.

Orlov nodded. 'Good. But the poison is preferable. Silent

17

and anonymous. It will look as if he died of natural causes. They will suspect foul play, but the relatively long time it takes this particular poison to achieve its effect will confuse them. Suspicion will fall on many people. That is good. You will be able to make your plans accordingly.'

One of the KGB colonels said something in Russian to Orlov. He listened carefully and then burst out laughing.

'Give me your pistol, please.'

Abdul handed it over with a smile. He knew what was coming.

'Here, Colonel Vimov, show us what is so special about this pistol.'

Colonel Vimov's movements were deft. He stripped the pistol down to its basic component parts in about thirty seconds, laying barrel, butt, magazine and ammunition neatly on the table in front of him. He picked up the butt, tapping it with his forefinger. 'If you look very carefully, you can see that a section of the base plate has been cut out and rewelded.' He held it out for inspection. 'You can just see a faint line ... there.

'The workshops in Moscow made it up to our specification. Inside, it's packed with high explosive which will detonate when the pistol's fired. Enough to blow the firer's hand off and quite possibly kill him. A very nasty surprise for our friend.

'But it can be operated normally. If you look very carefully at the butt plate again, you will see there's a small safety catch here. Can you see? It's very stiff to operate for obvious reasons.' He struggled with a ballpoint pen for a few seconds before finally forcing the catch over. 'There. When it shows red, it means it's operational. When it shows black, it's just a normal pistol.

'Obviously you must always have it on black until you make a present of it to the bandit Durran.'

Orlov stood up. The meeting was over, but he had one last point to make. 'If you succeed, Abdul, a golden career awaits you in KHAD. But if you fail and survive ...' The blue eyes had no hint of human kindness. 'We will track you down wherever you are.' The words hung for a moment in the silence of the still hot afternoon. Then Orlov turned on his heel and strode out of the room.

Outside the engine of his bullet-proof Zil was running. The street was empty. The war, for the time being, was quiescent.

M16 (Personnel) has the name of every member of the Special Forces, past and present, on computerised file. Everyone who has been in the SAS, the SBS and the Commandos, from Lord Lovat who led No 1 (Special Service) Commando Brigade in the Second World War and David Stirling, who started the Long Range Desert Group which eventually became the Special Air Service (SAS), down.

Because he knew this and it appealed to his sense of humour, Fulford took the Head of Personnel, Giles Ponsonby, to lunch at the Special Operations Club, which, with its photographs of distinguished past members on the walls, has about it an almost theatrical air of cloak and dagger, World War Two vintage. Upstairs the bedrooms are named after heroes of the French, Belgian and Dutch Resistance and of the American OSS, like 'Wild Bill' Donovan. It also has the advantage of being fairly quiet at lunchtime.

They had a drink in the bar where the only other occupants were two old ladies in tweeds waiting for their brigadier (retd.) husbands. They had ordered gin and tonics and were talking about the funeral that morning of an old friend they had served with in India. He seemed to have been called Stuffy and had been keen on polo.

The dining room, which is not much bigger than the bomb bay of a Lancaster, was empty. They ordered fried plaice and a bottle of Sancerre and Fulford, who had already outlined his project to Ponsonby in the office the day before, asked, 'Any luck with your search yet?'

The bar steward brought the wine, opened it at the table and poured two glasses.

Ponsonby took a sip. His tone was casual. 'I think I've found the chap you're looking for.'

'Really! That's terrific news. And bloody quick.' Fulford found himself talking rather more loudly than he meant to. 'Who?'

'Chap called Mike Wills. Was a very good officer. Brilliant. First-rate career. Went into the SAS from a cavalry regiment.

Did extremely well in the Iranian Embassy siege. Then the Middle East and Africa. The usual sort of thing. Unfortunately, he got mixed up with his CO's wife at one point. There was a nasty scene and he ended up punching the colonel. I would say there were distinctly mitigating circumstances for Wills, but the court martial saw it in strictly black and white terms. So they found him guilty of serious misconduct and he was dismissed from the service at the age of thirty. Found himself on the scrapheap. That was two years ago.'

The coloured waitress brought the plaice and a dish of chips. The two old ladies, chattering animatedly, made their entry, followed by their husbands, two cheery old men with the light step and pink cheeks that old soldiers somehow manage to retain, nine times out of ten, however old they are. They were in full flow about India and took not the slightest notice of Fulford and Ponsonby.

'And since then?' Fulford drank some Sancerre and found it enormously better than the house white which he had recently had at Whitehouse's club and whose derivation was almost as closely guarded a secret as Ponsonby's files.

'Odd jobs. The current one running a down-market country club near Woking. Bit of tennis, bit of golf, squash, snooker and a dance on the last Saturday of every month, with a special party at Christmas. That sort of thing. I think he hates it. But it is a job.'

'Not drawn to the City or business? After all, you did say a cavalry regiment, didn't you?'

'Yes, the Blues actually. Younger brother, so there was no room for him on the family estate. Anyway, I gather he didn't get on very well with his rather pompous elder brother. I imagine he could have got something in the City but he didn't seem to want to. Perhaps he felt the ignominy of his discharge pre-empted that. Very good plaice by the way. And Sancerre. My favourite white wine. Very kind of you, Roger.'

'Pleasure, my dear chap. Don't see enough of you. You said this fellow hates the country club job. Do you think he'd be interested in our thing?'

'I've taken the liberty of making a preliminary sounding. I simply said it was a government department looking for a chap like him for a job taking six months to a year. Abroad, adventurous, reasonable pay, and was he interested? He hummed and hawed a bit at first, asked a few shrewd questions, but when I mentioned a couple of names, and said he'd been recommended, he immediately changed his tune. Said yes, he'd be very interested. So I said he was on the short list – to give it a bit more authenticity – and could he come to London for interview. He said any time. His tone of voice suggested tomorrow, if necessary. I imagine he's dying of boredom and not being paid very much either.'

'So?'

'Well, you'd better read the file and, if you agree, we can get him up fast.'

'Sounds perfect. How does he strike you, overall?'

'Well, I've not met him, of course, but from his file and that very brief conversation, I would say a rough and tumble expert, even by SAS standards. A hard man. But with strong principles. In fact, without them I would have thought by now he would have turned to a profitable life of crime.'

Fulford rolled the Sancerre round his tongue and thought for a moment. 'Does he meet Whitehouse's criterion of expendability?'

Ponsonby laughed. 'Don't we all? No, I'd say he does, *par excellence*. Not married, apparently no steady girlfriend. Only one estranged brother, parents dead, few friends now, it would seem. A real loner since his disgrace.'

Fulford speared the last chip on his plate and munched it ruminatively. 'Any suggestion that he's been approached by the other side? After all, disaffected ex-SAS man. First-class record in the field. Make a good hit man, wouldn't he?'

Ponsonby sucked his teeth. 'We thought of that. Of course we don't know if he's been approached or not, although he certainly hasn't reported it to anyone. Also, as a man of principle, I doubt very much if he's fertile ground, even twenty per cent.'

They adjourned to the bar for a glass of Kummel on the rocks.

'You keep talking about Wills being a man of principle. Exactly what do you mean?'

'Well, he could have saved his skin at the court martial by ratting on the girl.'

'What exactly does ratting on the girl mean?'

'She apparently started the affair. She was known for sleeping around. She led him on and then when the husband, Wills's boss, found out, she shopped him. Said Wills had seduced her whereas really she had made all the running. In court she told a long sob story about how she was infatuated by him and he had treated her like dirt. Whereas in fact it was exactly the opposite way round. Of course he was too proud and too much of a gent to argue his case. The court, gallant officers one and all, took her side and wrote Wills off as a total shit. They decided the sooner he was run out of the service the better.'

'Pretty nauseating stuff. How do you know all this?'

'One of our people who knew Wills well was a member of the court martial. He was the only dissenting voice.'

Fulford paid the bill and they walked out into the spring sunshine to hail a taxi.

'You can't help feeling a bit sorry for the poor sod,' Fulford said. 'And now to be in Whitehouse's expendable tray. Life can be pretty unkind, can't it, hmm?'

The four big Mi24 helicopters took off in the evening from their base at Bagram and headed north-east. Bagram lies in a great desert bowl surrounded by the massif of the Hindu Kush to the east and the mountains of Kabul to the west. With the sun setting behind them, every jagged ridge and pinnacle was as sharply etched as a Durer: beautiful, majestic, but savage and forbidding. The Mi24s looked deceptively slow and ungainly but they flew fast, keeping low and hugging the contours of the land to minimise the risk of being shot down by Stinger missiles. As they swooped over the first ridge, the pilots looked down on a scene of unparalleled splendour, a vast panorama of mountain ranges climbing to the horizon with the long green furrow of the Panjsher Valley bisecting the mountainous mass to their right. A few minutes later they crossed the main road from Kabul to the north, marked by the lights of an occasional lorry. It runs through the dusty ruins of deserted villages which were long ago destroyed by the repeated offensives of Soviet tanks and motorised infantry.

Just as the light was beginning to fade, they came to the southern approaches to the Salang Tunnel. Two of the Mi24s started to lose height, eventually landing in a great cloud of dust, while the other two rode shotgun above them, ready to strike if any mujahideen tried to oppose the touchdown. As the dust whirled a hundred feet in the air from the rotor blades, a stream of heavily armed Spetsnaz jumped from the open doors and ran across the rough ground to take up covering positions on the perimeter. It only took about a minute for the whole group, about thirty strong, to drop clear and for the Mi24s to lift off again. Russian pilots in Afghanistan did not like to linger on the ground once they left the safety of their bases: apart from the deadly Stinger, the mujahideen had enough Chinese 107- and 122-millimetre rockets, with a range of five to ten miles, to make a stationary helicopter an inviting target.

It was almost dark by the time the young Soviet captain in charge of the Spetsnaz began to move off to the rendezvous in an empty village four miles from the road, in the foothills that climb eventually to the Salang Pass. The Russian unit travelled well strung out, twenty paces between each man, with two scouts a hundred yards in front of the main body, in case of ambush.

Although the Afghan landscape, which is extremely mountainous and barren in the east and centre, looks empty, it is almost impossible to move through it without being observed by someone: a herdsman or peasant farmer scratching a living in a fertile pocket of an otherwise stony valley, or another traveller. So now, although the Russians had deliberately landed at last light, the arrival of the helicopters and thus of the troops had been observed by a small boy herding a flock of sheep and goats further up the hillside. After watching, with eyes as sharp as a bird of prey's, the direction the '*Shurawi*' had taken, he ran a mile uphill to his father's stone and turf bothy to announce his discovery, the words tumbling out as he fought for breath.

'*Shurawi, Shurawi!*' he shouted as he came within earshot. 'The Russians landed from two helicopters ... they're going towards Abdullah Khel ... very fast ... almost running!'

His father appeared in the doorway of the bothy, where the family lived during the spring and summer, grazing their animals on the sweet upland pasture.

'How many *Shurawi*?' he shouted, strapping on an ammunition belt.

The boy had counted. 'Twenty-eight.'

The father lifted an old British Lee Enfield 303 from inside the door and spoke to his young wife who now appeared nervously.

'I must warn Panna that the *Shurawi* are coming in his direction. If I run fast I will reach him before they do.' He swung the rifle over his shoulder and started up the mountain at a very fast walk, a pace which an Afghan hillman can keep up for hours on end across the most murderous terrain. The family, including two little girls who had appeared behind their mother's skirts, watched him go until he was lost on the mountain in the fading light.

The Russian scouts reached the village in under an hour, moving silently between the darkened houses, listening for any sign of occupation. But the place was empty. Not even a dog barked. One scout went back to give the captain the all-clear. Then the main body moved in, searching through the ruined houses, looking for something to loot and muttering angrily when they discovered that their compatriots had been there before them and had picked the place as clean as the bones of the dead horses that lay beside the arms trails.

The captain, a blond young six-footer from Volgograd, made his HQ in a big, half-bombed house at the far end of the village. It had a well in the dried-out and trampled garden. This was the rendezvous as specified in his orders, and they were to wait here for the Afghan contact.

It was shortly before midnight when the captain, half dozing on a dirty carpet in the corner of the only un-damaged room in the house, heard the sentries challenging someone. A few minutes later two Afghans were led in at bayonet point. One spoke English.

'Please tell your soldiers we are friends.' The smaller of the two Afghans said it with a smile but he looked nervous.

The captain said a few sharp words in Russian and the sentries withdrew. There were half a dozen other Russians in the room, one a very fresh-faced young lieutenant and four or five hard-looking NCOs who had made themselves immediately comfortable with the practised skill of the professional soldier. They had just eaten a meal of tinned Bulgarian meat and vegetables and had lit a fire to make tea. The smoke made the newcomers' eyes smart.

The captain waved his hand to indicate a corner of the dirty carpet, which was too old and tattered to have tempted even Russian soldiers' insatiable appetite for looting. The two Afghans sat down. The one in charge had a pock-marked face and restless, suspicious eyes.

'Captain, I am Ahmed. This is Mohammed. We are both from KHAD.' Mohammed was clearly the bodyguard.

The captain nodded. He had been told that two agents of KHAD would rendezvous with him.

'This *dushman*, Panna. Do you know where he is?'

Ahmed, who sat cross-legged facing the captain, nodded. His eyes flickered sideways to cover the rest of the room and then came back to the captain. 'Yes. We know he is tonight at his main village, where he usually stays. He has been there since he carried out the big attack on the Salang.'

One of the sergeants came over with cups of tea for the captain and lieutenant but did not offer any to the Afghans. Ahmed's eyes strayed to the steaming cups and stayed on them, but he said nothing. He had worked too long with the Russians to expect equal treatment.

'Do you know where he stays in the village?' The captain sipped his tea noisily.

Ahmed hitched himself to the edge of the carpet and started to draw a rough circle representing the village on the mud floor. 'Here is where Panna is staying when he is in Abdullah Khel.' He made a cross near the top left of the circle. 'This is the road. There will be no one on it at night. We will come by this way and then when we get to the village, I will lead you to the house.' He marked two smaller crosses between the edge of the circle and Panna's house. 'These two houses are empty. We will walk past them and then you will have Panna in your grasp.' Ahmed snapped shut his outstretched hand to make a fist.

The Russian captain studied the drawing on the floor for a moment in silence and then leant back against the wall.

25

'Provided you take us to the right house, we will do the rest. The bandit is as good as dead. How long will it take us to reach the village from here?'

'An hour. Maybe less.'

The captain consulted his watch. 'We will leave here in one hour. Get some rest, everybody.'

At a quarter to two, an NCO shook the captain and lieutenant awake and went outside to take a roll-call. The lieutenant, the two Afghans and the scouts moved off first, followed by the captain and a couple of the NCOs, and then the rest of the party numbering about thirty in all. It was so dark that even walking on the path was difficult and several of the young Russian soldiers tripped and fell, cursing, among the stones. But as they neared Abdullah Khel, the track grew smoother and the going was easier.

Ahmed made a wide detour through the fields which brought them to a clump of willows on the edge of the village, roughly level with Panna's house. A noisy stream flowed through the middle of the group of willows, its rush masking the sound of their movements. Ahmed led the way to the stream and pointed into the gloom. 'Panna's house is just over there. Can you see?'

The captain strained his eyes, trying to make out one shape significantly darker than the others.

'How far?'

'About a hundred metres.'

The captain gave whispered instructions, first to two of the NCOs. 'You will come with me, plus two machine-gunners and the two marksmen. Are they here? The rest of the party will wait outside under your command, Lieutenant. Be ready to move fast if we need you. Look out for the dogs. And, Ahmed. . .' he switched to English, 'you and your friend will be in front. And no tricks, eh, otherwise I'll blow your heads off.' He clicked the safety catch of his Kalashnikov sub-machinegun to make sure there was no misunderstanding.

They waded through the fast-flowing but shallow stream and squelched their way up the slope towards the village. The first of the empty houses loomed in front of them, and a dog started to bark some distance away. The Russian captain swore under his breath, but there was nothing for it but to go on.

26

'Go quickly!' he ordered Ahmed in a hoarse whisper. They passed the second house: Ahmed put his hand on the captain's arm and pointed.

'You can see Panna's house now, there.' Through the darkness, aided only by the radiance of the stars, the Russian could just make out the high walls and rough castellations of a *qala*, a fortified house. They crept closer. Another dog started to bark, closer this time. The Russians fingered their weapons nervously. Some of these village dogs were savage, particularly the mastiffs, and liable to attack strangers.

The captain, his men close behind him, moved slowly towards the entrance to the *qala*. The big wooden door was closed. But the first-floor windows, as in most Afghan village houses, had no glass and were unshuttered. The captain sent one of the NCOs to the other window. Then together they unhooked grenades from their belts, drew the pins and lobbed them through the dark rectangles, hearing the thuds as they landed inside. The captain lifted his Kalashnikov and, firing from the hip, sprayed the front door. The sound of the burst was overtaken by the roar of exploding grenades, the flashes lighting up the interior with a bright orange glare. The Russians fired another couple of bursts into the door and then the two young soldiers put their shoulders to it. It was strongly made and it took them several minutes to break it down. The captain led the way up the steep earth steps to the first floor, firing a burst into the darkness at the top. Here, several rooms branched off the passageway. Torches flashing, the Russians burst into each one, spraying bullets into the darkness. The noise was deafening.

Finally the captain shouted: 'Stop firing!' The sudden silence was unnerving.

'Nothing here,' someone called.

'Empty,' another voice said.

Torches flickered through the rooms. They were all empty. Panna was gone. When the squad had reassembled by the front door, the captain seized Ahmed by the collar of his dirty shirt.

'You said the *dushman* was here! Someone must have told him we were coming!' He let go of Ahmed's shirt and

27

the terrified KHAD man staggered backwards. 'You deserve to be. . .' The captain stopped in mid-sentence.

From the edge of the village came the sound of automatic weapons fire: as they listened it grew louder and seemed to spread across the whole village.

'God above.' The young marksman's voice was shrill. 'We are surrounded!'

Now they could hear the party on the road shooting back. Some of the bullets went hissing over their heads.

'Damn fools,' the captain swore. 'Let's get out of here. You go first and show us the way.'

He prodded the two Afghans with his Kalashnikov. They started to make their way hesitantly towards the edge of the village. As they moved clear of the last house, making for the stream and the trees, one of the Russians in the main party let off a star shell. It fizzed up into the night above their heads, opened like a poisonous flower and lit the scene below with a pale green glow. The two Afghans and seven Russians were starkly revealed in the middle of the open space that separated the edge of the village from the trees.

A mujahideen machinegun began to cough tracers at the little group. Suddenly, in a ragged bunch, they were running for their lives and had almost reached the trees when the gunner found his range. Three dropped straight away, falling like sacks off the back of a lorry, then another. The last five disappeared into the trees.

The flare died and the darkness grew doubly intense, and then another flare rose with a whoosh. As it burst at its apogee and started to float down, the firing became more intense, puncturing the darkness, the mujahideen keeping their bursts short to avoid giving their positions away. The Russians began to panic, with their captain and three men dead and the lieutenant and several NCOs badly wounded.

The senior remaining sergeant was radioing for an emergency pickup. It took him five minutes to get a response. There were four dead, including the captain, he told base, and possibly a dozen wounded. That meant ambulance helicopters in addition to the troop carriers. The duty officer promised to get them to the rendezvous point as soon as he could. They both knew that if they waited until daylight, the mujahideen would shoot down the rest of the party like so many rabbits in a field.

Three

It was a very big room and Michael Wills had to walk twenty paces from the door to the table, which gave the men round it a chance to have a good look at him. What they saw impressed them. Wills was six feet tall, weighed about thirteen stones and moved with the poise and ease of an athlete. He looked and no doubt was extremely fit. His shoulders were slightly too broad for the old but well-cut dark grey pin-stripe, a relic of better days in the army. He was handsome in a truculent way, with his thick dark hair worn longer than the army likes, strong nose and regular features. But his eyes were the most striking, large, slate-grey and very direct, and they stared back hard at the three men at the other end of the table: Woodhouse, his pipe, tobacco pouch and matches lined up ship-shape beside his blotter; Fulford, spectacles glinting with a hint of menace in the pale sunlight that filtered through the window from the Horse Guards; and Ponsonby, donnish, withdrawn. Wills took the chair Woodhouse indicated and sat down, his eyes watchful.

Woodhouse lit his pipe and temporarily disappeared behind the wreath of blue smoke.

'We've all read your file, Wills, so I'll ignore that for the moment unless there's something you want to say?'

Wills shook his head, tight-lipped. 'Absolutely nothing.'

'Right. In that case and before I tell you exactly what we have in mind, let me ask you a couple of questions.' He fiddled with the matches. 'First, do I gather that you're not exactly deliriously happy in your work?'

'I hate the stinking job. In fact, whatever you decide today, I'm going to pack it in.' There was a controlled

29

violence in his voice which was not lost on the three SIS men.

'Have you anything else in mind?' Fulford asked.

'Nothing definite.'

Woodhouse blew a smoke ring down the table. 'My second question is this. Given the, er, past, would you be prepared to do something which is completely unofficial, but at the same time has a government connotation?'

'Depends what it is.'

'Quite.' Woodhouse tapped the stem of his pipe on the table. 'But in principle would you have any objection to being, however remotely, connected with a branch of government?'

'No. I've already told your colleague that.' He looked at Ponsonby.

Woodhouse kept his voice bland. 'Good. I'm glad we can establish that at the outset because what I have to tell you is secret. Top secret.' He paused for a moment to let the words sink in. 'By the way, I presume you signed the Official Secrets Act when you were in the Special Forces?'

'Yes, I did, when I started doing special ops.'

'When you, er, left the Service, did they refer to that?'

'Yes, they did. Reminded me that I was still bound by it.'

Woodhouse looked round at his two colleagues. 'Well then, that saves us a lot of trouble.' He pointed his pipe-stem at Fulford. 'Roger, would you like to begin?'

Fulford gave Wills a headmasterly stare over the top of his spectacles and then launched into his lecture without a glance at his notes.

'As Commander Woodhouse has just said, this is officially an unofficial project. That's to say, it's been approved at the very top, but is something the government doesn't want to hear anything more about. In other words, if anything goes wrong, you're on your own. Now,' he gave another look over the top of his hornrims, 'if you don't like what I'm telling you, just stop me, would you, and then we'll save your time and my breath.'

'Go on,' Wills said. 'I'm listening.'

'Right, you know about Afghanistan. Ever been there?'

'No.'

'OK. You know about the conflict. It's been going a long

time now and indeed we believe is reaching a crucial stage. The Russians have said they're prepared to go, under certain conditions, and we – I mean the West – are trying to encourage them to fix a date with every means at our disposal.' He waved a small square hand. 'Diplomatic pressure, withholding high technology, and supporting the Resistance as best we can. That means arms and equipment. The Americans, the Saudis and the Gulf States supply the money, China ships in the hardware and we try to give back-up and advice in special areas.'

'Is that where I come in?'

'Precisely. This project is a perfect example of the sort of help we try to offer. Let me explain. Recently, the mujahideen in the Salang area, that's the big tunnel through the Hindu Kush that links Kabul to the Russian border, carried out a spectacular operation against a big Russian convoy. Mined it at night when it was parked and then blew it up. The Russians were carrying a lot of 1,000-kilogram bombs. It must have been quite a sight.

'Their success led us to think more constructively, or destructively if you like, about the Salang Tunnel supply line to Soviet forces not only in the capital, Kabul, but in the whole area south of the Hindu Kush. Here, take a look.'

He walked over to the wall and pulled down a large detailed map of Afghanistan. He held up a pointer. 'Here's Kabul.' Fulford indicated the centre right of the map. The pointer moved upwards. 'And here, just to the north of it, is the Salang. And here's the Soviet border. Now, come down here again to the Salang, move east and south a bit,' the pointer moved a couple of inches to the right, 'and you have the Panjsher Valley. As you can see,' the pointer moved left and right, 'the end of the valley is only eighty or ninety kilometres east of Kabul. And what's the significance of that? The significance of that, let me tell you with all the emphasis at my command, is that this whole, very strategic area is dominated by one man, called Durran. It was his people who blew up that convoy I was telling you about. In our judgement he is the most important guerrilla leader in the whole country. The Russians think so too. They've mounted a dozen or more operations against him, full-scale search and destroy missions, and have never succeeded in either

31

defeating him or even destroying a substantial part of his force. His intelligence is first-class and his people the best-trained. We want to help him and we want to help specifically by blowing up the Salang Tunnel.'

There was silence in the room for a moment, and then Wills leaned forward.

'Blow it up. How?'

'We're not sure yet. Plans are working on it and hope to have an answer soon. So far, they've discovered more don'ts than do's. For example,' Fulford also leaned forward, the light catching his glasses, 'trying to plant explosives in the tunnel itself is not on: too many Russian patrols. We did think about infiltrating the Afghan labour force that does all the running repairs to the tunnel, but they're very carefully screened. They're brought in from Kabul by bus, housed under Russian guard while they're there and then bussed back again when they've finished.

'At the moment, we're working along different lines, because we've had a bit of luck. We've discovered a young Russian defector who has served in the Salang and knows the whole set-up. We've thought of dressing you up as a Russian officer and sending you in with him. How's your Russian, by the way?'

'Non-existent.'

Fulford grinned. 'Don't worry. His English is rather good, by all accounts.'

'Where is he? In London?'

'No, he's in a sort of no-man's land on the Afghan-Pakistani border. What they call the Tribal Areas. Our people have debriefed him and have given him a very good write-up. He's a paratrooper, was in the Spetsnaz, Special Forces, guarding the Salang, and saw a lot of action, quite a blue-eyed boy, in fact. But then his brother, a poet, ran foul of the system back home. Refused call-up for Afghanistan and was sent to a psychiatric hospital. They shot him so full of dope that he died. They were very close and this upset Anatoly very much. So one night he walked out of his quarters near the Salang and kept walking until he met some mujahideen. Luckily they didn't shoot him. Once he got to one of the senior commanders they realised he was rather special. Eventually, we got to hear of him.'

'So it would just be the two of us?'

Woodhouse chipped in. 'We haven't come to any decision. What do you think?'

'Well, in an operation of this kind, there's a lot to be said for the standard SAS system of the four-man team. Then you've got a bit of support if one of you gets into trouble. Or if you have to carry out a complicated piece of sabotage. I think it all ultimately depends on what we've got to do when we get there.'

Woodhouse looked across to Fulford. 'Roger?'

'I'm sorry to sound so unhelpful, but we just haven't got a final plan yet. But in essence, you've got to get a large amount of high explosive into the tunnel undetected and blow it up without getting blown up yourself. We've debriefed Gradinsky – his name is Anatoly Gradinsky – and the synopsis is here.' He patted a folder beside his pad. 'I can let you have a copy. He's in favour of a lorry bomb. Beirut-style. In fact two. He says if we can get two lorries loaded with HE into the middle of the tunnel and blow them up, together, we might collapse the whole thing. If we can block the tunnel for a long period, we will disrupt the whole Soviet logistic system and bring it home to the Russians that the sooner they get out the better.'

'Sounds a pretty tall order,' Wills objected. 'Are the Russians just going to stand idly by and allow these two lorries to drive right in to the middle of the tunnel? And are we supposed to blow ourselves up as well, Beirut-style?' His tone was sarcastic.

Woodhouse's was placatory. 'No, no, of course not. That's exactly what we're beavering away on right now. How we can successfully carry out the mission and get you both out safely.' He looked hard at Wills. 'You have my assurance on that. We want you both out alive. What do you say? Will you do it?'

Wills took his time, frowning with the effort of trying to assess the chances of success.

'Well, obviously it's got to be an extremely hairy operation. A lot depends on the Russian. If he's all you say he is, if he's committed to us and a first-class operator, we might pull it off. But even then, the chances of coming out alive aren't very good in my opinion.' He looked round the three

33

faces watching him impassively. 'But why should you care about that? Despite what you say.' There was no response. They were watching him. Wills leaned back in his chair. 'OK, why not? What else have I got going for me? Nothing. But on condition, gentlemen, that I am involved in the planning from now on and that you bring the Russian back so we can see if he's any bloody good. If he isn't, then the deal is off.'

Woodhouse let out a little hiss of breath. 'Right you are, Wills. I think we can accept your conditions. As a matter of fact, we've already taken steps to bring Gradinsky over. He should arrive in a couple of days. We thought – provided you accepted our offer of course – that you and he should get acquainted at a place we have in the country, not too far from London.'

'A weekend would be OK.'

'Understood. Shall we say next weekend? Roger'll be on hand for advice. There'll be somebody from Planning and a couple of analysts. In fact James, our man in Peshawar, will be travelling with Gradinsky and he'll have the latest information on the mujahideen situation. So by the end of next weekend you should have a pretty fair idea of the possibilities, even maybe a tentative plan. And you should know by then whether you and the Russian can make a go of it.' He put down his pipe and shot an encouraging look at Wills.

'I very sincerely hope you can, because I think this is the best chance that's likely to present itself. I really do. The combination of your skills and his inside knowledge seems to me an irresistible one. I feel in my bones it's going to work.'

Woodhouse stood up. The interview was over. It was six-thirty and dusk was creeping across Horse Guards. 'Care for a drink before you go?'

After pouring Scotch all round, Woodhouse held out his glass. 'Here's to the success of your venture. We'll all be rooting for you. And ...' he swirled the brown fluid round his glass... 'I can hardly tell you how terribly important, vitally important it is that this show goes well. And is seen to be a success.' He locked eyes with Wills. 'One last word. If you pull this off, we will show our gratitude in a fitting manner. You won't regret it. Cheers.'

Wills brought them back to earth. 'I said I'd go only if the conditions are right, remember? I stick to that. Cheers.'

Woodhouse took a generous pull of his whisky. 'Now that we've got this far, I'd like to hear your side of the story from your own lips. I mean your leaving the service.'

Wills froze for a moment, his face shuttered. Then he shrugged. 'Why not? You might as well hear it the way it was, not the way it is in the file.' He took a deep breath. 'I suppose you could say I was a fool. She was bloody attractive and I didn't realise that I was simply the last in a long line. Nymphomaniac is a nasty word but it's hard not to use it. She shopped me to her husband. He and I had always got on well. I apologised immediately and said I would resign.' Wills looked round the faces of his inquisitors but, trained to hide their feelings, they returned his glance without expression.

'He said, "Don't resign. We'll get you a transfer. You're too good a man to lose." But then she must have got at him. Told him all sorts of lies about me. Judging by what he said later.'

'But was there any need to assault your commanding officer?' Woodhouse's face was hard.

'I didn't, sir. We had a row and he hit me. Once was OK. It was when he tried to karate chop me that I had to defend myself. I didn't mean to hurt him. But you know how these things are. I hit him very hard. I was fitter and ...' Wills drained his glass and put it down. 'You know how these things happen.'

Fulford promptly filled his glass.

'Then she came in. I think that's what did it. If it had just been the two of us we'd have shaken hands and had a drink. But she came in and sort of screamed. He had quite a lot of blood on his face and shirt. She kept on screaming until someone came. The duty warrant officer. That made it official. He couldn't settle for anything after that but a court martial. The rest you know.'

Woodhouse took a sip of whisky. 'You obviously feel pretty bitter about the whole thing.'

Wills's eyes were hard. 'I know I behaved foolishly but I think the punishment was heavier than the crime. A lot heavier. Not only my service career ruined, but my prospects outside as well.'

'In what way?'

'Well, the old-boy network. They passed the word everywhere. The City, business, all the sorts of places that are normally open to former Special Forces people. Security, that sort of thing. I found myself up against a blank wall. After dozens of letters and interviews I gave up. Obviously everybody had been told, don't touch this bloke with a barge pole. What impresses me now is how efficient the system is. Until then I had no idea you could blackball someone as thoroughly as that.'

'They knew your background and your contacts. That made it easier.' Fulford squinted sympathetically through his heavy spectacles.

'They knew bloody well everything. I thought I was all set for one job, acting as bodyguard and security adviser to an African potentate. It had all gone extremely well and I was due to sign the contract the next day. Then I got a telephone call saying the whole thing was off. Another candidate had been chosen, because he was better qualified. I got angry. I said I'd like to know who was better qualified than myself for that particular assignment. They became very evasive at that point. No names, no pack drill. Finally they offered me a hundred quid to cover expenses and loss of face. I told them to stick it up their jumpers.' Wills took a big mouthful of whisky. 'To me there was no question at all they had been got at. Their whole attitude changed totally overnight. That's when I gave up.'

Outside they could just hear the dying roar of London's traffic. It was nearly seven.

'Give us all one for the road, would you, Roger?' Woodhouse struggled to light his pipe. 'Well, you don't have to worry about the problem any more.'

Wills grinned. 'I'm sure you have better-qualified candidates. I can't imagine I'm the only one. Unless you're looking for someone really expendable?'

There was a moment of silence in the big room. Then Woodhouse spluttered into his pipe, 'No, no, not at all.'

Wills grinned at Ponsonby. 'Just before you telephoned I had decided to go west. To the States. There was an advert in *Soldier of Fortune* asking for people to fight in Nicaragua. Good money, too.'

'Did you actually apply?' Woodhouse put down his pipe.

'I filled out the coupon and was about to post it when you rang. It's still at home.'

'Tear it up when you get back.' Woodhouse's voice sounded terse for the first time.

A week later, Wills caught the train from Charing Cross to Ashford in Kent, an attractive journey once you are past Sevenoaks, with the oaks beginning to flaunt their spring glory across the slopes of the Downs. Kent was well named the Garden of England, Wills thought as he gazed out of the window at the oast houses and hop fields flashing past, the small fields and neat hedges, a magical, enclosed world. Ashford is only fifteen miles from the sea, but it could as well be a hundred.

A man in a chauffeur's cap sauntered up to Wills as he paused by the exit from the station.

'Mr Wills? The car's here, sir. Let me take your bag.' He lifted Wills's modest suitcase and strode towards an inconspicuous black Ford Granada. There were only half a dozen other travellers at the station and none of them showed any interest in Wills.

'Pleasant journey, sir?' Wills grunted noncommitally. 'The drive'll take about twenty minutes, sir.' Wills said nothing and the rest of the journey was completed in silence.

Hidbrook Manor stood on the top of a hill ten miles from Ashford, part Georgian and part much older, Jacobean or even Tudor. As they drove through the entrance, Wills noted the electronically operated gate, the watchful face at the window of the lodge and the high wall that disappeared into the trees. A broad lawn swept up to the big white house and the drive zigzagged up the hill, ending in a flight of shallow steps that led to the front door. An extremely thick, knotted wisteria covered half the house and an early-flowering clematis made a splash of blue on the other corner. In between, climbing *Danse du Feu* would later be a mass of orangey-red blooms. It was late afternoon and there was a distinct chill in the air, which made the fire crackling in the marble fireplace in the big drawing room doubly welcoming. The driver disappeared upstairs with his suitcase, leaving Wills a chance to admire the sweeping view from the west windows.

'Hallo, had a good journey?' A tall grey-haired man advanced into the room, hand outstretched. 'Brigadier Bowman, Jack Bowman. Welcome to Hidbrook. I run this place, for my sins, or try to. Would you like a little tour outside, while there's still light, and then I'll show you your room?'

Bowman led the way through the French windows along a terrace of York stone to the back of the house, where in brisk succession he showed off a squash court, an all-weather tennis court and a handsome, old-fashioned swimming pool.

'Still a bit chilly in the mornings, but certainly gives you an appetite for breakfast.' Bowman laughed. 'I usually come down at about seven.' It sounded as if Wills would be expected to do the same.

They were joined in the drawing room for a drink before dinner by a tall man with jet black hair and very white teeth called Guy Jackson. He was the main analyst on Afghanistan and had been brought down from London to brief Wills. After dinner, which reminded Wills almost nostalgically of many hundreds of similar meals eaten in British Army messes in various parts of the world, the brigadier left them to their port, pleading that he had to catch up on his paperwork.

Jackson passed the decanter and offered Wills a cheap cigar. He accepted the first but declined the latter.

'How much do you know about the war?' Jackson began.

'I've read everything I could get my hands on in the last week, but the answer is not much. There's precious little in the papers, for example.'

'That I'm afraid is very true. No, you won't get much information from the media. That's the way the Russians want it, of course, and when you take into account the difficulties of operating in Afghanistan − the language, terrain, lack of organisation on the part of the guerrillas and so on − it's not surprising.

'I'll give you a reading list tomorrow. I've got one or two things with me, and I'll get you the rest in London. But in the meantime, would it help if I gave you a quick break-down of the situation as we see it?'

Wills replenished his glass and pushed the decanter back to Jackson. 'It's a bit difficult passing the port to the left when there are only two of you. But fire ahead.'

Jackson topped up his glass and took a sip. 'I'll try not to use too many long names and obscure details. The first thing is that the war started well before the Russian invasion on Christmas Eve, 1979. It really dates from the coup mounted by a Communist called Taraki the previous year. Taraki overthrew a government which had originally been pretty sympathetic to Moscow, but by the time of the coup was trying to extricate itself from the Russian bear hug. In fact, what triggered the coup was a decision by the President, a chap called Daoud, to arrest a number of Communist or pro-Communist ministers. That's when the Russians told Taraki to move. Daoud and his entire family were murdered in the presidential palace. A very bloody business, but then Afghan politics have always been pretty bloody.

'Taraki, with the Russians right behind him, took over in the spring of '78 and within weeks rather than months, as Harold Wilson said about somewhere quite different, the opposition began to grow. Very soon the whole country was literally up in arms. You know how every Afghan carries a gun? Well, in every town and village, people formed themselves into armed bands and attacked the new regime. By the summer of 1979 the Communists were in a bad way, facing a national rebellion, and so they turned to Big Brother. Or, more probably, Big Brother told them, move over, we're coming in.

'We know for a fact that the Russian occupation wasn't a sudden decision. All through the summer of '79 they were massing troops in the staging areas north of the border, in Samarkand, Tashkent and so on. When they did strike, on Christmas Eve, it was a pretty impressive operation. They moved in 85,000 men virtually overnight, a lot of them by air, and took all the big towns and key installations. No doubt they thought, rather like the Americans in Vietnam, they would have it all buttoned up in a few months. After all, what could a bunch of *dushman* – that's the pejorative word meaning bandits that the Russians use for the guerrillas

39

– do against the might of the Red Army?' Jackson laughed, topped his glass up and pushed the decanter back towards Wills.

'Well, it's ancient history now, but they got a very nasty surprise. The war has escalated year by year and Russian casualties have mounted steadily. So have not so much the mujahideen's, but the Afghan people's. There must by now be well over a million Afghan dead and wounded, let alone the millions of refugees.'

'Who's winning, in your estimation?'

'The 64,000-dollar question. Well, we certainly don't think it's the Russians. In fact, all the indications from Moscow are that they are prepared to go. There's a lot of opposition from the army, of course. They would lose a useful training ground and they don't like the idea of defeat any more than the Americans did in Vietnam. But other voices are increasingly making themselves heard. The KGB is worried about the effect on internal security and the growth of the anti-war movement, thanks to the horror stories brought back by the lads from the front and now common talk in every factory and communal farm. We think that at the Geneva talks Gorbachev may set a time-table for their departure. What we hope is that your mission will make it certain he does.'

Wills drained the last of his port. 'It's an exciting thought. It's not often, after all, that one feels part of the historical process.'

'Even rarer when it's something one actually approves of, namely the defence of freedom.'

'Late-night talk.' Wills's voice was sarcastic. 'Look here, Jackson. I'm no starry-eyed idealist, just an out-of-work soldier, a glorified hit man. Only difference is that I'm a respectable hit man, working not for the IRA or Colonel bloody Gaddafi, but for the British government.' He raised his empty glass mockingly. 'I give you the Queen, Jackson.'

The analyst forced a careful smile. 'Come on, time for bed.'

Four

Next morning, on the dot of seven, Wills dived into the swimming pool, shattering the smooth surface into a thousand shimmering wavelets. The sudden shock of the cold made him gasp but when he had swum ten lengths with a steady crawl, the blood was pounding in his veins. All traces of a port hangover had gone by the time he climbed out, to be confronted by Brigadier Bowman.

'Ah, there you are, Wills. I warned you it would be a bit parky, didn't I? By the way, let me introduce our new arrivals, Colonel James from Peshawar and Mr, er, Anatoly Gradinsky.'

Jimmy James, ex-Irish Guards, was tall and tanned with a soldier's steady gaze. 'Hello,' he said to Wills. 'Pretty impressive stuff, at seven in the morning.'

But Wills was more interested in his companion, a muscular blond man with a ready smile and striking blue eyes. He stepped forward and grasped Wills's damp hand.

'Gradinsky. Good to meet you, Wills.' The newcomer had a marked American accent, but it was clear English was not his mother tongue. 'There are people in Moscow, you know, who take a swim every day of the year. They even break the ice to go in on what you call Christmas Day. I think they're crazy.' He gave a deep, infectious laugh.

Bowman touched his arm. 'I'm sure you're hungry, both of you. Let's go and see what they've got for breakfast. Join us when you're ready, Wills. The others should be here shortly.'

Ten minutes later, Wills found Gradinsky in the dining room tucking into a huge plateful of bacon, sausage, tomato, mushroom and egg while James was doing justice

41

to a kipper, tea and toast. Wills helped himself from the sideboard and sat down opposite the Russian. 'This is the small breakfast, today. Usually we have kidneys as well.'

Gradinsky's eyes narrowed and then he burst out laughing. 'The English sense of humour. I keep getting caught out. That's what comes of spending too long in the States.'

'How did you come to do that?'

'I was in our embassy there, as an assistant military attaché. For two years. From there, I went to Afghanistan.'

'That must have been quite a change.'

'You can say that again.'

'You certainly speak very good English, or should I say American?'

'Thank you. I became very interested in American slang. Through my brother, really. He's a poet. Was a poet, I should say.' Gradinsky's voice changed and, glancing across, Wills saw his face harden. Then, without another word, the Russian rose from the table abruptly and left the room. They heard his feet clumping up the stairs.

James put his cup down. 'He was very close to his brother. It came up all the time in his debriefing, as you probably know.'

Wills nodded. He kept his voice low. 'Tell me, do you think there's a chance that he's a KGB plant? He seems too good to be true.'

'We're pretty sure, no, we're bloody sure he's exactly what he says he is. We've checked his story and it all fits. I mean his army career, his time in the Washington Embassy, even his brother and the way he died. We've checked the whole lot. But why do you raise it? Is there anything that bothers you in particular?'

Wills finished his coffee. 'I can't put a finger on anything specific. It's more a gut feeling. It just all seems too damn neat. The answer to an MI6 man's prayer. A Russian defector from Afghanistan who's got everything: impeccable reasons for defecting, perfect military background, perfect English, or American. He's even served in the Salang. Doesn't it sound too much like a coincidence to you?' Wills's laugh was sceptical.

'Obviously he can't be a plant in the conventional sense,' James objected. 'He had walked across the line into the arms of the mujahideen long before we'd even thought of the Salang idea.'

'I realise that, but his defection may have been a KGB stunt in the first place. Jackson was telling me last night, I think ...' he grinned ... 'that the KGB have tried to infiltrate agents into the Resistance in the past. One was sent to Durran with orders to find out everything about him and then escape, make his way to Pakistan and give himself up to the Soviet Embassy. From there, he would have been flown back home and debriefed.'

'Oh, you mean Kristov?'

'Was that his name? Jackson never finished the story. What happened to him in the end?'

'Apparently Durran liked him and talked to him a lot. But the second time he tried to escape, they shot him. They decided he wasn't the innocent defector he pretended to be.'

'So isn't it just possible that Gradinsky is a second, more high-powered attempt to penetrate the Durran organisation? The whole thing carefully prepared and planned? And, as luck has it, I appear on my white charger and the castle gates swing open for him?'

'I doubt it. Badly as they want Durran, I don't think they would expend a senior major with top qualifications on such an assignment. But I suppose it is just a possibility.' James sucked his teeth as if doubt had suddenly assailed him. 'We'll have to see. In any case, he's very much on probation here. We'll all be watching him like hawks. You do the same and let me know if you spot any flaws in his cover, if cover it is.'

They heard the sound of wheels crunching over the gravel to the front door. Car doors banged and voices approached, erupted into the front hall and passed on. Bowman put his head round the door. 'The others are here. Come through to the morning room when you're ready.'

'Right.' Wills rolled up his napkin, inserting it into the bone ring Hidbrook Manor had thoughtfully provided. His bore a silver 'C' on one side. As he followed Bowman down the corridor, Wills idly wondered what the 'C' stood for. Chump, probably, he concluded as they reached the morning room.

Like the sitting room, it too had French windows and the

morning sun was flooding in, gilding the faded carpet. The furniture had been rearranged for the informal conference: a table and chair in front of the French windows, with a view of the lawn sloping down to an ornamental pond below; a Knole settee against one wall, opposite the empty marble fireplace; and four club armchairs, their leather rather cracked, facing the windows.

Roger Fulford was standing in the middle of the room, a cup of coffee in his hand, explaining how he had spent the weekend tending the roses in the garden of his Sussex cottage. He shook hands with everyone, affable but business-like. 'Help yourselves to coffee, everyone, and then we'll get started. Glad you're here, Jackson, to keep us straight on the background. What with you and Colonel James we should at least get our facts right. Perhaps you would kick off, Colonel James, with an update on the war? Then Jackson might like to take us through the plan for the Salang operation. It's pretty sketchy at this stage, I'm afraid, and any bright ideas will be welcome. Then I'd be very interested to hear from you, Major Gradinsky, about general security in the Salang area and any comments you might care to make?' Fulford gazed quizzically at Gradinsky over the top of his spectacles. 'And finally, Wills, your ideas and sugges-tions would be most welcome, of course.' He sat down behind the table and looked expectantly at James.

Wills listened to James's crisp résumé of the war, and then Jackson's brief outline of the Salang operation. The analyst said that although they had not yet come to any definite conclusions, they were 'leaning positively' to Gradinsky's idea of using a couple of lorry bombs, or more specifically, tanker bombs. Tanker convoys ran through the Salang regularly to pick up fuel north of the tunnel and this might be the best way of penetrating tunnel security and 'beating the system', as Jackson put it. If they did decide to use tankers, they would then have to establish which of several types of suitable explosive could be found locally. Wills watched him, his mind partly on Gradinsky and his first impressions of the man. With his blond good looks and vivid blue eyes, there was something appealing about him: a mixture of naughty boy and crazy Slav. But when it was Gradinsky's turn to speak, he had to admit that he was listening to an intelligent, highly professional army officer.

'I'd like to make two comments, if I may, Mr Fulford. First, when Colonel James talks about the apparent failure of the Soviet army to interdict the mujahideen's supply routes, he may not be aware that we were doing so very successfully in 1986 when orders came from the Kremlin to reduce our vulnerability and above all to keep casualties to a minimum. It was the casualties that they suddenly got worried about. You know, all those tin coffins coming back on the "black tulip" flights from Kabul. The people at home didn't like it. And once the politicians start running the war, as the Americans found to their cost in Vietnam, the generals may as well pack up and go home.

'The second thing is this. When we carry out the operation in the Salang, we have only one chance of getting out alive, that I know of.' There was an immediate stillness in the room, as if all of them were holding their breath. 'It is imperative, I repeat imperative that if we go for the tanker option, we stop the vehicles and stage a breakdown opposite or very near an emergency exit in the tunnel. This is a small steel door set in the outer wall of the tunnel. It is usually locked, so it's essential that we arrange for it to be unlocked on the day...'

'Or we blow it,' Wills interrupted.

'Yes, of course. But we won't have much time and if we had a couple of local helpers who could unlock the door in advance and cover our rear, that would be a great help.'

'How do you know about this door?' Fulford's eyes were hard.

'I discovered it by chance when I was on an operation one day near the tunnel. We were chasing a band of *dushman* – in the winter. There was a lot of snow. We lost track of them on the mountain and, to return to base, we decided to take a short-cut through the tunnel. My sergeant knew about the emergency exit and said we could ski down from there.' Gradinsky gave a short laugh. 'Well, I can ski all right but it was bloody steep and there were lots of rocks sticking up out of the snow. I can tell you, it was no joke. But it got us down the mountain pretty fast.'

45

'Sounds like a lucky break,' James said. 'I was wondering how the hell you were going to get away in one piece.'

'Where would you get away to, though?' Wills's voice was sharp. 'Where would we be heading for?'

'Either the Panjsher, across the mountain, or the road. It's about half a mile below. If we chose the road we'd have to have a back-up vehicle waiting for us there.'

'Wouldn't your people, I mean your former people, stop all traffic and grab us? After all, they could hardly miss us if we go clambering down the mountainside after the tunnel goes up.'

'Not if we're in Spetsnaz uniforms.' Gradinsky smiled. 'I've still got mine. The mujahideen gave it back to me. So as you say in the British Army, I believe, "I'm all right, Jack".' He gave a huge laugh, and Wills could not stop himself laughing as well. If this really was a doublecross, if Gradinsky really was a KGB agent, at least he was an amusing bastard.

'I think Gradinsky's door is a good bet, but keep all your options open.' Fulford brought them back to order. 'Now, this afternoon, you two will have a technical briefing. We've got one of the great experts coming to talk to you so pay attention. That's all.'

It was a morning of breathtaking beauty, the sky an enormous and perfect dome of heraldic blue, against which the stark mass of the mountains stood out in awesome array. The air was so pure that every tree and every rock was delineated with extraordinary clarity. But there was a sense of emptiness and desolation in the air. Here, in the lower part of the Panjsher Valley, a long series of Russian offensives, involving hundreds of jets, helicopters, tanks and armoured personnel carriers, had ground the villages to dust and left the land barren and empty. The villagers had long since fled the bombing and now only the guerrillas moved through the desolation of what had once been their homes, usually at night and on their way to or from a military operation. The Afghan army, stiffened by a smattering of Russian advisers, held a number of posts in the lower part of the valley and at the entrance. The rest of the eighty-mile defile through the Hindu Kush was for them enemy territory

46

and the home of their redoubtable enemy, the guerrilla leader Commander Durran.

The three men, each carrying a Kalashnikov and wearing the flat Chitrali cap of Durran's mujahideen, black Russian combat boots and khaki trousers, walked the length of the deserted village street and turned down to the river. A long narrow bridge, just wide enough for a man on horseback, spanned the fast-flowing, diamond-clear Panjsher river, which rises in the snows of the Anjuman plateau. It was four years since Abdul had been in his home valley, and he was silent in the face of the destruction caused by the Russian bombing.

On the far side of the river the other side of the village, less damaged but also empty, lay half hidden among huge walnut and mulberry trees, some of them a couple of hundred years old. The houses were spread out, fifty or sixty yards apart, most of them with their roofs caved in or their walls gutted by a bomb or rocket. Some were mere piles of rubble. They had reached the far end of the village when a hidden voice challenged them to halt.

Abdul immediately stopped, his Kalashnikov dangling loosely by his side.

'Who are you? What do you want?' the voice asked in the rough Persian of the Panjsher.

'I am Abdul Mohammed. We are mujahideen from Kabul and we have come to see Commander Durran.'

The owner of the voice appeared at the window of the ruined house above them. He was no more than fifteen, but he looked older and he handled his Kalashnikov with assurance.

'Stay where you are until I come down.' The young mujahid disappeared from the window and they heard him clumping down the mud stairs.

'Show me your papers.'

Abdul took an identity card with his photograph from his breast pocket. All mujahideen were supposed to carry these cards to prevent infiltration by agents of the KHAD.

The young man appeared to have some difficulty reading but he studied the picture closely and recognised the green Resistance stamp of Jamiat-i-Islami, the same organisation as the one to which he, and all the other mujahideen in the Panjsher, belonged.

The two younger men travelling with Abdul held out their cards in turn. They had been well forged by the KHAD and carried the signatures of one of the Jamiat commanders in Kabul. The young sentry handed them back after a lengthy perusal.

'Where have you come from?'

'I told you, Kabul.'

'I mean today.'

'From Astana.' Astana was near the bottom of the valley and was occupied by an Afghan army garrison.

'You had no trouble?'

'No. We saw the *Shurawi* and the Afghan soldier dogs inside the village, but no patrols. We slept in an empty house about one kilometre away.'

'Which side of the river?'

'This side.'

The young mujahid nodded. 'Did you see any other mujahideen this morning?'

'Yes, we saw some on the other side of the river, about five kilometres from Astana, and we waved. They waved back.'

The next question was friendlier and part of the ritual of traditional Afghan hospitality. In times of peace it would have been almost the first question asked. 'Would you like to come into the house and drink tea?'

'With pleasure,' Abdul said and followed his young host inside.

The young man led the way up the solid mud steps to a big, empty room above. The window from which he had accosted the three strangers had no glass or even a shutter and there was a gaping hole in the roof where a shell or rocket had passed through. The floor was bare, made of dried mud, and as hard as concrete. Normally it would have been covered with rugs, but the Russians had looted the place thoroughly and the small carpet beneath the window had been brought in by the young sentry to make his guard room slightly less spartan. He now disappeared outside on to the balcony and came back a few minutes later with a blackened kettle from which he poured pale China tea into

48

three cracked and rather dirty cups. A small pewter tin of sugar was produced. Abdul and his two companions declined, out of courtesy; sugar was a scarce commodity.

The rigid laws of hospitality discharged, even if only in token form, the young man put on his stern face again.

'You said you wanted to see Commander Durran?'

Abdul nodded. 'Yes. I have a message for him. A very important message.'

'What is the message?'

'I am ordered to disclose it only to Commander Durran personally.'

'Who sends it?'

'Commander Khalili in Kabul.'

'Commander Durran is not here.' The boy's voice was gruff.

Abdul put down his cup, which was immediately filled up again. 'It is important that I see him as soon as possible. Can you send him a message?'

There was a long pause as the young man tried to assess the older and more confident man sitting opposite him. He was undoubtedly a Panjsheri, from Rokha, the main town of the valley and the main Russian base in the Panjsher. He knew that from the way the stranger spoke. And to delay the man's message might have serious consequences. He came to a sudden decision.

'When you have drunk your tea, we will go to find the local commander. He is in the next village.'

'We are ready,' Abdul said, putting down his cup and getting to his feet. 'The message is very urgent and it is important I should see Commander Durran tonight.'

The young mujahid went outside again and they heard him shouting for someone to take over his sentry duty. Eventually a voice answered and a few minutes later an equally young replacement appeared. At the far end of the village, they left the trees behind and climbed up to a path which ran along the mountainside above the river. Once there had been an irrigation channel here from which all the small terraced fields had drawn their water supply but with the bombing and neglect it had fallen into disuse and was now broken and dry. Below them, the fields lay brown and fallow. They walked fast and in silence along the twisting

49

path. The sun was overhead when a small cluster of brown mud houses came into view in a fold in the hillside. They were empty. They skirted these and climbed up again to another, smaller hamlet which was perched almost against the rock. Here, they could see smoke and signs of occupation. As they approached, several men appeared at the entrance to one house. They greeted the young mujahid with loud shouts and much embracing, all talking at once until a tall man appeared in the doorway and quickly surveyed the new arrivals. This was the local commander.

'Come inside. You must be tired after your journey.' There followed the traditional phrases that all Afghan travellers exchange. They sat down in the usual big, bare peasant room, the rough walls unadorned except for a poster displaying a blurred black and white photograph of the bearded Professor Rabbani, the leader of Jamiat. As they settled themselves cross-legged on the dusty carpet, the commander ceremoniously tucked a fat cushion behind Abdul's back, a gesture of an older courtesy that had remained unaffected by the war. The owner of the house performed the same service for Abdul's companions.

The commander appraised Abdul with his grave dark eyes. 'You say that you have a message for Commander Durran?'

'Yes. It is extremely urgent. For the ears of Commander Durran only. From Commander Khalili in Kabul.'

The local commander, whose name was Sayed, stroked his long, curly black beard. He knew Khalili.

'How is my old friend?'

'He is well, and fighting hard. Almost every night he leads his men in a rocket or mortar attack on the infidel dogs of *Shurawi*. We have killed many in the past two months.' Abdul's eyes glistened with pride.

There was a pause in the conversation as tea was brought and served. Abdul knew better than to rush his fences.

'You yourself are from Rokha?'

'Yes. I was at school with Commander Durran, in the class below. He may not remember me, but I remember him very well.'

'Ah, you must be the same age as his younger brother Ahmed?'

'Yes, we were exact contemporaries. What's happened to him now?'

'He's in Peshawar, running our offices there. He was badly wounded in the leg, so he cannot fight any more.'

A man came into the room, and, after embracing the commander, went round the room shaking hands with everyone. Then he sat down beside Sayed and in a low whisper began to recite what seemed to be a long message, Sayed interrupting him occasionally to ask a question. When they had finished the local commander turned to Abdul.

'He has just come from Commander Durran. We will go tonight, you and I, to a place further up the valley. It's a long way and will take several hours. We will see Commander Durran tomorrow, *inshallah*. Your friends will stay here and rest.'

After they had eaten a simple meal of grilled goat, yoghurt and flat, unleavened wheat bread, called *nan*, they drank tea and dozed. At ten o'clock Sayed got to his feet and buckled on his pistol belt. Abdul, who had not slept, walked across the room in his stockinged feet and pulled on his boots by the doorway. Each man selected his automatic weapon from the pile that stood against the wall and was ready for the march.

Outside the night was completely still, the silence broken by the rush of the stream below the houses. The moon had almost disappeared behind the mountain crest; they would have only starlight to guide them. Not that it mattered to the mujahideen, for they could have found their way up the valley blindfold.

Sayed had waited until now to lessen the chance of ambush by Russian Spetsnaz. This was not a particularly big risk, he believed, but there was no point in giving the Russians the advantage of good visibility. Sayed made his dispositions standing outside the house. Up the valley, the fields and river were already in deep shadow; only the tops of the mountains were still bathed in the cold light of the setting moon.

Sayed detailed four mujahideen to form the advance party and spring any trap that might be waiting for them. Then fifty yards behind them he placed himself, his deputy and Abdul, with Abdul in the middle, and finally a rearguard of two young mujahideen.

In a few minutes they had crossed the river and were heading up the valley, dwarfed by the vastness of the landscape.

Two hours later, they turned off the main valley and started up a steep tributary, climbing steadily for another three hours. The last mile or so was almost sheer, the river cascading down between great slabs of rock. They could feel the damp despite their sweat and the spray clung to their beards and hair, like dew on a spider's web. Near the top of the gorge, a broad ledge jutted out over the dimly perceived chasm below, painstakingly terraced and with every inch cultivated.

Here Sayed stopped and gave some instructions in a low voice to his deputy. 'You stay here,' he told Abdul. 'I will go forward and see where Commander Durran is.'

They dozed for perhaps two hours, the roar of the river numbing their senses, the cold creeping into their bones. Sayed finally reappeared at dawn with three men, one of them older, well over six feet and barrel-chested. Behind them, the rising sun was flooding the valley a deep furnace red, throwing every pinnacle of rock into sharp relief.

'You must be hungry,' the big man said politely. 'You had better come and have some food.' He led the way to a dry-stone lean-to built against the rock. Inside, there was a carpet on the ground and a kettle simmered on a brush fire in the corner. A dark-eyed girl of about fifteen slipped past them, drawing her veil across her face at the sight of strangers.

They sat down, cross-legged, and the big man took off his cap, revealing an almost bald head tonsured like a monk's.

'I am not sure if Commander Durran is still here. I have sent a message to the house where he was staying. If he's not here, you will have to give me the message.'

Abdul kept his voice polite. 'Alas, my friend, I cannot do that. Commander Khalili commanded me on pain of death to deliver the message personally to Commander Durran. And it is very urgent.'

The big man scowled. 'If he is not here, I tell you, you will give the message to me. Otherwise we will cut your tongue out and send it back to Khalili. You we will feed to the vultures.'

'I would willingly tell, my friend, but I am sworn to silence. Commander Khalili makes all his mujahideen swear the oath on the Koran; in case we fall into the hands of the *Shurawi*, or the KHAD. So even if you torture me, even if you tear my tongue out of my mouth slowly and painfully, I cannot reveal my message.' He smiled a wry smile. 'And if you tear my tongue out, I will not be able to tell Commander Durran something that is of the utmost importance to him.'

The big man turned away and held a muttered conversation with the three mujahideen who, Abdul had not failed to notice, had kept their Kalashnikovs with them, cradled in their laps, instead of leaving them at the doorway when they came in. They stared now at Abdul suspiciously as they listened to their instructions.

The big man faced Abdul with hard eyes. 'You will stay here, under guard, until I come back.'

He had been gone less than half an hour when there were voices outside and a slim, almost delicate-looking man of about thirty, with quick, intelligent eyes and a small beard, came in, followed closely by the big man. It was Durran. Abdul rose to his feet and he and the newcomer stared at one another for several seconds. Finally Durran, speaking quietly but with unmistakable authority, told the three mujahideen to leave. To the big man's surprise, he then advanced, arms outstretched, and embraced Abdul, three times, as is the Afghan custom.

'What a surprise, my brother. Have you come from Kabul?'

'Yes, with a message of the greatest importance.' Abdul hesitated, with a sideways look at the big man.

Durran waved his caution away. 'Azim is my right hand. You can speak freely.'

Abdul took a step closer and then, very slowly, took the black fountain pen out of his pocket. Azim watched him like a cat about to spring.

'The Russians gave me this to poison you with.'

For a moment there was absolute silence in the lean-to. Outside, very faintly, they could hear a man shouting to his oxen as they ploughed one of the terraced fields, their heads yoked low to a heavy wooden pole.

'Is that why you have come?'

'Yes, I was sent by the KHAD, on the instructions of the Russians. They not only recruited me but made me the leader of the assassination group. To kill you.'

'They recruited you? You of all people. I can't believe it.' Suddenly Durran burst out laughing. After a few moments Abdul joined in and, in some curious release of tension, what had been a joke became a paroxysm of laughter. Durran had to bend forward to relieve the pain of so much mirth. Eventually he straightened up.

'You came alone?'

'No, I have two men with me.'

Durran turned to the big man, Azim, who had remained woodenly uncomprehending throughout. 'Azim, my friend, you must think I am mad. But this man here, Abdul, is one of my oldest friends. He is our most senior and trusted agent in Kabul. Or was. Ever since the Russians invaded our homeland in 1979, he has been my secret eyes and ears in the capital. He is "Buzkashi".' At the mention of the codename, understanding flooded Azim's face.

'Buzkashi! This man is Buzkashi? Now I understand everything.'

Durran tilted his head. 'The other two. They must be arrested.' He looked at Abdul. 'What sort of men are they?'

'Parchamis. Dedicated Communists. Sons of Communists. And trained in the Soviet Union.'

Durran thought for a moment before looking at Azim. 'Give them the option. Either they join the mujahideen and fight for the *jehad* or they die tomorrow.'

Azim stood to attention to show that he understood the order and would carry it out.

When he had gone out, Durran motioned to Abdul to sit down on the carpet beside him. 'This poison, who gave it to you?'

'General Orlov. Apparently it was developed by the Syrian Secret Service and made available to the KGB. I was told to put it in your tea or food when I had an opportunity. I was to make sure there was an opportunity.' Abdul's laugh was sardonic. 'Only three or four drops are enough to kill you. It is slow but death is certain. And it leaves no trace. The symptoms are like those of a heart attack.' He held up the fountain pen and unscrewed it. They could see the level of the deadly contents through the thin plastic. 'There is enough here to poison the whole of your entourage.

'And there is something else I have to show you.' He pulled the Makarov from the shoulder holster. 'This is also not quite what it seems. Let me show you...'

The drumhead court was composed of Durran, Azim, Abdul and a dozen other mujahideen and members of Durran's inner circle. The two young Parchamis, disarmed and with the fear of dying shadowing their eyes, stood before their judges.

'Why did you betray Allah and the land of your fathers?'

The older of the two curled his lip. 'We are modern Afghans. We do not believe in feudalism. We look to a future guided by our friends and allies, the great Soviet people.'

Azim thrust forward his great bull neck. 'Your friends and allies, the Soviet people. Those friendly allies who bomb and destroy the men, women and children of Afghanistan, your fellow countrymen who believe in Allah. You march at the side of the Infidel against your own blood and your own religion. I say this to you.' He spat on the ground with theatrical force and drew back his arm as if to strike. The two prisoners stood, eyes down, no blood in their faces now, awaiting the inevitable.

An old man rose to his feet at the back of the group and, his voice quavering with rage and anguish, shouted, 'Parchami dogs. You have killed my brothers and sisters, my sons and daughters, my grandchildren. You have slaughtered my sheep and goats and desecrated my land. You are worse than the infidel *Shurawi* because you were born in the sight of Allah. You learnt to pray in the mosque. You were taught the words of the Koran. You were brought up in the land of Babur and Shah Jehan, of Abdur Rahman and Ahmad Shah. And yet you have forsaken the way of the Prophet. You should die like dogs. Bullets are too good for you. I say, brothers, stone them to death!' His voice rose to a thin scream demanding retribution.

Durran cut in. 'Do you renounce the murderous Kabul regime and ask Allah's forgiveness?'

Still showing no sign of emotion apart from their rapid breathing, the two young prisoners stayed silent.

'Do you abandon the Communist cause and join the *jehad*? To fight the invader and restore our homeland to freedom and independence?'

The one who had spoken before lifted his eyes and said in a low voice, 'We believe in the teaching of Marx, in the great and glorious Bolshevik Revolution and in the world leadership of the mighty Soviet Union which...'

Angry shouts drowned the rest of the speech. Hands gripped them, propelled them out of the circle and up the slope. Prisoners and escorts disappeared among a group of trees surrounded by huge rocks on the edge of the field. A few seconds later there was one shot, then another. The two reports fused into one and, amplified by the wall of mountains, reverberated thunderously from one rock face to another. A flock of startled choughs flapped wildly into the air and went wheeling away across the valley, chattering querulously.

Five

Wills and Gradinsky, who was travelling on a British passport under the name of Anthony Grade, took the afternoon flight on British Airways from Heathrow, arriving in Islamabad the next morning. After England, the air was warm and the sun strong. By the time they had fought their way through the elbowing mass of passengers to the immigration desk and then back again to the baggage claim and customs, they were sweating and bad-tempered. Clutching their bags, they struggled towards the exit, surrounded on all sides by jostling Pakistanis. A row of taxi touts waited to pounce.

'Taxi, sir? Nice taxi, yes please, this way.'

'Where you go, *sahib*? You like good car? Me have very good car.'

'I have better car, *sahib*. You come with me.' Hands reached out trying to wrest the suitcases from the victims' grip.

But behind this wall of importuners, Wills could see a bespectacled, undoubtedly English figure. He wore a blue open-necked shirt, a crumpled pair of jeans and scuffed brown shoes. Hardly in the classic colonial mould, thought Wills, but sure enough, as they came within range, he stepped forward. 'Hello, Michael Wills? And, er, Anthony Grade? I'm Dawlish. Hugo Dawlish. Good trip? I've got the car over here.'

He led the way in bright sunshine across the road where buses and Vespas honked and spluttered great clouds of blue smoke. Dawlish's car was in fact a large white Range Rover with a driver who obligingly piled their bags in the boot. He manoeuvred them skilfully through the traffic jam and then drove at speed along a dual carriageway planted with tall oleanders.

'By the way,' Dawlish said. 'Jimmy James would have come to meet you himself but he's been called away on some pretty urgent business. So I'm afraid you'll miss one another. I'm a colleague of his, so I'll do my best to stand in for him.'

'OK,' Wills said. 'Thanks for coming.' After half an hour the white high-rise garden city of Islamabad came into sight above the trees. Dawlish had a comfortable bungalow in one of the quiet streets in the diplomatic quarter in the northern part of the city, not far from the huge Feisal Mosque, said to be the largest in the world after the Great Mosque in Mecca. The house was built on stilts and the hall and large sitting room were open plan. Dawlish, whose wife also worked in the Embassy and was still at the office, showed the men their rooms, apologising for the teddy bears, Mickey Mice and ETs which adorned beds and dressing tables, and explaining that these were the children's rooms in the school holidays.

A white-coated servant with bare feet padded almost silently across the parquet floor with a tray containing duty-free gin, tonic and a large bucket of ice.

'Thank you, Joseph. Would you tell Sulaiman we'd like lunch in half an hour? Now, Anatoly, would you like a gin and tonic?'

'Hugo, I certainly would. Now that Gorbachev has banned all vodka in Russia, we have to come to the capitalist West to get an honest drink.' He laughed cheerfully, displaying white teeth.

Wills grinned. 'I wouldn't say no, either. I gather where we're going the pubs aren't great.'

'So I'm told. Although, like you, I've never been there.'

Dawlish cast a watchful eye towards the kitchen quarters. 'We won't be able to talk at lunch, because of the servants. We'll settle down afterwards, though, and I'll take you through the immediate plans. Just to say now that we've done our bit at this end, as far as we can.'

'Does that mean not very far?' Wills kept his tone polite but there was an noticeable edge to the question.

A slight flush came to Dawlish's cheek. 'Well, we are not

58

in charge here, as you well know. But we've asked our friends, the Paks, to arrange various things and I've been down personally to see that they're on the right tack.' He stared, large-eyed, through his spectacles at Wills. 'I cannot guarantee that it'll be up to the standards of the Royal Ordnance... But the two, er, vehicles are being converted as you might say, and will be ready in a few days' time.'

'Well, that's very good news.' Wills's tone was milder. 'I didn't mean any criticism.'

'Have another gin,' Dawlish said briskly. 'And you, Anatoly, your glass looks pretty empty.'

'Always, it's a bad habit of mine.' The Russian produced another of his explosive laughs. There was the sound of a car drawing up and then of a light step ascending the outside stairs.

'That'll be Mary!' Dawlish moved with remarkable speed to the door. 'Darling, good that you're back.' He pecked her vigorously on the cheek. 'Come and meet our guests.' Mary stepped into the room, a slight, pretty woman with the freshness of England still in her cheeks, despite two years in Islamabad.

Lunch was rather formal, both as to content and conversation: indeterminate brown soup was followed by stringy lamb chops, mashed potatoes and fresh fruit salad with tinned cream. They talked about embassy life in Islamabad.

'There's tennis,' Mary said. 'And of course bridge, and Hugo takes part in hash whenever he can, you know that running thing. All the overweight diplomats charge round Islamabad once a week, to the amazement of the locals who can't think why they don't go by car.' She giggled attractively.

Joseph hovered throughout the meal, making any shop talk impossible. But after he had brought coffee and disappeared, followed by Mary who said she had things to do, Dawlish produced a bottle of brandy and waved his guests into the armchairs. He poured three generous tots.

Wills took a sip of brandy. 'Nice stuff, this. By the way, we'd like to see the conversion, if possible, Hugo.'

'That's all arranged. Tomorrow or the next day. I should get a call from our Afghan friends tonight. We need to be rather discreet about it, as you can imagine. In the last couple of years, since we've been here in fact, the Russians have stepped up their watching activities. Very considerably. So I thought we'd keep you here for a couple of nights to rest you up after your flight and brief you – as much as I can. Then after we've seen the conversion – it's not too far from here – I've arranged for you to stay at Mastuj Fort. It belongs to a friend of mine. He used to be in the British Army, many moons ago.'

'Wasn't there a famous battle at Mastuj?' Wills asked.

'Absolutely right. The British were besieged there in the 1890s for about a month by my friend's great-grandfather. They were relieved just in time. Very warlike people, the Pathans in that area. In every area, come to that.' Dawlish gave a self-deprecating laugh and took a sip of brandy.

Dawlish got his call that evening and next morning they drove to the outskirts of Rawalpindi, the old British garrison town only ten miles from Islamabad. Whereas Islamabad has been laid out with some semblance of planning, Rawalpindi is a sprawling conglomeration of old wooden houses and cheap modern concrete abominations tacked on to a once elegant mall and cantonment area. As they drove past a rather grand-looking military outfitters, Wills squinted into the dusty sunlight. It was easy to imagine the days when the empty *maidan* would have been busy with British army officers exercising their polo ponies.

The Range Rover turned down a dusty street into the industrial quarter and threaded its way, horn blaring, past dilapidated lorries and ramshackle horse and donkey carts until they came to a high-walled compound. Above the gate was the legend: Khyber Transport Company. Dawlish's driver sounded his horn impatiently and after a few minutes an old man with a stick, the *chowkidar*, came running to open up. The rickety iron gates swung open to reveal what appeared at first to be a scrap yard. Old tyres, wheels, bits of lorries and even one or two whole chassis were scattered about. At the far end was a large building like an aircraft hangar with a tin roof. Its huge double doors were closed, but a small side door now opened and a piratical-looking Afghan with a large hook nose and piercing black eyes, wearing a dirty white turban, appeared. As soon as he saw Dawlish he strode towards them, grinning excitedly.

'Ah, Mr Dawlish, this great honour. Come inside, please, it is hot today, too hot.'

'Hallo, Hashem, how are you today?' Dawlish indicated Wills and Gradinsky, without introducing them. 'My friends were interested to see your workshop.'

The Afghan winked knowingly. 'Come on, please. It is fine workshop, very fine. Best in whole country.' He ushered them into the hangar like a tribal prince throwing open the gates of his palace. Inside, the neon lighting was subdued and the temperature cool, almost cold.

Dawlish gave a small gasp of pleasure. 'My God, Hashem, I didn't know you had air conditioning here.'

Hashem beamed, his teeth flashing. 'I installed it only a month ago. Already it has improved productivity no end. Come this way please.' He led them to the far corner of the workshop which was curtained off by plastic sheeting, pulled a flap aside and ushered them through. Inside, surrounded by scaffolding, were two Russian petrol tankers. Hashem led the way up some steps and along a gangway so that they found themselves looking down on the two vehicles. The Afghan lowered his voice. 'You see, each tanker is divided this way...' He chopped his hand down vertically several times. 'Each one has six tanks. Now all empty. Look here.' They leanë over the guard rail to peer at the tanker below them. Spaced along the top of the hull were six inspection covers, one for each of the six individual compartments. The one directly below them was open and they could see, as Hashem had said, that the tank was empty.

The Afghan tapped the side of his nose. 'When convoy goes to Salang, all tanks empty. Except...' He paused theatrically, holding each of them in turn with his mesmeric black eyes. 'Except for Tank Number One. Tank Number One will register empty. But will be full up to brim – ' he tapped the back of his hand under his chin – 'with methyl nitrate.'

Gradinsky gave a growl of surprise. They had been told methyl nitrate was their best option but might well prove impossible to obtain.

'How the hell did you get it?' Wills asked. Dawlish merely laughed. 'Let's just say that we have our suppliers, although sometimes they're involuntary ones, I must confess.'

Hashem was anxious to explain the properties of the explosive. 'Methyl nitrate is safe if handled OK. But can be dangerous if tank not full and – ' he made a swishing noise, moving his hand backwards and forwards – 'there too much gas inside. Then go boom!' He laughed as if it was the funniest thing in the world.

Wills knew enough about methyl nitrate to realise it was going to be a very risky business. The danger was not so much in the stuff itself as in the vapours, or gases, it gave off. But he tried to make a joke of it. 'We'll be bloody lucky if we're not sitting on a cloud playing our harps by the time the convoy reaches the tunnel.'

Dawlish chuckled reassuringly. 'You're in good hands with Hashem, you know. He's a highly experienced chemical engineer. He used to run the big explosives factory in Kabul before the war. And he worked under the Russians after the occupation for two or three years before they rumbled that he was passing a lot of the product to the muj and he had to do a bunk. The other point is that they'll do all the loading here. If they make a mistake they'll blow themselves up, not you.'

'Yes, but we're the ones taking the bloody thing to the Salang, aren't we?' Wills's grey eyes were hard.

'Oh, sure. But they're taking it by road through the Khyber to Kabul and that's arguably the worst part of the journey.' Dawlish's slightly owlish look had disappeared and his dry tone suggested the matter was closed. 'Hashem, what's the timetable?'

'Will be ready in one week. Then we drive to Kabul, *inshallah*.' Hashem showed most of his very white teeth.

'How much does the tank hold?' Wills asked matter-of-factly.

'One thousand gallons.'

'*Bozhe moi*.' Gradinsky gave an involuntary shudder. 'And both tankers will be like this? Two bloody great tankers like this?'

The Afghan grinned. 'You need this much to blow up the Salang Tunnel. Maybe more.'

'OK, Hashem, we'll leave you to it.'

As they drove back through the gates, Dawlish asked Gradinsky, 'What are the chances of a snap inspection *en route*? To see if the tanks are all really empty?'

Gradinsky shrugged his big shoulders. 'This is a question I cannot answer. Maybe one smartass KGB cop with a nose for trouble will take it into his head to give us the works. Tear the whole truck to pieces. OK, that's a chance we have to take. But these tankers are always running through the Salang to pick up gas in the north and bring it back to Kabul. It's the only way they can keep the wheels turning. And, you know, the men don't care any more. They just want to get out of the goddamn place and go home. That's all they're thinking of, counting the days and hours and minutes until they've completed their tour of duty and can cross the border. That's our best hope. Their minds aren't on the job. What do you think, Mike?'

'I agree. I think if everything else is OK, if the drivers' papers, the papers for the trucks, our papers, everything else, are OK, there will be no problem. Quite frankly, I'm much more worried about something quite different.'

'Tell us.' Dawlish twisted in the driving seat to look at Wills.

'It's quite simple. If a burst of AK fire or a mortar or whatever hits that tanker, then it's goodbye. We won't have to worry about anything else ever again. And given the nasty habit some of these lads have of ambushing everything that moves along those roads, well, frankly, I think it's going to be a very scary ride.'

'Yeah. All we need is some fool of a muj who wants to shoot up every passing tanker for the hell of it. They're the obvious target, after all. We've lost more tankers than anything else. They make such a nice bonfire, eh?' Gradinsky's belly laugh made the back seat heave.

'I remember one occasion. We were coming south in a big convoy. We had just come through the Salang Tunnel when we ran into this ambush. They hit one tanker right at the front of the convoy. It exploded. *Voosh.*' Gradinsky threw his hands out to demonstrate. 'There was this terrible explosion and then a whole row of tankers following behind also went up. It was like what the Jews call the holocaust, eh? Luckily we were far enough behind to be able to stop in time.'

'Did the Russians carry out reprisals?' Wills asked.

'Yes. Although we did not wait to see for ourselves. As soon as we could we bulldozed the tankers off the road and carried on as fast as we could to Kabul. If you are caught on that road at night ... bad luck. But I heard later that they sent the Mi24s and ground troops to some villages near the Salang Highway. They killed everyone they could find and burned the houses. They killed a lot of civilians but missed the mujahideen.'

Dawlish drew up outside his gate. The gardener was cutting the lawn with an ancient push mower, bent almost double with the effort.

Dawlish got out to open the gate, beating the *chowkidar* to it by several lengths. 'Lazy sod,' he said casually as they drove in. 'But at least he's honest.'

Even under ideal conditions, the road to Mastuj is a rough cart track and after rain it becomes a near-impassable riverbed. Luckily it was dry for the time of year and Dawlish's Range Rover, although bumping and lurching horribly, safely negotiated a series of dizzying bends before finally drawing up in front of the square, stone-walled fort. The three men got out and stretched. It had been a long and uncomfortable ride, but the view was some compensation. To the east stretched the great mass of the Karakorams, although Nanga Parbat and K2 were hidden in the cloud that covered the far horizon. To the north, less high but almost as impressive, rose the massif of the Hindu Kush, the snow-capped peaks shining like silver in the evening sunshine. The air was clear and cold and sounds carried a long way. A small group of men came hurrying to greet the new arrivals.

'My dear Hugo, welcome to Mastuj. Come along inside, you must be tired after your long journey.' Jackie Mastuj, the owner of Mastuj, descendant of the Amirs who had once fought the British, was a man of about fifty, not very tall but broad and with a natural air of command. He led the way past a pair of British cannon that had defied the Pathan besiegers for many weeks and into a courtyard that looked as if it hadn't changed for a hundred years. They climbed up a grim stone staircase, the walls hung with old shields and swords and enormously long-barrelled *jezails* which had undoubtedly peppered many British in the past. At the end of a passage they entered another world. Here, furnished unspectacularly but comfortably, rather like a set of rooms in an Oxford college, was Jackie's own private domain. A grand piano stood in one corner, and a CD player in another. Sofas and armchairs in faded chintz covers completed the feel of an English country house and only a magnificent Bokhara rug in pale blue and beige and a suit of Persian armour suggested they were not in the Home Counties.

A turbaned servant appeared with a tray and despite the government's ban on alcohol the visitors were relieved to see the unmistakable label of a well-known brand of whisky. Jackie poured generous measures.

'The nights are always pretty cold up here. You need this after your long journey.'

Nursing his glass, Wills walked to the window. A sprinkle of lights was coming to life in the gloom of the valley below them. 'Is that one of your villages down there?'

'Not one of mine. It's an Afghan encampment. A mujahideen transit camp. They moved here a few months ago to get away from the bombing on the border. They didn't ask my permission, of course, but what can you do?' Jackie shrugged.

'Are they running guns from here?' Wills was counting the lights. He got up to thirty.

'I haven't actually been down there. They don't exactly encourage visitors. But my people tell me that a lot of weapons are stashed there and at any one time there will be something like a thousand horses in the surrounding valleys, waiting to ferry supplies in over the border.'

Jackie pointed above the encampment, to the massive barrier of the Hindu Kush, sharply silhouetted against the setting sun. 'There are plenty of passes through the mountains that they can use. The Russians can try as much as they like, but they'll never be able to block the infiltration routes.'

'They could give them a really bad time. We did for a while.' Gradinsky swirled his whisky round his glass and drained it appreciatively. 'But then Moscow got nervous and we gave up.'

'But you did drop a lot of anti-personnel mines?' Wills turned to Jackie. 'Do you still get a lot of wounded?'

'Yes, mostly civilians, coming over with wounds from these mines. The Russians scatter them from helicopters and also from a kind of mortar, isn't that right?'

Gradinsky nodded. 'Yeah, they're very nasty things. They can blow off your foot if you step on them. But in the end, they're really just a nuisance. They'll never stop the mujahideen, not even if you laid a solid carpet of them all the way from here to Kabul.'

'What about another drink, everybody?' Jackie held out his hand for the Russian's glass. 'Then we'll go in and have dinner.'

Next day Dawlish, Wills and Gradinsky, accompanied by Jackie's *malik* or head man and two bodyguards, rode out from the fort on Jackie's best horses, small hardy animals reared in the mountains of the North-West Frontier. The men looked ridiculously big for their mounts, but the horses carried them with sure-footed ease. They trotted down the road they had driven up the night before with a great deal less bumping and then cantered across the stony fields to the bottom of the valley where they had seen the lights of the Afghan camp. Smoke from the cooking fires was rising in the still air against a sky of magnificent virgin blue. As they reined back to a walk, dogs started to bark fiercely and people drifted out of their tents and shanties to investigate.

A man with a hawk nose and dark eyes like daggers came out of a black camel-hair nomads' tent. He carried a pistol in a holster at his waist and wore the flat Chitrali cap of the northern mujahideen. He advanced to meet the new arrivals, his glance taking in everything: the state of the horses, their weapons, their dress and above all the fact that three of them were Westerners. He spoke the traditional greeting, '*Salaam Aleikum*'.

'*Aleikum Salaam*,' the *malik* replied. 'The two *sahibs* are guests of the Amir. Since they were riding past they were curious to learn about the Afghans who are camped here.'

The Afghan replied in what seemed a friendly voice. The *malik* translated. 'He invites you into his tent to have some food.'

'That is extremely kind of him, but we will have food when we go back to the fort. Perhaps we could drink tea instead?'

'He wants you to have food, and these people are very hospitable. You may have to eat something. Come, we will go inside.'

They dismounted, leaving the horses with the two body-guards, and shook hands with the Afghan. He was as tall as Wills and his handshake was immensely strong. He showed very white teeth. 'Please, you are my guests.' He swept aside the flap of the tent and motioned them into the dark interior.

It was much roomier than Wills had expected. Two women stood up at the sight of strangers and veiled themselves, but not before the men saw that the younger one was strikingly beautiful, with eyes as dark and direct as her father's. Their host gave his orders and the women retired to the back of the tent and busied themselves with cups and a teapot that sat on the embers of a fire. Some of the smoke drifted outside but most of it seemed to stay in the tent.

'It's better when you sit down.' Dawlish demonstrated by sitting down promptly on a thick, dark-red carpet with blue markings. 'In fact, if you don't, you soon choke.'

Their host fussed about, tucking cushions behind their backs, making sure they were as comfortable as possible.

'He says he is sorry for the poor hospitality,' the *malik* interpreted. 'He says it is the war. If you had come to his house in the north before, he would have entertained you properly.'

The hospitable Afghan poured the pale green tea with a courteous flourish and then sat down opposite his guests.

'He asks what brings you here,' the *malik* said.

'That's a bit of a poser,' Dawlish replied. 'Tell him we are friends of the Amir and spending a few days with him.'

'Where will your friends travel to next?' The *malik* nodded at Wills and Gradinsky. The Russian laughed. 'This one is smart. He must think we look different to Hugo.' Dawlish adjusted his specs with a donnish gesture. He looked even more owlish and Foreign Office than usual.

'They will probably stay some time up here, seeing

the country and travelling round...' It sounded a bit lame.

The Afghan's eyes looked sceptical, as he put another question in Farsi. 'He says he thought you might be representatives of the British government seeking to help the Afghan Resistance in its *jehad* against the infidel *Shurawi*.'

Dawlish cleared his throat pompously. 'No, they are not members of the British government. But of course we are all interested in the cause of the Afghan Resistance. Are you directly involved?'

The Afghan took his time to reply, watching them over the rim of his glass as he drank.

'Since you are friends of the Amir and you are British I will tell you. But you know one must be careful here. There are too many spies. Yes, we are from the Resistance, like every other good Afghan. We come from Badakhshan, in the north. We have just marched for two weeks to come here to get more weapons and ammunition. We have been fighting all winter and our supplies are running low.'

'What sort of weapons do you need?'

'We need everything. RPGs, recoilless rifles, Kalashnikovs, mortars, 107- and 122-millimetre rockets, and of course more missiles. British or American. Blowpipe or Stinger.'

'Thought you had Stingers,' Wills said.

The Afghan laughed. 'Yes, we do. But not enough. We need more Stingers, otherwise...' He spread his hands in a gesture of resignation.

'Otherwise, what?' Wills asked.

'Otherwise we will not be able to win the *jehad*. The *Shurawi* still have control of the skies. If you want us to win this war, which is the West's war too, you must send us more weapons. Please tell your leaders, my friends. We cannot fight with our bare hands.' He smiled, but his eyes were hard.

Six

The wind that blew off the mountain tops surrounding Kabul had a chilly freshness to it. Orlov looked through the bullet-proof windows of the big black Zil limousine at the bleak landscape beyond the city. How he hated this place and its accursed people. Only yesterday the bastards had rocketed the Soviet Embassy compound, killing six guards. The 122-millimetre rockets had landed on the guardroom and blown a bloody great hole in the place. A fluke, of course, but every night there was a shower of rockets on the city. They tried very hard to keep the *dushman* out, but it was virtually impossible. The damned Afghans they were supposed to be helping were so unreliable that they let the bandits slip past the checkpoints. Probably took the money and then turned their backs. They had shot one or two of the bastards to remind the rest of their duty but it still went on. Treacherous. That was the only word for them. Downright treacherous. General Maximov was right when he said in the Officers' Club the other night that they should drop the Bomb on the blasted country and kill the whole bloody lot of them. Then they could start again from scratch. *Tabula rasa*, old Maximov had said. How long would it take before the radiation subsided, though? Ten years, twenty years? Who cared? The place made more sense as a no-man's land, a buffer zone. That would teach the Afghans.

The car swung in through the heavily guarded gates of the headquarters of the Soviet Army in Afghanistan, threading its way through the double chicane built to stop suicide bombers. Orlov had an appointment with the Commander-in-Chief to which he was not particularly looking forward. The old man had obviously been having a hard time recently with the Ministry of Defence in Moscow. And he was in a particularly filthy mood over the failure of Abdul's venture to the Panjsher Valley. Orlov still didn't know what had gone wrong. Abdul captured, the other two shot, according to their latest reports.

Orlov got out of the car and walked swiftly towards the heavy steel front door which swung open as the sentry snapped out a stylish 'present arms'. He was met by a blast of hot air and the door whined shut behind him. The Commander-in-Chief's ADC was waiting in the hall to escort him to the first floor and General Ustinov's office. They went up in the lift in silence, Orlov running over in his mind the details of the plan that he had been instructed to prepare.

The ADC knocked and opened the door. 'General Orlov to see you, sir.'

'Come in. Good to see you, Sergei. Sit down.' Ustinov pointed to an armchair placed at the corner of his desk so that the light from the big window behind the Commander-in-Chief shone straight into the visitor's eyes. They were alone, as was Ustinov's rule when the head of the KGB in Afghanistan called to discuss an operational plan.

Ustinov's face looked as if it had been carved from granite – all flat planes and hard edges. Even his eyes were granite grey.

'So. What have you got for me? Good news for a change, I hope.' The smile was bleak.

'I hope so, Vassili. We have just recruited a girl who has a sister in the Panjsher and this sister, called Fatima, is very close to the bandit leader himself. To Durran. Now, our girl has been working in KHAD for some time and they in fact introduced her to us. We've checked her out thoroughly and she seems to have very sound credentials. There's only one real question mark about her.'

'Oh, what's that?' The grey eyes scanned Orlov's face suspiciously.

'Well, she comes from a very privileged family – in fact she's related in some way to the old Royal Family.'

Ustinov frowned. 'I don't like the sound of that. I hope we're not being taken for another ride by these blasted KHAD people.'

'They swear she's one hundred per cent OK but I've had our own very exhaustive vetting done. What we've come up with is this.' Orlov took a sheet of paper from his briefcase and slipped a pair of gold pince-nez on his nose.

'She is the second daughter of the old King's nephew, called Shahnawaz, who worked as assistant court chamberlain. She went to the French Lycée where she came under the influence of a Marxist French language teacher called Prevost and by the time she went to Kabul University at the age of eighteen, she was a convinced Marxist. She joined the People's Democratic Party of Afghanistan three months later and became a dedicated member, with a first-class record of attendance at meetings. She was elected a member of the Central Committee the year of our intervention, in 1979, at the age of twenty-one.'

'Hmm, a meteoric career. That makes her twenty-seven or twenty-eight now. What's she been doing in the meantime?'

'She was a supporter of Taraki and a member of his Khalq faction. When he was overthrown by Hafizullah Amin, she was arrested and given a bad time. Tortured. She is said still to bear the scars. Then, after the 'intervention', when Babrak came back, she was released and reappointed to the Central Committee. She joined KHAD about this time and has been active in Kabul since then. She is now a colonel in KHAD and her main job is to monitor Durran and his organisation in the Panjsher.'

'Was she responsible for the Abdul fiasco?'

'No. She knew nothing about that.' Orlov's voice was clipped. It had been a purely KGB operation.

'Well, that's something, I suppose.' Ustinov's tone was sarcastic. 'So what's the plan with this girl?'

'We send her in to see her sister. Through the sister she gets to Durran. Then, when she's with Durran, she switches on her little toy.'

'Don't mess about, Orlov. What toy?'

'A tracking device. A transponder. It's a tiny little thing, transistorised, Japanese, of course. It sends out a continuous signal on a specific wavelength to which we will be permanently tuned. She will have the transmitter switched on as long as she's with Durran. We will scramble the

71

snatch squad as soon as we get the signal and, with any luck, your man will be in the bag soon afterwards.'

Ustinov rubbed his jowl with the back of his hand, making a noise like sandpaper on wood. 'Will you scramble right away?'

'It will depend on what time of day we get the first signal. If there's time to do the operation in daylight, we'll go right away. But if we're going to arrive in the Panjsher in the dark, we'll wait and go in at first light.'

'And she'll have instructions to stick to him like a burr?'

'Absolutely. She'll stick to him or to the sister and the sister will not be far away.'

General Ustinov drummed his fingers slowly on the top of his desk and stared morosely out of the window at the distant, snow-capped mountains. 'Despite her background, the girl sounds as if she might be just the right operative.' He swivelled round to look Orlov in the eye. 'And anyway, I can't think of any other way of getting to him. He's very elusive, blast him.'

'He is. We've tried damned hard, as you know, to penetrate his entourage but without success. I think this gives us our best chance so far.'

'I hope so. It had better be.' Ustinov's voice was a growl. 'But surely the sister knows that your one is a member of the Party, even if she doesn't know she's in the KHAD?'

'I agree. They must know she's a member of the Party. But the plan is that our girl will contact a Panjsheri representative here and explain that she wants to defect. She'll ask him to send a message to her sister saying that her life's in danger and that she has to get out in a hurry.'

'What are the risks to us?' Ustinov didn't want to get his fingers burned again. Moscow thought Durran should have been liquidated long ago. 'Either they'll rumble her as soon as she arrives and put her through the mangle and get the whole truth out of her. Or, once there, with her sister and the bandits all round her, she'll defect. Or third, even if her bit works, the snatch operation will be a balls-up. Is that right? Have I put it fairly?'

Orlov coughed. 'Correctly, if a little pessimistically.'

Ustinov glared at Orlov, his face giving nothing away. Then he burst out laughing. 'Don't look so bloody worried,

72

Sergei.' The laugh disappeared as abruptly as it had come. 'Tell me one thing. You can pinpoint the exact position of the transmitter?'

'Yes, of course.'

'Well, then, we could bomb the place flat, couldn't we?'

'Yes, of course, Vassili, but I thought you wanted to take Durran alive?'

'Yes, I do. But it's always another option, isn't it? Just suppose that you get the first bleep at dusk. If you scramble the Spetsnaz, they'll be falling over themselves in the dark half way up some God-forsaken mountain. Too bloody impractical. They'll end up shooting one another. But if you wait for first light, that's the best part of twelve hours gone. All sorts of things can go wrong in twelve hours. Durran might smell a rat and do a sudden bunk, leaving the girl behind with the bleep going. So when the snatch squad arrives, he's miles away and all they get is the girl and a bellyful of lead. See what I mean? If that was the option I might go for an airstrike instead.'

'He's survived those before. Unless you get a very lucky shot, it's the weakest option.'

'I know, I know. Well, it's up to you, Sergei. This girl had better come up with the goods, or both of us will be looking for winter quarters in Siberia!' It was a standing joke, but Ustinov's laughter was a little forced, Orlov thought.

Ustinov looked at his watch and stood up. 'You'll stay for lunch? Good. Come and have a drink with your colleagues, and to hell with Afghanistan. And with Comrade Gorbachev too.'

General Ustinov still wore his spurs from his morning ride and they clinked defiantly as he strode across the parquet floor to his private dining room where they joined several other officers.

Over lunch the talk turned, as it did increasingly these days, to the morale of the forces and the possibility of withdrawal. Ustinov waited until the mess steward had left the room. 'I received a personal letter this morning from our boss, General Oblonsky himself. As you know, he's an old friend. He says we'll be out within the year. That's his own guess, mind you, but he's better informed than anyone outside Gorbachev's personal entourage.

73

'By the way, that was a nasty incident the other day at Bagram, when the rifleman went berserk and shot up the mess hall. Was he drunk, on drugs or just mentally deranged, Sergei?'

Orlov took a sip of the good red Georgian wine Ustinov served his friends. 'I think he was certainly the latter but it was caused by drugs, not booze. He's still being interrogated, by the way, but it seems he was a regular purchaser of hashish and also heroin, although to a lesser extent, from the locals at Bagram. There's a thriving trade, as you well know, all round the bases, with suppliers operating right up to the perimeter and sometimes inside it.'

One of the other generals, Lev Grishin, who commanded the air force, gave a snort which Orlov interpreted as disbelief.

'You don't believe me? I'm telling you the absolute truth and it's time everyone woke up to the fact, including you, Vassili! Well, this young sergeant either had no money that day or he tried to get the stuff for nothing and the pusher wouldn't play. Whatever the reason, when he couldn't get it he worked himself up into a terrible state, went back to his hut and reappeared with his Kalashnikov. From there to the mess hall was only a hundred metres or so and nobody took any notice. Not until he opened up in the middle of the mess hall. As you know, he killed eleven and wounded twenty others before he was shot and overpowered.'

'Badly hurt?' Ustinov demanded.

Orlov shook his head. 'Flesh wound in the leg, I think. He's in hospital but he'll be OK.'

'OK for the firing squad.' Ustinov's voice was like a death sentence.

'It's not the first time, nor will it be the last.' Grishin was a tough, pockmarked veteran of Ethiopia and Angola. He was in charge of the heavily armoured Mi24 'Hind' helicopter gunships and the supersonic SU25 'frogfoot' ground attack squadrons.

'I thought you and the GRU were trying to clean up this mess? I thought we were putting these bastards up against the wall and shooting them?' Pyotr Fodorovich had the knack of upsetting Orlov. He was the head of the armoured corps and, like Ustinov, was continually frustrated by the fact that he could not deploy his tanks in massive sweeps, grinding the opposition into the dust as he would have done in Europe. In Afghanistan, tanks were at best an irrelevance, and at worst a death trap.

A slight flush appeared on Orlov's cheeks which had nothing to do with the wine. 'We're running a big campaign against drugs, and you bloody well know it. But it's not just an Afghan problem, it's a worldwide problem and most of the world's heroin at this moment comes from Afghanistan and Pakistan. Heroin is the real threat. Hashish is bad enough but we'll never stamp that out. Every other field in this damn country is growing the stuff. But on the heroin side, there's been a worrying new development. Until now, the Afghans ran the trade in the traditional way, as they have for centuries, growing the opium poppy as a cash crop, using it themselves as a stimulant instead of alcohol and selling what they didn't need. But with the discovery of how to refine opium into heroin, and the simultaneous discovery that there is a large and hugely lucrative world market for the stuff, especially in the United States and western Europe, all sorts of entrepreneurs have moved in. The Mafia we've known about for a long time, of course. But there are very strong indications that the CIA is encouraging them not only to produce the stuff but to give it away. To our boys! And they're grabbing it like crazy.'

Orlov rapped his knuckles on the table. 'What we're facing, comrades, is the possibility of a heroin crisis, a heroin epidemic in the Soviet Union.'

'Come, come, Sergei. I think you are being melodramatic.' Ustinov's face was grim.

'I'm not being melodramatic. I'm trying to be realistic. Do you know, the other day we broke up a gang of soldiers, our boys, running a heroin ring in the Salang? We'd been watching them for some time, but we could never pin anything on them. All we knew was that truckloads of stuff were going missing. Ammunition. Weapons. Fuel. Food. Even boots and army belts. Then one day, about a week ago, one of my undercover teams came on this unit, on highway patrol. They'd just stopped a couple of trucks at the end of a convoy. One was full of weapons, the other of ammunition. The sergeant orders the drivers out and sends them off to the guard post. Then, with my boys looking on from a discreet distance, the sergeant gives a signal and up saunters a bunch of bandits. They have a chat and there's a pay off. Afterwards the *dushman* climb aboard the lorries, drive them a couple of hundred yards down the road and start off-loading them. Meanwhile my boys arrest the sergeant and the rest of the patrol and guess what had been changing hands? Money? No. Hashish? No. Heroin? Yes. A couple of kilos of it, one for each lorry. I mean that's enough to blow the minds of every kid in Moscow. It's a lethal amount, worth millions of dollars if you sold it in New York. So we take them and grill them and the sergeant says, "Oh yes, we've been doing this for months. We sell it to a ring in Kabul." "Who's in this ring?" "Oh, friendly diplomats. Arabs, South Americans, Bulgarians, Yugoslavs. They pay good money. Dollars." When we turned over this boy's quarters, we found a quarter of a million dollars. In greenbacks! Waiting for the day when he could get back to Moscow.

'My people asked him what he was going to do with it. He said he wanted to buy jewels and furs for his girlfriend, and of course a *dacha*. He wants to become a part of society in the Lenin Hills. My God, it's terrifying.' Orlov crashed his fist down on the polished table, making the glasses rattle.

'Steady on,' Ustinov barked. 'You'll spill the wine. But what you're telling us is a straightforward story of greed and criminal corruption, based on drugs. That's hardly going to undermine the youth of the Soviet Union.'

'Yes, it is. Because those diplomats and their middlemen are selling some of the stuff in Moscow. To Russians. To the *jeunesse dorée* and their young friends in the pop and film world. It's the same disease that we were so pleased to see afflicting the West. Now it's coming home to roost right here, with us. If we don't do something about it soon, we'll be a nation of junkies. And all because of this damned country, a country that we in the KGB always said we should never invade. I don't need to remind you of that, gentlemen.'

There was an awkward silence, broken by Ustinov. 'Have some more brandy, comrades. The way things are going, I might not be able to get another shipment for quite a long time.' He took a generous gulp.

'The onus is very much on us, Sergei. We've got to catch the heroin gangs and stop these shipments getting to the mother country. You've done well to arrest those criminals in the Salang. But what we need, comrades, is vigilance on all fronts, on every base and in every unit. The alert must be redoubled in the whole of the expeditionary force. I'll draft a new order this afternoon. This thing must be brought under control, stamped out, once and for all! Is that understood?'

They all nodded non-committally. They had heard these speeches from Ustinov before. Usually it was about dealing a final, mortal blow to the bandits. To the *dushman*. They had learned to take them with a pinch of salt. Only Orlov had the rank and authority to query the Commander-in-Chief. It was a reflection of his own power and of the power of the KGB.

'I agree, Vassili, we must have the biggest ever drive against the drug rings. I've made my dispositions and, throughout the country, my men are concentrating all their energies on it. Even at the expense of some of our other priorities. But I must warn you in all honesty that I simply haven't got enough people. I could do with twice as many drug squad officers as I've got. Three times as many. Think of it this way.' He took a swig of Ustinov's VSOP brandy and held the eye of each of his colleagues round the table in turn. They were all listening intently.

'These heroin-for-guns rings are operating all over the place, not just in the Salang. In Herat, Kandahar, Jalalabad, Shindand, Mazar – you name it, on every base, the pushers are there. And they're not just ordinary pushers, they're working to a pre-arranged plan. Somebody's supplying them with good-quality heroin, number one pure, which they know will fetch a high price on the world market and in Moscow. Who's supplying them? My guess is not only the CIA but also SIS through their Pakistani contacts. The middlemen in Kabul and Moscow are getting fat on the profits and most of them have diplomatic immunity. The stuff goes out from Kabul to Moscow in the diplomatic bag and no questions asked. Unless I can deploy a lot more agents, I just can't keep pace. We'll catch one lot here and another lot there. Put them on trial and then up in front of

77

the firing-squad. That'll scare off a few of the windier ones. But they soon forget, and with the temptation of that kind of money ...' Orlov shrugged.

'We know where it's coming from, the Tribal Areas between the Afghan border and Pakistan.' Ustinov's voice was a thoughtful growl. 'We've tried to burn their nests out before, haven't we? Well ...' His hard grey eyes went from one to the other of his subordinates. 'We'd better mount another operation fast. Sergei, I'll need the locations of all suspected heroin factories. The Dir Valley is still the main source of supply, isn't it?'

'Yes, but there are so many little factories producing the stuff now that you're talking about virtually the whole Tribal Zone. From Dir in the north to Waziristan in the south. A distance of roughly 450 kilometres. And all mountain.'

The other generals sipped their brandy gloomily. Every conversation about the damned country tended to end in this way, with talk of hundreds and hundreds of kilometres of damn-all except mountains.

'Trying to find these heroin factories is like looking for a sober man in the sergeants' mess on a Saturday night. Bloody impossible.' Fodorovitch's joke fell flat with the Commander-in-Chief.

Ustinov glared as if he hoped he might scare the problem away.

'You, Sergei, will make a list of the most important ones and you, Lev, will go and bomb them. Is that clear?'

Orlov coughed. 'Don't forget, Vassili, the Tribal Areas are the other side of the Durand Line, and therefore inside Pakistan. If you bomb the factories, you will kill not Afghans but Pakistanis. They'll kick up a hell of a fuss. Do we want that?'

'What the hell do I care if we kill a few Pakistani heroin smugglers? Do you see any other possibility of stopping what you have just called a concerted plan to turn us into a nation of junkies? Not just the army, but the whole bloody nation, you said. For God's sake, if the situation is critical, let's do something about it. We'd be failing in our duty if we allowed a handful of Pakistani drug pushers to stand in our way. Get the plans drawn up without delay, gentlemen.' He pushed his chair back noisily. Lunch was over.

Orlov drove back to his office. It was easy for Ustinov to call for a list of heroin factories in the Tribal Areas, but he was not at all optimistic that it would mean very much. The information would have to come from KHAD agents and he did not trust them. Most if not all of them would be in the pay of the heroin bosses. They had penetrated KHAD just as KHAD had penetrated the heroin gangs. The richest and best-organised barons would be tipped off and have time to move their stocks and equipment. They might blow a few factories to bits but the rest of them would be back in business in new premises a couple of days later. And then the protests from the Pakistanis would be in every paper and on every radio broadcast. You could get away with border raids, but bombing well inside the Tribal Areas was quite a different matter. And it would alienate the tribal chiefs, whom Orlov had been trying to cultivate for a considerable time now, turning them against the Pakistani government with gifts of arms and cash. If they bombed the Tribal Areas, they wouldn't have many friends left. But he knew Ustinov was adamant. The pressure from Moscow to halt the drug traffic outweighed any other considerations.

Orlov brightened up as his headquarters came into sight. It reminded him that he had an appointment with Colonel Shahwanaz of the KHAD that evening. He had not, of course, bothered the Commander-in-Chief with the information, but he had already taken quite a fancy to his latest recruit. In fact as a ladies' man he considered his seduction of comrade Colonel Zarina Shahwanaz one of the KGB's few recent successes in the wretched place.

Orlov's villa was on the far side of the compound which housed his headquarters, and had once been the dower house to the palace; it was surrounded by trees and had a fine view of the distant Hindu Kush. The lights burned in welcome as the big Zil bumped past the sentries and purred up the drive. Another KGB man, in civilian clothes, was waiting at the steel door for his master. As Orlov got out of the car, the guard pressed a buzzer and in response to his signal the door clicked open. It could only be opened electronically from the inside. Orlov gave instructions to the driver and disappeared into the house, which still retained something of the grandeur it had known in the days of King Zahir Shah.

The driver cursed the Comrade General as he bumped out of the gate again and headed for the other side of Kabul. Why couldn't he keep his floozie in his villa like the rest of them? He hated these night-time excursions through the deserted city. It was so badly lit, you never knew when you were going to lose your way or run into something. The last thing he wanted to run into was a bloody bandit ambush. That had happened to a couple of the other drivers in the past few months. Hello, what was that ahead? The driver pulled the big car hard over nervously but relaxed when he saw it was a stationary Russian armoured-car patrol, lights dipped. Relieved, he accelerated again. Those two drivers. They'd hushed it all up but everybody knew they had been ambushed by the bloody bandits. Shot them up good and proper and left them at the side of the road. Nasty mess they had made of them too, by all accounts. Slit their bellies and cut their balls off. My God, it didn't bear thinking about.

The driver pressed the accelerator down and the big car bounded along the empty road. Even the centre of Kabul was dead after sundown. Who'd want to go out, anyway, in this bloody place? No bars, no clubs, nothing. Just flea-bitten coffee and tea shops and the smelly old bazaar. Far better to stay in and drink in the sergeants' mess. At least you could get a decent drink at a decent price and know that you wouldn't be stabbed in the back on the way home.

The driver made a right turn into a tree-lined street with some big houses set well back in large gardens. He stopped outside the only house with a light on above the gate and sounded his horn. He wasn't getting out of the car for all the vodka in Kabul, that he bloody well wasn't. He hooted again impatiently, conscious that he presented a tempting target to any bandit skulking around with a gun in his hand. As the blast of the horn echoed along the empty street the gate squeaked and a woman, wearing a long cloak and with a scarf half across her face, slipped out of the shadows and came towards the car.

She brought a whiff of expensive perfume into the car with her, and the slithering of silk. She greeted the driver in Russian and he grunted a reluctant reply. Then, after making a U-turn, he sped back the way he had come, depositing the Afghan tart, as he described her to his mates in the sergeants' mess, at the front door of the villa just twenty minutes later.

A KGB man took Zarina's coat and escorted her across the hall, its walls hung with trophies of the chase, including some magnificent heads of Marco Polo sheep, with long, curving horns. He knocked, and when a voice responded, opened the door deferentially.

Orlov got up out of a chair and advanced to meet his guest. He was wearing a velvet smoking jacket and a silk shirt open at the neck.

'Ah, Zarina, how beautiful you are tonight. Come over here to the light so that I may have a proper look at you.' He drew her over to the wood fire that crackled comfortably in the grate and kissed her. She chastely offered him her cheek in case the bodyguard was watching.

As the door closed behind the bodyguard-cum-butler, Orlov lifted Zarina's scarf from her hair and pulled her towards him. She was almost as tall as he and he hardly had to bend to kiss her on the lips. They were cool and soft. He spent a long time kissing her.

Finally she broke away with a little laugh. 'Sergei, you are so passionate.'

'Don't you like me to be passionate?'

She laughed again. 'Of course, it's just that you make me out of breath.'

She had a soft, slightly husky voice which Orlov found extremely attractive. He held her at arm's length and studied her. She had an almost perfectly oval face, with arching black eyebrows above huge dark eyes which could flash imperiously but which, now, were as soft as velvet. Her mouth was another perfect, slimmer oval and her teeth, when she laughed, which she did often, were small and very white. Her body was concealed in a long silk dress, midnight blue slashed with red, made in New York and a present from Orlov. But he knew from their previous encounters that it was also perfect, young, firm and very voluptuous. For one so young and undoubtedly of good family – whether royal or not – she was also an adept lover. He had been pleasantly surprised. Very pleasantly. And as for calling him passionate, she herself had been extraordinarily passionate. He smiled at the recollection

81

of past delights and the promise of more, much more, to come.

'But I nearly forgot. Darling Zarina, I have a present for you. Close your eyes. Are they shut? There.' He pressed a small packet into her hand and stood back. She unwrapped it with little cries of delight like a child.

'Oh, Sergei, how kind of you. My favourite perfume.' She threw her arms round his neck impulsively and kissed him full on the lips.

'Come,' Orlov said. 'We'll have dinner. Are you hungry, *dorozhka*? I have some caviar specially for you. Flown in from Moscow today. Fresh. You know how difficult it is to get fresh caviar in this God ... in Kabul, I mean.' Orlov pressed a bell by the fireplace and the butler reappeared.

'Bring in the food,' Orlov told him. They ate in front of the fire, from a low table, sitting together on a sofa covered with a fox-skin rug. Orlov took a spoon and helped Zarina to the shiny red grains of the fresh caviar. Then he helped himself and filled their glasses with his best vodka – specially manufactured for the KGB. He lifted his glass in a toast. 'To your beauty and my passion.' They clinked glasses.

'You know,' Orlov said, 'your company gives me such great pleasure – of course it's always a pleasure in itself, but especially after a day like today.'

'Why, was today very bad?'

Orlov sighed. 'Yes, we had more problems than usual. We managed, but as soon as you solve one problem, there's another waiting. And when you solve that, there's another, and another. And so on.'

'My poor Sergei,' she said softly. 'I will do my best to cheer you up after dinner.'

Orlov ran his hand lightly over Zarina's thigh. 'You darling girl. I am all impatience, I assure you. But there is something I wanted to ask you, a little favour.'

'What is it, Sergei? Anything.'

'Do you not have a sister in the Panjsher, Zarina?'

'Yes, I do.'

'Is she as pretty as you?' Orlov was stroking Zarina's thigh gently.

'She is much prettier than me.'

'Impossible, my darling. Older or younger?'

'One year older.'

'How delightful. Well, my sweet, I want you to visit your sister. Listen carefully, it is a very important assignment.'

After a few minutes he stood up and pulled her to her feet. 'Come upstairs,' he ordered.

Seven

The sun rose behind their right shoulders, sending their shadows leaping ahead of them along the path and drawing a rich scent from the ranks of pines that marched up the hillside. All morning they rode at a brisk pace, climbing steadily, the track getting steeper and rougher. Before the final approach to the top of the pass, they halted for a breather. The great barren southern flank of the Hindu Kush rose up before them, an impressive and intimidating barrier. Beyond lay Afghanistan, the war and, as Wills reminded himself, an adventure that seemed more hazardous the more he thought about it. The plan was to reach the Panjsher Valley, north-east of Kabul and about 250 miles from the border, where they would pick up the converted petrol tankers and some of Durran's men. The mouth of the valley was roughly half way between Kabul and the Salang so they were in effect taking a short cut and avoiding the risk of entering the capital. Security round it, they had heard, was extremely tight, with Soviet and Afghan Communist troops manning roadblocks and stopping and searching all traffic.

The party had been kept small for speed of movement and to attract as little attention as possible. Large parties, especially arms convoys and long straggling groups of refugees, were easy to spot in the barren wilderness of the Afghan countryside and therefore prone to bombs or ambushes. The Spetsnaz had been increasingly active in the border area recently, successfully ambushing one arms convoy and several parties of refugees. So there were only five of them: apart from Wills and Gradinsky there was Panna, the commander who had blown up the Russian bomb convoy in the Salang a couple of months earlier, and two tough-looking boys, Ali and Mirza, obviously brothers, dressed in khaki trousers and black Russian army boots. Each carried an AK47 and wore a black imitation leather jacket with 'Kung Fu' stencilled on the back. When they had met at Mastuj the night before, Gradinsky had muttered to Wills, 'They have nice smiles but they look as if they would happily shoot their own grandmothers.'

Wills told him, 'But only after they had shot yours first.'

Panna, who had been chosen as their escort because he was a close confidant of Durran and also spoke excellent English, having been educated in America, squatted down beside Wills and Gradinsky while the brothers lit a fire of twigs and brushwood and put their blackened kettle on to make tea.

'At the top of the mountain, up there,' Panna indicated with a lift of his chin, 'we come to the first pass. It's about 13,000 feet and quite easy, really. I want to get over it early enough for us to make camp in the valley by dark. We will probably meet some of the Badakhshani mujahideen you saw at Mastuj. There is a big party of them going in. We won't travel with them but they may have some up-to-date intelligence of the route farther in.'

'If we let them go first, they'll spring any ambush that the Russians have set up.' Wills was ever practical.

Gradinsky laughed approvingly. 'If it's a big convoy I think it would be wise to stay well away from it.' He peered up at the empty blue sky above them. 'We want to stay clear of the choppers; they're always bad news near the border, they're usually looking for people like us.'

They finished the refreshing pale green tea, liberally laced with sugar, and ate a handful of dried mulberries, called *tut*, which the mujahideen carry on long journeys. They are light and keep well and give them, at any rate, enough energy to cover vast distances without any other apparent means of sustenance.

The climb now became harder and Wills and Gradinsky dismounted and led their horses up the stony track, which zigzagged exhaustingly in a series of steep hairpin bends. Wills, stopping to gulp air into his unacclimatised lungs, saw a flash of yellow and found himself looking down on the great planing shape of a lammergeier vulture. He had a fleeting impression of a piercing yellow eye and majestic wingspan above the yellow ruff which gives the bird its Latin name of *Gypaetus barbatus*, or bearded vulture. At the same time, and no doubt explaining the vulture's interest, they smelt the strong putrid stench of decaying flesh, strong enough to make Wills jerk his horse's reins and hurry upwards.

'There, beside those rocks. You can see. A dead horse.' Gradinsky pointed to their left. As they climbed higher, the carcase came into view, spreadeagled across the rocks, its ribs straining the rotting brown hide. The eye sockets stared blindly at the sky, picked clean no doubt by the lammergeier which came swinging past again on its great, silent, outstretched wings, the cruel beak silhouetted for a moment against the blue of the sky.

'Yes, there are many sights like that on these mountains.' Panna was waiting for them, his breathing untroubled by the long pull to the summit ridge. The brothers had already reached the top and were sitting happily on a rock surveying the scene beyond. 'Sometimes when the horses become too weak to carry on they simply wander off the path and wait to die.' The Afghan was matter-of-fact. All war is by definition cruel, and he was inured, after eight years of fighting, to much greater cruelties than the death of a pack horse.

The panorama before them was vast, a great sea of mountain ranges with soaring snow-capped peaks and saw-toothed ridges stretching as far as the eye could see. Wills turned to look into the sun.

'Over there, somewhere, must be Everest.' They shaded their eyes against the brilliant light, but the haze and the distance defeated them. To the north, they knew, lay their destination. 'My God, Anatoly, you see what we've got to cross? Another four passes like this one. Two or three hundred miles of rock and blasted heath. That's Shakespeare swearing, by the way, not me.'

They went down fast, their heels jarring on the hard ground, the horses slipping and stumbling, the mountain unfolding beneath them like a vast *terra incognita*, the far side of an undiscovered planet, empty of all life except for

86

the shadow of the lammergeiers and the quicksilver flash of
an occasional lizard disappearing from its lookout position
on a warm rock. It was a surprise when Panna, twenty yards
ahead down the slope, stopped and waved his arms.

'Hurry. Helicopters ahead. We must get to the shelter of
those rocks.'

Wills and Gradinsky stopped and listened. They could
hear nothing and the vast bowl of the sky seemed empty.
But the two young Afghans, who were further ahead, were
gesticulating excitedly, their hearing twice as sharp as
Wills's and Gradinsky's. Panna shouted again. 'Hurry, they
are coming this way and they travel fast.'

It was only when they had descended another twenty
yards or so that Wills caught for the first time the faint beat
of the rotor blades and, stopping, strained his eyes in the
direction of the sound. After a few seconds, he made out a
tiny speck, and then, some distance behind, another. Panna
was shouting more urgently now from the slabs of rock that
stood out on an otherwise bare mountainside.

'Quick, run, take cover.' Wills bounded down the last few
yards, tugging his horse behind him, his boots skidding on
the scree. Panna and the two young Afghans were sheltering
behind the rocks.

Wills spoke in angry jerks, between gasps for breath.
'Don't be bloody silly ... they couldn't possibly see us ... at
that range.'

He peered upwards. The helicopters were clearly visible
now, two of them in line astern, but still small in the sky. If
the helicopters looked that small to them from the ground,
Wills knew, they would be microscopic dots to anyone in
the air, and if they were not moving, virtually invisible. But
Wills still did not know how terrifying the mujahideen, even
veterans like Panna, found helicopters.

Panna was equally angry. 'They can see you from a long
way away. They have special devices, like telescopic sights,
and they can easily pick up the horses. It is the horses that
are easy to see,' he said half accusingly. Only Wills and
Gradinsky had horses.

Gradinsky said nothing, as if this was a quarrel that did
not concern him. He was watching the helicopters closely,
shading his eyes with his hand.

'Mi24Ds, probably from Bagram. Carrying a full load of rockets and bombs.'

The lead helicopter was menacingly large now, heading towards them but slightly to the left. It changed course as it neared the ridge behind them, and started to fly along it. Wills wondered what the lammergeiers would make of this unaccustomed and noisy competition. The young Afghans, keeping one eye on the helicopters and the other on the horses, manoeuvred them round the rocks so that they were always behind cover, although it was difficult to keep out of view of both helicopters at the same time.

Suddenly they saw the first helicopter veer away from the pass and Panna guessed at once.

'They've seen something... It must be...'

The sentence was cut short by a series of sharp cracks. At the same time streaks of pale grey smoke shot from the Mi24D's belly, fore and aft. Then, muffled by the bulk of the intervening mountain, they faintly heard the rapid-fire crash of the rockets landing.

'The other bastard is going to have a go now.' Wills was watching the second gunship steadying itself above the ridge and then, when the pilot had lined up on the unseen target, they again heard the hiss of rockets being fired and the ripple of explosions.

Gradinsky leaned towards Wills. 'From here, it sounds nothing. But if you were underneath, I can tell you...'

'I know ... I was once on the receiving end ... in Angola. It wasn't funny.' Wills could still remember the vicious sound as the rockets had flown frighteningly close over his head and exploded, luckily harmlessly, in the bush behind.

The first helicopter by now had made a big circle and was coming in again for a second strike. As it wheeled at about 500 feet above the ridge it started dropping decoy flares.

'They're worried about ground-to-air missiles, Stingers.' Gradinsky turned his head slightly to watch the second helicopter. It was half way through its circle. 'You see, they are really too high to be fully effective. But the pilots have orders to keep above a certain height because of the possibility of missiles.'

Wills nodded. He was watching how the flares were fired almost horizontally.

'They don't want to take any chances. Everyone is under orders now to keep casualties to a minimum. Don't take unnecessary risks. That's the watchword, and that's why professional soldiers as opposed to political commissars are fed up with the whole thing.'

The Mi24D fired another salvo: first came the twin streaks of smoke and then a few seconds later the vicious crack of the rockets.

The second helicopter was coming in at a different angle.

'Look out, he's going to bomb,' Gradinsky warned. After shooting out half a dozen flares which went spinning away like shooting stars in the bright sunlight, the shark-nosed gunship steadied itself above the mountain and released two bombs. They saw them clearly in the bright air, two deadly black-finned cylinders, falling swiftly. The second helicopter had wheeled well away by the time they heard the muffled explosions, two bursts of distant thunder. Minutes later the first mushroom of dirty brown smoke rose above the ridge and was whipped away by the wind.

The helicopters circled once more without firing and then beat their way back to the north-west, the way they had come.

Panna was on his feet. 'I'm going back to see what happened. I think they were attacking the Badakhshanis.'

He started to race up the mountain at a pace that Wills and Gradinsky could not match, and was already near the scene of the attack by the time they reached the top of the pass again, gasping for air.

At first they could detect nothing, then they began to see a few heads moving among the rocks. The mujahideen had scattered when they heard the helicopters and were still spread out, in case the gunships came back. Wills saw there was a small group just off to one side of the path.

'It looks as if someone's hurt, let's get down there.'

It took them only a few minutes to scramble down the stony slope that they had struggled up with such effort an hour or two before.

A small knot of men was clustered round two figures on the ground. Panna straightened up as Wills and Gradinsky approached.

'It was the bombing. You see...' He pointed to a shallow

crater near the path. The explosion had gouged out what little earth there was and carved white scars across the grey bedrock.

'The splinters must have acted as shrapnel.' Wills could well imagine the deadly effect of the bomb blast on that bare surface.

'Yes. Just like shrapnel. One young mujahid was killed on the spot, the other one is wounded. I don't know how badly. We are treating him now.' The group of mujahideen made way when they saw Wills and Gradinsky, and there was a low chorus of 'Doktor, Doktor': the only Westerners most Afghans ever saw here were the French doctors who provided virtually the only medical attention that was available in the 'liberated' or guerrilla-held areas, which covered roughly eighty per cent of the country.

A young man lay on the ground, half wrapped in a thin woollen *pattu*, his face pale with shock and pain. A medical orderly was bending over him, trying to pick the bits of jagged rock out of his chest and side.

'He's had an anaesthetic?' Wills asked Panna.

'Yes, luckily they had just picked up fresh medical supplies from the other side of the border.'

The leader of the group, the hawk-nosed man they had met earlier at Mastuj who was kneeling beside the boy, stood up to shake hands. Panna translated.

'He says he is sorry to meet you again in such bad circumstances.'

Wills bent his head. 'We are sorry too for the loss of one of his men. Can we do anything to help the wounded man?'

Hawknose shook his head, Panna translated his reply. 'We are doing what we can for him now and tonight he will go back to Pakistan. Luckily he has come only a short distance and, Allah be praised, he is not badly hurt. But it is better we don't stay here, in case they try to attack us again. Why don't you come with us tonight? We will have scouts in case the Spetsnaz are watching this route. Then tomorrow we will move first and you can follow. That way, it will be safer for you.'

As they climbed back up the mountain to the pass, Panna recounted an incident he had witnessed a year or so before.

'We were approaching the Panjsher from the Nuristani

side. We were just climbing the last pass, at Chamar, when we saw four helicopters rocketing and bombing just like today. We got to the pass an hour later and found that the victims were all refugees, women and children and old men. No mujahideen at all. They had been surprised near the top of the pass and it was very bare. The helicopters shot them down as they ran about on the side of the mountain. It must have been like shooting rabbits. They killed about forty, and also many horses and donkeys. We met some of the survivors. They were so frightened they could hardly tell us what had happened. Now we try and send always some mujahideen with refugees, so at least they take cover when they hear the helicopters.'

'I remember the Chamar massacre,' Wills said. 'Some journalists happened to be going the other way, otherwise we would never have heard of it.'

By the time they reached the foot of the pass on the far side of the mountain, another fifteen miles or so on, it was nearly dark. Hawknose ignored the first village, where the river gurgled quietly between dark willows and a few cows grazed peacefully on the wide meadows. This was the obvious stopping place for caravans and it would be the obvious target for a surprise attack. Instead they pushed on for another hour until the valley narrowed and another, smaller village appeared out of the dusk, the houses clinging to the hillside like the mud nests of a colony of house martins. A few lights flickered in the dusk and voices came towards them.

The headman, a thick-set, talkative figure, arrived and embraced Hawknose and then led them to their lodging place for the night: the mosque. It was dry, relatively roomy and there was fresh hay on the floor. They would be comfortable here and welcome, despite being infidels, Panna explained. No, they would not interfere with the prayers. Wills and Gradinsky unrolled their sleeping bags in one corner and lay down to rest.

Panna, who had disappeared with the headman, came back in half an hour and said they had been invited to supper. It had not been easy to arrange and money had changed hands. 'These people have very little food now. The Russians kill all the animals and destroy the crops, although there has not been too much bombing here. Other villages are much worse.'

'I'm surprised they allow the mujahideen to stay here.' Wills stood up and dusted the hay from his jacket. 'It's an invitation to the Russians to come and bomb them, isn't it?'

'Yes, you are right. Many villagers, now, do not want the mujahideen to come near them. They are too frightened. But others, like this man here, say it is their patriotic duty to look after the fighters in the *jehad*, our Holy War. So they take the risk. But it is becoming more difficult.'

Gradinsky forced his great shoulders into the old combat jacket which he still wore, but without insignia. 'It is the policy, as you know. Scorched earth, we called it in the Great Patriotic War. But that was while we withdrew. So the Germans would find nothing as they advanced. Now we have adopted the same policy in Afghanistan, but this time to drive out the Afghans. When the country is empty we will resettle it with new Afghans, Communist Afghans, and they will build another new Afghanistan. God forgive us, my friends.'

'You are right. But we will fight to the last breath to stop that happening. Come, let us go, the headman awaits us in his house.'

Panna led the way between the houses and up a steep cliff to the last house perched on a rock at the top of the village. It was almost dark, but they could just see that the house was built of great timber beams and the mud walls were several feet thick. Inside there were carpets on the floor and the smell of cooking. After removing their boots, they were ushered into a big room full of men, including Hawknose and his lieutenants. They were made to sit down on the carpet and plump cushions were thrust behind their backs. The room was noisy with talk and extremely hot. Wills, unable to understand the conversation and tired after the day's long march, found himself dozing off.

Panna shook him by the shoulder. 'Come, wake up, they are bringing the food.' The host and his sons proceeded to spread a long cloth on the floor, between the squatting men. Then while one young man expertly threw a flat piece of *nan* in front of every diner, the others brought in a series of dishes which they placed, as directed by the host, in front of the guests, starting with Hawknose and the foreigners and then the others, in descending order of importance. The foreigners, being infidels, and therefore thought by the more devout to be unclean, were served separately. The food was copious but simple, mostly rice and vegetables, and the Afghans at least ate with gusto.

After dinner, the host was questioned by Hawknose and Panna on the state of the route north and the latest signs of Russian activity and Panna relayed his replies to Wills and Gradinsky.

'They bombed several villages not far from here last week. They killed about ten people and a few cows and donkeys. Four houses were destroyed. One little girl had her arm blown off. But apart from that it has been quiet.'

'Any recent Spetsnaz activity?' Panna asked.

'No, not here. But farther north, we are getting reports of a big action.'

'Where was that?'

'In the Laghman area. They say the mujahideen attacked a big convoy, killing a number of *Shurawi*. So they came and bombed all the villages the next day and then they sent in the soldiers and killed a lot of people.'

'Civilians?'

'All civilians.'

Wills looked at Panna. 'Do we go that way?'

Panna consulted with their host. 'He says maybe. It will depend on the latest information. It is one way to go. Why? You want to see?'

'Not particularly, but if that is your route, then I would be interested to see how they operate. And the people might need our help?'

'If they are not all dead.' Panna's voice was matter-of-fact but Wills could hear the bitterness behind the words.

To see them home, their host lit a couple of cedar branches, the resin in the wood crackling and flaring, casting a brilliant orange light, bright enough for them to negotiate the steep path down the rocks back to the mosque. Wills looked up at the stars. They were by contrast utterly remote and pure, giving the night a majestic calm and beauty.

Hawknose left before daybreak, sending scouts out well

ahead and splitting the main party into three separate sections, each of between twenty and thirty men.

'They're beginning to learn, not before time.' Wills wondered as he spoke what Hawknose's reaction would have been if he had known that Gradinsky was a *Shurawi*, and a former Spetsnaz into the bargain.

They left an hour later, just as the sun was coming up over the eastern mountains, its appearance preceded by a delicate wash of the palest pink which lasted only a few minutes. At first the valley opened green and peaceful before them, but soon began to grow narrower and rougher. The track became brutally hard on the horses, the jagged rocks cutting their fetlocks and the overhanging crags threatening to send horses and riders tumbling into the river which dashed itself against the boulders a hundred feet below.

For four days they climbed up and down through alpine scenery of a beauty that under normal circumstances would have been a constant source of delight but which now, in the light of what was happening ahead of them, seemed almost obscene.

They eventually came to a small cluster of houses, gilded by the late afternoon sun and perched on a hilltop like a medieval Italian village. Here Panna embarked on a lengthy discussion with local greybeards while Wills and Gradinsky sat down to rest under a leafy arbour hung with long, green, half ripe grapes. The two young mujahideen went into the village to forage for food, eventually returning with some goats' cheese and small yellow apples. Shortly afterwards Panna too reappeared.

'They say the normal route is too dangerous. They have reports that the Russians landed commandos on the top of the pass a few days ago and they may have ambushed the mujahideen.'

'Did they go through here yesterday?'

'Two days ago.'

Wills looked at Gradinsky. 'I thought we had been travelling fast.'

'They go at what we call mujahideen pace. For us it is different.'

Both Wills and Gradinsky laughed. 'So what do we do?'

'We take that other route we talked about before.'

'Where you said there had been a Russian operation against some villages? Won't that make things difficult for us?'

'The old men here tell me that they have gone. You know, they come in their tanks and trucks and make their sweeps through the villages and then they go back to barracks. They know if they stay too long the mujahideen will cut them off and kill them. We will sleep here tonight. They have food for us and the horses. Tomorrow we leave early.'

After the gruelling steep climbs and long forced marches of the past few days, it was a luxury for Wills and Gradinsky to eat well and loll at their ease. But Panna was nervous. Curious village boys who came to stare at them were quickly shooed away by the brothers.

'Please come into the house. Everywhere you go these days, there are spies. You cannot trust anyone.'

Wills wondered if Panna was exaggerating. 'Spies? Who are all these spies that everyone talks about?'

'KHAD. Kabul has people everywhere. Because they pay a lot of money.' He held up his forefinger and thumb and rubbed them together. 'They get the money from the Russians. They are always trying to find out what Durran is doing, where he is, who is with him...

'They even send young boys to spy on him. Yes, young boys. We caught one aged twelve the other day. He had been trained in the Soviet Union, in sabotage and all kinds of intelligence work. You know that?' he shot at Gradinsky.

'Yes.' Gradinsky sighed. 'It is how the bloody KGB operates. In Russia, too.'

Eight

They came to the plain of Laghman in the late afternoon, and stopped on a low ridge overlooking what had once been a fertile expanse of wheatfields and orchards. The westerly sun gave the villages scattered across the plain an air of calm and well-being, but it was an illusion. Wills, who had slipped his rucksack on to the ground and was sitting with his back against a rock, shaded his eyes.

'Is this the place, Panna? These villages all look deserted.'

'Yes, this is the place. That village over there used to have maybe thirty families – that's 300 people. Now there are maybe ten. If you look carefully you can see that nearly all the houses are in ruins. And over there, that village, is the same. And the village beyond. There are ten or twelve villages in this area and it is the same in every one.'

Gradinsky had a small pair of binoculars with which he was studying the scene intently. 'Yes, you are right. I can see that the houses have been bombed very heavily, or else destroyed by tank fire.'

'Both,' Panna replied. 'They bombed first and then they sent in the tanks. But you will see for yourselves. In five minutes, when you have rested, we will walk to the first village. Maybe we can find someone who is still living there.'

They set off down the last slope, crossed a small stream and walked along the edge of the untended and empty fields. Even at this time of year, the winter wheat should have been showing green in the cold ground. But the fields were parched and dead. Their feet, almost silent on the dry earth, kicked up little spurts of dust. An irrigation ditch which in normal times would have been brimming with

96

clear water was empty, the earth at the bottom caked and cracked.

They came to what had been a large farmhouse standing at the edge of the fields. It looked as if it had taken a direct hit, with shattered wooden beams lying among the rubble and the pathetic remnants of a peasant household scattered about: a woman's blue and red dress; a single laceless shoe; a broken teapot. No dog barked, no animal moved. They passed another group of houses. These were less badly damaged but the doors stood disconsolately open and they had the same air of abandonment.

Panna went to one doorway and looked in. 'The Russians have been here. Look, you can see the bullet marks.'

Gradinsky pointed to a window. 'And also the burn marks. They were probably using incendiary grenades. They fire them into the house and the whole place goes up.' Inside, a few wisps of charred cloth and some smashed crockery were trampled into the earth floor.

Crossing another dry irrigation channel, they skirted a huge bomb crater and another empty house. The door into the courtyard was wide open and as he passed Panna saw a small flash of movement. He stopped, AK74 at the ready, and advanced, alert for trouble. Something flickered again among the branches. It was a hand, the hand of an old man half hidden behind a trellis.

'Hallo, old man, what are you doing there?'

The old man's face appeared, terror in his eyes. He made as if to turn and run, but Panna called in Farsi, 'Don't run, old man, we are friends.'

After a long, doubting look the old man finally came towards them. His voice quavered as he tried to control his fear. 'God be with you. Where do you come from? Did you see anyone on the outskirts of the village?'

'You mean villagers? No, you are the first person we've seen.'

'No, I mean ... *Shurawi*.' His voice trembled so much he could hardly pronounce the word.

'*Shurawi*? No, not a sign. Why, are you expecting them to come?'

The old man began to tremble, first his lips, then his head and finally his whole body. The spasm lasted about a minute. One of the two young mujahideen offered the old man a drink from his water bottle. After hesitating, he took it but his hand shook so much, that it spilled down his chin.

'Someone's really put the fear of God into this old boy.' Wills had understood only the word *Shurawi* but he could guess the drift of the conversation. 'What's his story, Panna? Why's he so frightened?'

'He hasn't told me yet, but I will ask him when he has calmed down.'

The old man led them to the back of the courtyard and through a small wooden door set in the corner behind the enormously thick stem of the vine that covered the trellis. On the other side of the mud wall was a small inner courtyard, with a shed or stable built against the highest part of the wall.

Panna questioned the old man. 'He says the Russians looted his house and set fire to it but they did not find this courtyard and so he escaped. He thinks he is the only one who stayed in the village not to have been killed. Some of the people ran away before the Russians came.'

The old man looked wonderingly at the two foreigners. His reedy voice questioned Panna while his watery eyes appraised the strangers. Panna's reply contained the word 'Angrez'.

Wills looked at Gradinsky. 'He says you're English. That's quite a compliment. If he told him the truth, the old man would get his flintlock and shoot you dead.'

Gradinsky grinned. 'Panna's a good diplomat. He'll go far, this boy.' Panna, who had overheard their conversation, smiled rather sheepishly. 'The old man wants to offer you hospitality. He has a little food and will make some tea.'

'We can't take his food,' Wills protested. 'Let's get some of our own provisions, for God's sake.'

Panna shook his head. 'No, the law of Afghan hospitality would not permit him to accept. But don't worry, I will give him something privately tomorrow when you are not there. Please go inside.'

Amazingly, the old man had salvaged a modicum of order and even comfort from the thunderbolt which had struck his home, scattering his possessions and destroying his family. He boiled a kettle and poured tea with a shaky hand.

'What happened?' Panna prompted.

The voice quavered and then got stronger as he warmed to his tale. 'The mujahideen attacked a big convoy north of here about a week ago. They blew up many lorries and killed many *Shurawi* and puppet troops. Then they went away. Next day the Russian bombers came. All morning they bombed. My house was hit and my wife and sister-in-law were killed. Praise be to Allah my two grandchildren and their mother had fled the day before. I sent them away. I feared what might happen. In the afternoon, the soldiers came. I heard the noise of the tanks as they approached across the plain. Then we heard shooting in the next village.

'I went up to the roof. Half had fallen in, but I managed to climb up in one corner. I saw the tanks, a hundred, two hundred. They were drawn up round the village and were shooting at the houses. Then they stopped shooting and the soldiers, the *Shurawi* soldiers, went in.'

'How does he know they were *Shurawi* and not Afghan soldiers?'

Panna grinned as he translated. 'The old man says you can tell by their uniforms, which are a lighter colour. And they do not walk like Afghans. You could never mistake a Russian soldier if you had once seen one, he says.' Wills caught Gradinsky's eye and winked.

'Go on.'

'There was a lot more shooting from inside the village. After half an hour or so, the soldiers started to set fire to the houses. First they looted and then they burned.'

'How do you know they looted?'

'I saw. They came out carrying clothes and carpets. They always take watches from the men and jewellery from the women. Everyone knows that. Then they came to this village. First the tanks shot at the houses, and then the soldiers came. I heard them talking here, right outside.'

'Where were you?'

'I stayed up there in the corner of the roof. I was too frightened to move. I saw and heard everything. I heard the soldiers looting my own house. When I buried my wife later, I saw her hands. They had cut off her fingers to take her rings.'

99

The old man broke down and cried, wiping his tears with his ragged sleeve.

'And they never came in here?' Wills looked round at the spartan furnishings of the little room.

'They never found the inner courtyard. They took what they wanted in my house and then there was shouting from next door. They had found someone and the soldiers left my house and went there.'

'What did they find?'

'There were two young boys there who had not run away in time. They asked the two boys: "*Dost* or *dushman*?" Friend or foe? The smaller boy who was only about ten, said "Friend." But the other boy, who was twelve or thirteen, said "*dushman*", meaning he was on the side of the mujahideen.

'They hit him with their rifle butts, on the face and across his shoulders. They broke his teeth but still he refused to give in. His face was all bloody and cut but he did not beg for mercy.' The old man gulped, his eyes recalling the horror of what he had witnessed. 'Then after a while they led him out into the field beyond the houses. There was an old water pump there which belonged to my neighbour, Ahmed. It was not working properly and he had been trying to repair it. It was lying on the ground, so the Russians made the boy pick it up and carry it round the field. It was very heavy, the pump, and they made him carry it round and round for an hour, maybe two hours. When he fell down they kicked and beat him until he got up again. In the end he fell down and he could not get up again. He was unconscious.

'They threw water in his face and when he was able to stand again they took him and tied him to a tree in the corner of the field. They also placed a mine in the ground at his feet. They left him there all night and in the morning, they came and offered him bread and water. He was so weak that he could hardly lift his head but he still refused to take anything, even the water. So they hit him again with their rifles and then they started to shoot at the mine from a distance. Some of the bullets hit the boy. One in the leg, another in the foot. Because the mine was only a few inches from his feet. Once he called out to Allah...'

The tears came to the old man's eyes again and he had to clear his throat several times before he could continue. 'He called to Allah the All-Merciful to come and take him to Heaven. And to give him strength. Then one bullet hit the mine and it exploded with a big noise and a cloud of dust. And when the dust settled I saw the boy was dead. Allah be praised. The Russians left him there. When they had gone, and when it was dark, I cut his body down and buried him. I will show you his grave, if you like.'

There was a long silence in the little room. Wills suddenly felt cold.

Gradinsky got up and stood in the doorway, looking out. 'They are animals. I can hardly believe it. This terrible war, how I hate it...' Then he said, so quietly that only Wills heard, 'My country, my country, what are they doing to Mother Russia, these new barbarians?'

It was nearly dark when the old man ventured out into the fields. The beam of a torch showed them a freshly turned patch of earth which was the boy's grave. The old man had placed a few stones at one end to hold a stick, to which he had tied two scraps of cloth, one green, one white, to show this was the grave of a mujahid, or as the old man said, 'the resting place of a martyr'.

They left the next morning and, as he had promised, Panna gave the old man some money. They heard him protesting but finally he accepted, saying he would stay in his house until Allah sent for him. His whole life was here and he was too old to make the long trek to Pakistan and the chaotic new world of the refugee camps.

They walked north through the deserted country, avoiding the villages themselves, keeping to the edges of the fields and the empty irrigation channels. They saw no one, although there may have been a few survivors like the old man, too terrified to show themselves by day and too old to want to leave. The sense of a great disaster lay over the villages, as if some volcanic eruption or plague had struck without warning and left a landscape devoid of human or animal habitation. The only thing that moved was a kite planing on stiff wings, hunting for small rodents.

They marched hard for two more days, reaching the southern approaches to the Panjsher Valley late one evening.

Panna left them with the two young mujahideen while he went ahead to reconnoitre, coming back half an hour later to say they were welcome to stay the night in the head-quarters of the local commander, a cave on the side of the mountain. No one used their houses here any more. They had either been destroyed or were considered too dangerous. In the Panjsher, where there had been so much fighting over the years, they had learned the lesson which the villagers of the Laghman plain had learned so disastrously late.

It was dark by the time they had climbed to the commander's outpost, the stars huge and brilliant in the blackness of the sky. While they waited for food, Gradinsky, who had been lying on his back on the floor, turned on one elbow and looked straight at Wills.

'What we saw in those villages, the other day. There has been no time to talk about it. But I cannot get that old man's story out of my mind. You must think we are savages, criminals!'

Wills took a deep breath. His voice was quiet, placatory. 'It was terrible, Anatoly. But all armies do these things, when discipline breaks down. This is a cruel war, on both sides, and by all the signs getting crueller.'

'Yes, I knew such things were happening, but never quite as bad as what we heard the other day.'

'You believe what he told us, about that boy?'

Gradinsky let his breath out in a long sigh. 'I'm afraid so. You see, there's despair now in the army about this war. The young soldiers, the conscripts, do not want to fight in Afghanistan. They say this is not our war. They no longer believe the propaganda they hear that we are fighting the Americans, the Chinese, the Pakistanis, that we are protect-ing the Afghans against outside intervention. They know that this is all lies. Too many young Russians have fought – and died – here now for the propaganda to be believed except by a handful of committed Party members or simpletons. And they cannot escape the call-up. So they opt out in the only way that's open to them. By taking drugs: hashish mostly, but also opium and heroin now. Heroin is the big worry. The High Command is extremely alarmed at the increase in heroin taking.

'So when these boys know they are going on an operation,

they smoke. The officers do too. I have seen whole companies, officers and men, stoned out of their minds. So when they go into a village, where there may be opposition, they kill everything in their path. They no longer care if they are women, or children, or old people. They would kill their own brother or sister. They are crazy. They are literally out of their minds.' The sweat was beaded on Gradinsky's forehead and his voice had risen.

'Take it easy, Anatoly. You must be careful. Someone might overhear you and though hardly any of them speak English...'

They were interrupted by the curtain which hung at the entrance to the cave being swept back. It was the commander, with Panna and several other men. One spread a cloth on the floor, another carried a bowl of water for washing and Panna distributed the *nan*. 'The commander apologises for the poor meal he is setting before you. But he has been away fighting for many days and he has had no time to organise things. He says next time you come he will make a proper feast.'

'Tell him his hospitality is doubly welcome for being so unexpected,' Wills said.

At three in the morning, the dogs started barking in the courtyard and Wills woke to find Panna bending over him.

'Someone very special has arrived to see you.'

Wills sat up and rubbed his eyes.

'It is Durran himself. Get up quickly. He will be here in a moment.'

A few minutes later the commander respectfully ushered in three men, the first of medium height, with a thin intelligent face and a slight stoop of the shoulders which gave him the look of a falcon. The next man was huge, with a great barrel chest and a few strands of grey hair sticking out beneath his cap. The third man was young and watchful and Wills put him down as the bodyguard.

Despite the hour and the fact that he had probably travelled some distance, Durran looked fresh. He came forward with a springy step, hand outstretched to greet the two foreigners, and then sat down cross-legged in the corner, his back to the wall. When he began to talk everyone listened. Wills imagined that few people would have dared to interrupt him. He had an effortless way of establishing his ascendancy and although he spoke quietly, the voice was dynamic, commanding attention.

Panna supplied a running translation. 'The commander says first of all he welcomes you to the Panjsher and to the struggle of the Afghan Resistance against the Russian invader. He is grateful that some foreign countries at least are aware of what is happening here in our beloved homeland.' He paused and Durran, his dark quick eyes moving from one to the other, went on in his quiet, forceful voice.

'Next, he has two very important messsages for you. The first is that he knows from very good sources in Kabul that the Russians are planning a new offensive against the Panjsher in four or five days' time. He expects them to use helicopters to land commandos on strategic high points. At the same time they will send their tanks and armoured personnel carriers up the valley as they have done many times before. The commander says we are ready for them and key sections of the road are mined.

'There are other reasons, too, but for this reason, and because he is concerned for your safety, he wants you to change your plans and go to Kabul instead. You will meet the petrol tankers there and carry on with the original plan. But the commander says there will be some delay. The tankers will have to be registered and we need special documents for them. This can be arranged but it has to be done carefully.'

Wills and Gradinsky looked at one another, equally astonished. 'Go to Kabul? But isn't that more dangerous than staying here?'

'No, you will go to a safe place with me and another escorting officer.'

'You said there were other reasons?'

'Yes. It was originally planned, as you know, that the tankers would come to Charikar where we have a secret workshop and you would take over from there. But the Russians attacked the town again the other day and destroyed a lot of buildings, including the workshop. We have another place in Kabul which is safer. You do not believe me, but you will see. Our people are expecting you.'

'Where are the tankers now?' Gradinsky spoke for the first time. Wills studied Durran to see how he reacted to the Russian. Only he and Panna had been told that Gradinsky was a Russian officer. But Durran's face remained impassive and his tone as matter-of-fact as before.

'They are in Kabul, at our depot. It is a legal depot. They do not know that it belongs to us and it is safer there than in a place like Charikar which the Russians are liable to attack at any time. For this reason we are moving a lot of our business into Kabul, where we can either get protection because people on the government side secretly support us, or because we pay for it. The KHAD have penetrated the Resistance, but we have also penetrated the KHAD.' Durran leaned back and permitted himself a small smile. He had a wispy beard, and a curved, almost Semitic nose. Wills thought he had the most intelligent eyes of any man he had ever met.

'How long do you think we'll have to wait in Kabul?' Wills asked.

Durran shrugged. 'He doesn't know. Maybe some days. . .'

'There was an interruption while tea was brought and served, with dry *nan*. Durran was given a small pot to himself and, instead of a chipped mug, the commander's best cup and saucer. The milk had been already added to the tea in the pot.

'The commander gives us milk tea as a special mark of favour,' Panna whispered.

'For Commander Durran?'

'No, for you as well. Try it. It is very good.'

Durran looked at his watch like a man who does not have much time and fired a question at Panna, who translated. 'You have everything you need for the operation?'

Wills nodded. 'We have Russian uniforms in our rucksacks, a Kalashnikov each and our sidearms: Makarov pistols and ammunition.'

The door opened; a slim figure came quietly into the room and went round the circle shaking hands. To his astonishment, Wills found himself looking into the eyes of an attractive young woman.

'Hello, I'm Fatima.' Her voice was soft and musical but the handshake was strong, like a man's. Her English was strongly accented, but clear.

Wills found himself stammering. 'I did not know you had women in the Resistance.'

'Not many who fight,' Durran explained. 'But there are many women who work for the Resistance in other ways. Fatima is exceptional, as you will see. She speaks very good English and Russian. The two young mujahideen will stay here. She will be your escort to Kabul. One last thing.' He looked at Gradinsky. 'She knows who you are.'

Durran got up in one swift movement and held out his hand. 'He wishes you both great success and hopes we will meet on your return. You will need a few days' rest before you begin the return journey.' He turned and spoke urgently in Farsi to Fatima and Panna. Then, raising his hand in a gesture of farewell, stepped through the door, the big man and young bodyguard close behind him, and was gone.

Fatima picked up her AK74. 'Please follow me. We must reach another, safer place by dawn.'

In the next hour and a half, any doubts they may have had about the stamina of their new escort were rapidly dispelled. The mountain was still in darkness when they started and the going was rough, but Fatima, like all mujahideen, seemed to have the ability to see in the dark. Her stride never faltered and never slackened. When they came to the top of a last steep climb, Wills halted for a minute to catch his breath. 'Where did you learn to walk like that?'

Her voice had a trace of contempt. 'All Afghans can walk like that. We are born to it. Come, it is only another half a mile to the place where we will rest until evening.'

She led the way at a swinging pace, heading west. Before them the bottom of the Panjsher Valley began to take shape, a dim patchwork of fields and rivers rimmed with mountains. In the distance, across the plain, was Kabul, the capital of the Afghan kings, beseiged in turn by the Persians, Alexander the Great and, in more recent times, by the Imperial British: now it lay under the heel of an invader as ruthless as Genghis Khan, as cruel as Tamerlane. Would this invader also be driven out in time, or would he dismember the ancient kingdom and gobble it up as part of his already bloated empire? It was a thought that busied both Wills and Gradinsky as they hastened to beat the sun. For with the sun came the helicopters and danger.

Nine

They stopped beside a big outcrop of rock. Below them the hillside fell away steeply to the plain below. Between two great slabs, a dark crack opened into a large cave. It was as cold as a tomb but someone had uprooted several armfuls of bushes and scattered them over the floor in an attempt to make the place habitable. Wills shivered as the heat generated by their march evaporated and the cold began to seep into their bodies. He wrapped his *pattu*, a thin blanket, round his shoulders and sat with his back against his rucksack so that he could watch a patch of sky lighten through the crack in the rock.

'We're well hidden here,' Fatima said. 'There is a village just below and I have sent Panna down to get some food. We will keep our own supplies as long as we can.'

'I'd have thought all the villages round here would have been deserted.' Gradinsky lay stretched out on the floor, his head on his rucksack.

'Most are. But we keep a network of houses and supply depots in many of these villages. Since the Russian policy is to drive out the villagers and cut off their support for us, we have no alternative.'

'What about the KHAD informers?' Gradinsky asked. 'Don't they give away your hideouts?'

'Yes. It is a big problem. That is why we try to choose an empty village. That way there are no informers and the Russians don't bother us. They are only interested in villages with people whom they can loot and kill.'

Fatima unwound the scarf that had covered half her face and shook her hair free. It was long and curly, and suddenly Wills saw she was a desirable woman.

'Although the Russians have been successful in one way – by driving out the civilians – they have failed in another. They have forced the mujahideen to build up their own supply and intelligence network.'

'That can't be as effective as when you had a large civilian population all helping the mujahideen with food, shelter and information,' Wills objected.

'No, that's true. But, you know, the civilian population sometimes acted as a brake on our operations. In some areas the mujahideen wouldn't attack convoys or outposts because they knew that the Russians would retaliate by bombing the villages. So you got a kind of truce. Good for us but better for them. Now, we don't have that problem. If there are no more villages to bomb, no more civilians to rob and kill and drive into exile, we can fight wherever we want.'

They heard a scrape of metal on the rock and Panna squeezed through the entrance, carrying a battered, blackened pot filled with bread and rice.

Gradinsky sat up. 'My God, I've suddenly realised I'm starving.' Panna deposited the pot in the middle of the floor and they all sat round and scooped at the lukewarm food with their fingers. Wills noticed enviously that the Afghans could squeeze the rice into a ball with a deft movement of the right hand and carry it to their mouths hardly spilling a grain, while he and Gradinsky were lucky to get half the original handful to its destination. They ate in silence until the pot was empty, Panna scraping up the last few grains of rice with a piece of *nan*.

They left the cave in the late afternoon, having slept for most of the day, made their way down the steep hillside while it was still light and waded across the Panjsher river which at that point had five broad but shallow arms.

In the middle, where the current was very fast, Fatima stumbled and for a moment looked as if she would lose her balance. Wills put out a hand to steady her but she shrugged him off and splashed on, reaching the bank a good five yards in front of the others.

'What does it mean, Panjsher?' Wills asked when they had scrambled ashore and recovered their breath.

Fatima, who had waded the river barefoot, forced her wet feet into her boots.

'Some people think it means five lions, but they are wrong, it means five rivers, as you just saw. As in Punjab. *panj* means five in Persian and the Moguls took the word with them when they marched into India.'

A flare rose in a lazy arc half a mile away, burst into incandescence at the top and floated gently down. Fatima immediately gave orders in Farsi, then in English.

'A Russian patrol. We must move quickly.' Another flare rose as the first died, then a third. They marched in single file, first Panna, then Fatima, followed by Wills and Gradinsky, keeping the river on their left and the patrol away to their right. No more flares rose but in the distance they could see a glow in the sky.

'Bagram,' Fatima explained. 'It's a big Russian air base. We have often attacked it and so they have lights on all round it, all night long. And patrols. We do not go too close.'

They marched in silence now, Panna fifty yards in front acting as both guide and scout. After an hour or so the ground became sandy and then powdery, like loess, and as they trudged along their feet kicked up a cloud of dust which clung to their faces and clothing, covering hair and beards with a fine white film, finding its way into their ears and noses and even their throats.

The glow of Bagram grew gradually fainter as they headed towards Kabul, reaching the shelter of higher ground just before sunrise. A derelict village stood in a fold of the hills, the houses eerily empty, the doorways gaping open, like toothless mouths. Panna led the way past the last house, stopping finally by a pile of rocks among which was concealed the entrance to another cave. Wills could see it was well camouflaged and far enough from the village to be reasonably safe from bombing.

Within a few minutes of their arrival, Panna had started a small fire where a crack in the rock provided a natural chimney, and put the kettle on to boil. As if by magic he produced a small sackful of *tut* and *nan* and a small tin of sugar. They ate ravenously, in silence. Having just finished the tea, they were preparing themselves for sleep when Fatima sat up and said one single sharp word. '*Shurawi.*'

Gradinsky cocked his head to listen. It took him and Wills ten seconds before they heard it too.

'Tanks,' Gradinsky barked, scrambling to his feet. The steady rumble of diesel engines and the occasional screech of steel tracks filled the cave with menace.

'Come, we can see from the rocks.' Panna squeezed through the narrow entrance, the others close behind him. As they emerged from the interior of the cave, the noise of the engines was terrifyingly loud, the metallic roar of the powerful diesels reverberating off the hillside. They crawled on their stomachs to the top of the rock and peered cautiously across to the village below. The first thing they saw was a cloud of dust, rising like smoke above the deserted houses, and then beneath it the ponderous stream of Russian battle tanks and armoured personnel carriers, hatches battened down in case of trouble. Wills started counting the number of vehicles and had got up to eighty when he heard a warning from Gradinsky.

Wills followed his outstretched arm and saw that an army jeep had left the road and was bumping across the rough ground towards them. Wills ducked until only the top of his head was showing and watched the jeep drive straight towards the house below them and stop. Three Russians got out, one of them an officer, and walked towards it, fifty yards from the rock. It was one of the few buildings in the village that had not been seriously damaged.

'They are looking for loot,' Gradinsky said contemptuously. As the soldiers disappeared into the house, the Russian sat up and transferred his AK74 ostentatiously from one hand to the other. 'I have an idea.'

'I should keep out of sight,' Wills said sharply. 'We don't want your friends investigating up here.'

Gradinsky ignored him. 'We can take their jeep.'

Wills was taken aback. Was the man insane? He scanned the column. It was almost out of sight now, the engine roar muffled by the intervening hillside, leaving only a cloud of dust hanging in the still, dry air. There was a clink of metal on stone and Wills looked round to find Gradinsky gone. A few moments later, he saw him running in a crouch between the rocks towards the house, which stood in the remains of what had once been a small orchard, the trees now withered and leafless. Gradinsky was about thirty yards from the house when Wills saw him drop suddenly and take cover behind a bush. The Russians were leaving. The first one, the officer, was empty-handed, but the other two had their arms full: one carried a rolled-up carpet, the other what looked like a small chest.

Wills found himself muttering to himself, 'For God's sake, don't do it, you bloody madman.'

The officer walked the last few yards towards the jeep and just as he was about to climb in there was a single shot. He staggered, straightened up and then fell face down. Two more shots rang out. The soldier carrying the carpet lurched like a drunk and fell, half hidden by his booty; the third soldier dropped the chest he was carrying and ran. Gradinsky fired again but missed as the soldier dodged into the trees and made for the road as fast as he could. Wills, who had a better view, stood up and took aim. The man was seventy yards away. He fired in short bursts. The third one got him.

Wills scrambled down the rock, jumping the last six feet to the ground, and ran past the jeep, noticing that the two bodies lay motionless on the ground. It took him twenty seconds to reach the third body, but Gradinsky was there before him.

'You got him. Good shooting, Mike.' He pointed to the soldier who lay face down on the grass, red staining the back of his uniform.

Wills gasped angrily. 'You bloody fool. What the hell did you want to do that for? If he'd got away...'

Fatima and Panna appeared and Panna turned the dead soldier over. He looked very young, no more than twenty, his face unmarked, his mouth open as if in surprise. Gradinsky bent down and closed his eyes with an almost delicate movement.

Fatima's voice was harsh. 'That was very dangerous. Supposing some other Russians had been following them? We might all be dead by now. We must get out of this place, quickly.' Panna dragged the body into the shade of some trees and threw a few dead branches, cut down by the bombing, on top. There was no time to bury it. They

walked back to the jeep and disposed of the other two
bodies in the same way, first removing their weapons. The
officer had been carrying a Makarov pistol. His AK74 was
in the jeep.

Gradinsky got in to the driver's seat and turned the
ignition. The engine started immediately and ticked over
sweetly.

'The tank is full and it looks brand new. We can get to
Kabul by tonight.' He seemed unconcerned by the disapproval of the others and looked slightly mad, Wills
thought. But the reckless act having been committed, there
was nothing for it but to go on. He turned to Fatima, 'What
do you think? Are we likely to be ambushed by the
mujahideen?'

'It's a risk we have to take. We could fly Panna's green
scarf to let them know it's a captured jeep.'

'What about the Russian posts along the road?' Gradinsky
was trying out the gears.

'There is one, maybe two before Charikar. We would
have to hide the scarf and pretend to be Russians.'

'No need to pretend.' Gradinsky opened his rucksack and
pulled out his old Spetsnaz tunic with its major's epaulettes.

Wills examined him. 'You look pretty authentic to me. I'll
do the same.' He had a paratrooper captain's top which he
pulled over his head. 'What can we do about Fatima?' Wills
answered his own question by walking over to the trees
where they had dragged two of the bodies. After a few
moments he came back with the lieutenant's hat and khaki
combat jacket and held them up.

'Fortunately he was pretty small.' He passed the jacket to
Fatima. 'It's better than nothing.'

She made a face when she saw the blood stains but
Gradinsky held the sleeve for her and finally she tried it on.
It was a little too large but in the jeep no one would notice.
Gradinsky looked at Panna and laughed. 'There's nothing
we can do about you. You'll have to be my prisoner!

'Now the hat.' Reluctantly Fatima coiled her thick hair
into a bun and pulled it on. At a distance it would be hard
to tell the wearer was a woman. Her dislike for the disguise
came through in her voice.

'We must leave this place. Someone must know the three

of them left the convoy to search for loot. They may come looking for them.'

Gradinsky started the jeep and turned in the direction of the road. They bumped along the rough village track, past a score of almost totally ruined houses, back to the main road, which was not much more than a track itself. It was empty in both directions. Even the dust from the convoy had settled: all that remained clearly visible were the deep ruts caused by the tank tracks. Gradinsky turned the jeep to the west, towards Kabul, and accelerated sharply. Soon they were careering along at forty miles per hour, the jeep bouncing over the potholes and throwing up a thin stream of dust, like a jet trail, the green scarf trailing in the wind.

They had travelled west for about an hour when a noise like the roar of an express train coming out of a tunnel made Gradinsky swerve wildly, throwing Fatima against Wills in the back seat. Gradinsky braked hard and just got the jeep under control as two MiG 25s, travelling at 700 miles per hour, streaked above them, their jet engine roar drowning all other sounds.

'Christ,' Wills said. 'Just as well they weren't after us.'

'Is that Charikar ahead?' Gradinsky pointed to a fair-sized town in the middle of the plain before them.

Fatima leaned sideways to get a better view, her leg slipping against Wills's. He did not move away and she did not seem to notice.

'Yes, that is Charikar. We must take the scarf off. The first Russian post is about a mile outside the town.' She said something to Panna and he reached upwards as the jeep bumped along and untied the strip of green cloth fastened to the radio aerial.

Gradinsky flipped the switch on the radio and it emitted a piercing whine. He twiddled the tuning dials, found the local army net and listened attentively.

'Sounds like Bagram. They seem to have a strike on against the Panjsher. Could be related to the big convoy we saw.' He listened for a few moments and then tried elsewhere. A voice crackled, receded and then came back strongly. Gradinsky shouted out in surprise and turned excitedly. 'There's been a bomb at the airport. Sounds nasty.

They're calling for ambulances and blood.' He turned back to the radio, steering with one hand.

'Did they say how many casualties?'

'No figures, no.'

Wills could see what looked like a roadblock half a mile ahead. 'Panna, give me your hat. I'd better go in the front until we get past the roadblock. You come in the back.' Panna took off the stetson-like felt hat he had taken from one of the dead soldiers and changed places with him.

The country showed some signs of cultivation now and a few women were working in the fields. Gradinsky slowed down as he approached the roadblock. There was a guard post on each side and a Russian sentry sauntered into the road and casually held up one hand.

When he saw Gradinsky was an officer he straightened up and sketched a lazy salute. Gradinsky stopped and leaned out of the window. 'Morning, Corporal. Is the road ahead clear?' He jerked his head at the rear of the jeep. 'I'm taking someone into Kabul for questioning.'

The sentry's eyes scanned the back of the jeep without interest. He looked as if he were half asleep. Almost certainly on drugs, Wills thought, balancing his AK74 loosely across his knees. He could see two other Russian soldiers in the guardroom on the right but they seemed equally uninterested.

'The road's clear, as far as I know, sir. There was some shooting on the other side of Charikar last night and they say there's been a bomb at the airport. But you should have no trouble.'

'I heard about the bomb,' Gradinsky said revving the engine. 'OK, Corporal, thanks.' He waved a salute, let the clutch in, and drove steadily away.

'Looked as if he was stoned,' Wills said.

'Sure. All of them are. You can see how bloody bored they get, how homesick. Conditions are terrible. The officers get drunk and beat up the soldiers. It's really a terrible life. Why do you think I deserted?'

'I thought it was because of your brother?'

'Yes, that was the real reason. But I hated the whole thing about the war in Afghanistan. The bullying of the new recruits by the old guard. That's fairly normal in our army but it's much worse here. And some of the officers who've volunteered for second and even third tours are crazy. Absolutely crazy. I saw one, one day, shoot a young soldier because he wouldn't stick his bayonet into the belly of an Afghan woman with a baby.

'You mean she was pregnant?'

'Yes, pregnant. Well, he, the officer, did it himself. Stuck the bayonet right into her and then told the recruit to finish her off. When he still refused, he shot him. Just like that.'

'Was he court martialled?'

Gradinsky laughed. 'Court martialled? Are you serious? The whole system is based on killing. I don't suppose he even got a warning.'

Despite his lingering suspicion of the Russian's motives, Wills was impressed by the bitterness in Gradinsky's voice. But if he was working for the KGB, he supposed he would have plenty of stories like that – all of them part of his cover. The horror he had expressed at the old man's story in Laghman could also have been put on, although it had seemed genuine at the time. Doubt ebbed and flowed in Wills's mind, like a tide on the turn.

Charikar seemed to be half asleep, apart from the lorries moving in both directions and filling the main street with fumes and dust. Half of the shops that lined the main street were closed, but there was more activity in the bazaar which lay further back, down the narrow alleys. As they bumped along, to all intents and purposes Russians in a Russian jeep, Wills studied the faces of the shopkeepers and passers-by.

'Not too friendly, I would say, Anatoly. I don't think it would be a good idea to break down here.'

'In daytime it's OK,' Gradinsky said. 'But I tell you one thing; I wouldn't like to drive through here in this jeep at night.'

The Russian swerved to avoid a cart drawn by a scrawny horse. The Afghan driver gave them a malevolent glare.

'You wouldn't last long, I can tell you that. There are probably a hundred or more mujahideen in this town at any one time. During the day they are ordinary citizens, but at night they come out to play. Like the mice, no? And then no more jeep. No more Mike, no more Anatoly.' He laughed.

'You have a curious sense of humour, Anatoly. I'm not so sure we're safe even in the daytime, judging by the way some of these shopkeepers are looking at us.'

Gradinsky shrugged. 'Sometimes they shoot you up in the daytime, but not so often.'

They left the town behind them and approached another roadblock. This time the performance was less slipshod. The first guard sauntered up to the car and peered hard at Fatima and Panna. Fatima had the dead soldier's cap pulled down firmly over her hair, but the soldier ovbiously saw she was a woman. He started to speak to her in Russian but Gradinsky cut him short. The sentry stepped back as if he had been slapped and retreated, muttering to himself. Gradinsky rounded on the other soldier, barking at him in a parade-ground bass so effectively that the terrified man stood to attention and snapped up a salute.

As they roared away, Wills asked, 'What the hell did you say to that chap? Because you certainly put the fear of God into him.'

'I told him that if they didn't mind their own business I would arrest them, and take them to the GRU prison in Kabul where they would do thirty days in the punishment cells. And the punishment cells in the GRU prison make Siberia look like a picnic outing.'

'One seemed to be interested in Fatima.'

'Yes. He wanted to know who she was and where we were taking her. That's when I started getting nasty.' He laughed, but without his usual cheerfulness.

About ten miles from Kabul, they saw a dust cloud approaching.

'Convoy,' Gradinsky said. 'Looks like a big one.'

Five minutes later they saw the lights of the leading vehicles, huge MAZ trucks capable of carrying 1,000-kilogram bombs. Gradinsky pulled off the road, which trembled as the huge trucks went past. Wills counted twenty-five. Then came the tank transporters, all empty.

'Going back home for fresh supplies.' Wills counted twenty of those. Then came a mixture of ammunition lorries, petrol tankers and finally half a dozen huge lorries obviously designed to carry a heavy load.

'SS12 transporters.' Gradinsky gestured with his chin.

'What you call FROG missiles. Range of about thirty kilometres. I don't know what the Red Army High Command thinks they'll achieve in Afghanistan with those, but they always have some stationed round Kabul.'

The last vehicle thundered past and Gradinsky pulled back on to the road through the convoy's dust which hung in the still air like smoke.

'Ninety-five vehicles,' Wills said.

'Quite small, by our standards.'

Gradinsky put his foot down and half an hour later they were in the outskirts of the capital.

Ten

There were three checkpoints on every road leading into Kabul, the outer one manned by Russian troops, the inner two by the Afghan Army: the Russians did not trust their Afghan allies to keep out the mujahideen bomb and assassination squads which now made the Soviet occupation so nerve-racking.

'Everyone keep quiet, even if you're asked a question. Let me do the talking,' Gradinsky said as they rolled to a stop at the first barrier. It was fortified with barbed-wire and sandbags and a couple of heavy machineguns were trained on the approaching traffic. Wills wondered how trigger-happy the soldiers behind them were.

A Russian sergeant wearing a slouch hat stepped into the road and waved them down with his Kalashnikov sub-machinegun. But he did it nonchalantly, having seen the divisional markings on the front of the jeep and the officer's badges on Gradinsky's shoulder tabs. His eyes wandered without interest over Wills and only showed a sudden spark of life when he saw Fatima sitting in the back. Gradinsky did not wait to be questioned. 'I'm taking these people,' he jerked his head at the back of the jeep, 'to headquarters for questioning. And I'm in a hurry.'

'Can I see your identity card, sir? Sorry, sir, it's regulations now for everyone.'

Gradinsky fumbled in the top pocket of his tunic. The pass showed he was a staff major at Darulaman Head-quarters in Kabul. The sergeant was familiar with this type of pass, and the photograph was clearly of Gradinsky, looking almost as intimidating as in real life. Not wanting to appear inefficient but even less anxious to delay the major, the sergeant gave the identity card a cursory glance, stepped back and snapped up a salute, at the same time shouting to the soldier on the gate to raise the barrier. 'Thank you, Major. Safe journey, sir.'

'Safe journey, eh?' Gradinsky glanced across at Wills, who had feigned an appearance of total indifference throughout the proceedings. 'They must be bloody nervous to say that sort of thing, don't you think?'

'The lads behind the machineguns were pretty jumpy, I can tell you. One kept fiddling about with his safety catch while you were showing the sergeant your pass. He looked as if he expected a bunch of mujahideen to come tearing up the road at any moment, guns blazing.' Wills gave a hard laugh, as if he enjoyed the young Russian's nervousness.

'You heard what happened the other day?' Fatima was leaning forward, raising her voice above the whine of the tyres. 'A group of mujahideen dressed in Afghan army uniforms captured one of these checkpoints at night. Then when army trucks and things like that came through, they shot them up. They killed some Russians as well. Nobody knew what was going on. There was a lot of panic. Then when they saw some Russian tanks coming, they decided they had done enough and they escaped. I know the commander. This is typical for him. He is very brave. A bit mad too.' She chuckled in admiration.

They could see a second checkpoint half a mile ahead. 'This should be ROA Afghans, this time,' Gradinsky said. 'No sweat, I hope.' He braked sharply as they came to the barrier, forcing the sloppily dressed Afghan soldier there to jump back out of the way. Gradinsky grinned at him.

'Very sorry,' he said. 'We're in a hurry.'

'Pass, please.' The Afghan's face, with the slightly slanted eyes that betrayed Mongolian blood, was inscrutable. It was impossible to tell if he felt friendship, hate or merely indifference towards the two Russian officers sitting in the front of the jeep. After perusing Gradinsky's pass at some length, he handed it back, his face still expressionless. Then, without a word, he swung up the barrier and waved them through.

Gradinsky watched him in the rear mirror as they roared away, churning up a cloud of dust. 'I think these guys are all in league with the mujahideen, anyway. They hate our guts. And when we do decide to go home, just you watch. A few months, it'll all be over.'

'As quick as that? That's even faster than Vietnam.' Wills tugged his hat down over his eyes as they overtook a couple of rickety *gharrys* and narrowly avoided an oncoming bus which lurched across the road, horn blaring. The object of the bus driver's displeasure, a meandering bullock cart, continued on its way unrepentantly, its enormous unoiled wooden wheels sending out a high-pitched scream which pierced the traffic noise like a rusty knife.

The third and last checkpoint was even more of a formality than the second. A Red Army BTR 60 armoured personnel carrier with heavy-duty tyres had crashed into the side of the post and the Russian driver was arguing with the Afghan officer in charge. 'The Afghan is telling him he should be arrested,' Fatima said from the back.

'And the Russian soldier is threatening to shoot him,' Gradinsky added. As their jeep edged forward, trying to get round the APC, an angry-looking Soviet soldier, blond hair sticking out from beneath his leather driving helmet, jumped down and advanced angrily on the Afghan.

'To hell with them, let's go.' Gradinsky engaged first gear and they shot forward, leaving the two soldiers gesticulating at one another, past a line of lorries held up by the accident. The Afghan drivers were already sounding their horns impatiently, a convenient way of showing their dislike for the nationality of the soldier who had caused the delay.

'I think we're OK now, barring any accidents.' Gradinsky permitted himself a grin. He waved his hand at a dense array of cardboard and sacking hovels that crowded both sides of the road. 'These people are much more likely to give us trouble than the soldiers on the roadblock.'

As they drove past, Wills noticed that the majority of occupants seemed to be women and small children, with an occasional old man standing apart, staring at the passing traffic.

Fatima leaned forward between them. 'These are refugees. That is why they are mostly women and children. They come from all the villages round Kabul that have been destroyed by the Russians over the years. More come every day, of course. There must be between one and two million refugees all round Kabul. The luckier ones are able to stay with their relatives in the city. These are the unlucky ones who have nowhere to go except to the shanty towns where they live like the sheep and the goats.'

'I don't know which must be worse,' Wills said. 'The freezing cold in winter or the stench and flies in summer.'

They passed some women carrying old cooking-oil tins on their heads, one hand holding the tin, the other keeping their veil in place. 'See, they have to fetch all their water like that,' Fatima explained. 'Sometimes they have to walk a long way. The life is very hard for these people.'

They drove for another few hundred yards in silence and then Fatima's voice came from the back, tight with nerves. 'You had better stop soon. We have to turn right at the next crossroads into the bazaar, and that will be dangerous for you.' She pushed a bundle over the back of the seat to Wills. 'Here is your *pattu*, and one for your friend. Wrap them round your shoulders to hide your uniforms.' The road widened and Gradinsky pulled over on to an empty piece of ground. He and Wills jumped out quickly and got into the back while Panna and Fatima tied the green scarf on the aerial again and then climbed into the front. It took less than thirty seconds, but an old man driving a cart turned to stare at them and then, seeing the Russian uniforms, spat in their direction.

Panna, his flat hat at a jaunty angle, turned right at the lights and then left into a warren of narrow side streets jammed with carts, both horse-drawn and man-drawn. The crowds parted with ill grace and one or two pedestrians hit the side of the jeep with their bare hands as it inched forward.

Following Fatima's directions, Panna turned into a quieter street lined with old timber-framed houses leaning outwards into the street, like old friends stopping for a chat. The ground floor of each house served as a shop, open to the street and with its wares displayed to the gaze of passers-by: rice in huge sacks; spices in colourful, pungent mounds, the bright yellow of saffron, the deep red of chillis, green pepper, turmeric, coriander; and, much beloved by the Kabulis for their *palaus*, raisins and sultanas in sweet-scented profusion.

Then came the meat market: scrawny carcases of lamb and goat hanging on hooks, open to the breeze, the dust, the petrol fumes and the persistent attentions of the flies but in the eyes of the locals, apparently none the worse for it.

'After the mosque comes a little square and the house is there.' Fatima pointed down the street to where a small, white-painted mosque with a slim green minaret interrupted the procession of old dwellings which could not have been young when the British marched into Kabul for the first time in 1839. The house stood in the shadow of the mosque, invisible from the road, its high wooden gates unpainted and dilapidated. Panna opened a little wicket and slipped inside and a few minutes later the gates creaked open, revealing a surprisingly spacious tree-shaded courtyard with a big wooden house just visible at the back. They drove in and the man who had opened the gates shut them again quickly, then, smiling broadly, advanced to greet the new arrivals.

'This is Wali,' Fatima said, introducing a small, friendly, quick man of about forty, who led them inside the house. 'Wali comes from the Panjsher. He's one of our best people here in Kabul and speaks some English. He says he has some important news for you. Let's go upstairs.'

They walked up the wide wooden stairs to the first floor. The rooms were large, with carved panelling and even a chandelier in what must have been the main reception room. The house had a certain grandeur, but years of neglect had taken their toll and it exuded the musty, stale smell of somewhere that has not been lived in for a long time. Wills wondered who had lived here in the days before the Saur Revolution and the Soviet occupation had crushed the life out of the city. The room, which overlooked the courtyard and its trees, was empty except for a frayed and rather dirty carpet and a few cushions placed round the walls.

'*Bishi, bishi.*' Wali gestured, still smiling. 'Please, sit down.'

He spoke animatedly to Fatima in Farsi. 'He says there is some very big news. I will translate, it will be quicker. Gorbachev has just formally agreed to withdraw all Russian forces from Afghanistan by mid February next year.

'I wonder if he really will?' Gradinsky did not seem very impressed.

'Yes, but this time they have actually committed themselves by international agreement, haven't they?' Wills was excited. 'Where did he hear it?'

'On the BBC World Service. So it must be right.' Fatima giggled.

'We always believed we would be victorious,' Panna said proudly.

Gradinsky remained sceptical. 'Can you really believe the Soviet government when they say they'll pull out of Afghanistan? I think it's a trick. I've seen it too many times before.'

A boy, who looked like one of Wali's sons, came in with a pot of tea, five glasses and a plateful of hard, sweet biscuits. Wali poured the pale green *sabs* with a serious face.

Wills reached out for a biscuit. 'If the Russians are going to start withdrawing straight away, should we really be trying to blow up the Salang Tunnel? I should have thought it's the last thing London would want now, wouldn't you?'

'Bloody hell.' Gradinsky sat up with a jerk. 'Abandon our plan to blow up the tunnel? Just when the Russians are going to be at their most vulnerable, withdrawing through the Salang, your masters in London would want to call it all off? What the hell makes you think that, Wills?'

'They're your masters, too, don't forget.' Wills held out his glass automatically for more tea, his mind trying to digest this totally unexpected piece of information. 'Fatima, can you ask Wali again exactly what he heard on the radio. Word for word?'

When she had done so, she turned back to Wills. 'America and Pakistan have signed an agreement with the Soviet Union about finishing the war in Afghanistan, and the Russians will start withdrawing their troops next month.'

'Well, there's no doubt in my mind,' Wills said. 'If, after a lot of shilly-shallying, the Russians have finally made up their minds to go home, something the West has been urging them to do for a very long time, naturally we won't want to do anything to stop them. You can just hear the arguments

124

in Washington and London. "For God's sake, don't give the Russians an excuse for changing their minds about withdrawing. Get them out at all costs." Quite understandable, from a politician's point of view. It's lucky for them we were delayed and have heard the news.'

'But not for us.' Fatima's dark eyes flashed contemptuously. 'The Russians say lots of things but they are big liars. We know that from our own experiences, bad experiences. They may withdraw some of their troops and then change their minds and come back. Or they may decide to separate the north from the rest of the country and, how do you say, annex it. Or turn it into a sort of no-man's land, like the Israelis have done in the south of Lebanon. And even if they do leave altogether, don't you think they will try and keep control of Afghanistan through the puppet regime? Of course they will. The West is always ready to believe everything the Russians say. We are not so trusting. And one more thing.' Fatima's cheeks were pink with indignation. 'Whatever the West does, we will fight on. Our war started long before the Russians came in. It will go on long after they have left, until we have overthrown this puppet government and wiped the country's honour clean. If you are afraid to blow up the tunnel, I will go and do it myself.'

Wali, realising there was an urgent debate in progress but not able to understand all of it, had left the room. He now reappeared with a fresh pot of tea.

'She's right, you know,' Gradinsky growled, shifting his weight from one buttock to another and fixing Wills with his piercing blue eyes. 'After all the time we have spent on this project. All the training, the preparation, the planning. After all the bastard Russians have done to Afghanistan, all the thousands of people they have slaughtered, the villages they have bombed, the children they have maimed. After all that, we just let them go home without lifting a finger to punish them? Well, Mike, if the bloody English are too chicken to do it, I'll go with Fatima to the Salang. You can go home and tell your bosses that the mad Russian and the beautiful mujahideen guerrilla fighter blew up the tunnel themselves. And to hell with the English.'

'Now take it easy, Anatoly. You've made Fatima blush.' Wills's voice was cool, mocking. 'That's just how the

Foreign Office will react. I know exactly how their minds work. God knows, I've seen it enough times all over the world. If in doubt, do nothing. But supposing we do go ahead and end up by being captured? They'll really put us through the mangle, you especially. We don't need to kid ourselves about that. By the time the KGB has pumped us full of their latest truth drug, we'll be begging to tell them everything they want to know: from the names and descriptions of our recruiters and trainers to a sketch map of the safe house near Ashford where we first met. They'll soon nail us down as full-blown British agents, they'll never believe we're just a couple of freelancers. Then there'll be the show trial, live on television. The whole thing couldn't be more embarrassing for HMG. You must see that, Anatoly. It may be unadventurous, but it does make sense.'

'You call that sense? I call it a lot of balls. Letting the bully and the gangster walk away from the scene of his crime without even making him apologise. What sort of a man are you, Mike?

There was silence for a moment until Wills spoke. 'Fatima, can you ask Wali what has happened about the petrol tankers. Are they here and all ready to be driven to the Salang?'

Wali launched into a lengthy explanation.

'Yes, he says they are here and you can drive them any time.'

'Is that all he said? He seemed to go on for a long time.'

'Yes, these people often say the same thing several different ways, so it can take a long time.'

'Where are they, now?'

'They are near here, in a place which belongs to us. It is a proper garage which sells petrol and everything and it has a workshop behind. They are all ready for you to drive. But now, if you do not need them, we can get rid of them.'

Suddenly, before Wills could reply, they heard a cry from the street below. Fatima jumped up and went over to the window, Wills close behind her.

An army jeep had stopped below them and beside it, in the middle of the road, a bare-headed Russian soldier was furiously struggling with a young Afghan woman. As they watched he tried to lift the girl off her feet and force her into the back of the jeep. She fought ferociously, screaming at the top of her voice. Suddenly, a man of about fifty appeared from the house opposite and came running over, waving his arms and shouting. He tried to pull the girl away with one hand, punching the soldier with the other and shouting abuse at the top of his voice. The soldier let go of the girl, turned and reached into the open back of the jeep. When he swung round again he was holding a revolver. Seeing the gun, the Afghan immediately stepped back and half raised his hands. The soldier advanced unsteadily and then very deliberately started to shoot. The first bullets appeared to miss but, instead of running, the man, terrified, stood stock still. The next two bullets hit him full in the chest and he staggered back as if he had been punched. Two red splashes, as bright as poppies, flowered on his shirt. He stumbled again and then fell backwards, his head striking the road with a thump. A second soldier jumped out of the jeep and, ignoring the wounded man, went to help the first soldier overpower the girl. Together they dragged her to the side of the vehicle and bundled her inside. She had stopped screaming and was sobbing brokenly.

'Those drunken bastards.' Gradinsky leaned so far out of the window that for a moment Wills thought he was going to jump. 'I'd like to shoot them.'

Fatima pushed past and ran for the door, followed by Wali, as the jeep raced off up the street and swerved round the corner with a screech of tyres.

'Christ,' Wills exploded. 'Has your bloody army no discipline at all?' Even as he said it, Wills knew it was a stupid remark. Every army has its criminal elements but as a soldier he knew the smell of indiscipline and disintegration and what he had just seen suggested it was far advanced in the Red Army in Afghanistan.

As they watched, Wali and another man appeared below and hurried over to the figure which lay quite still in the empty street. Wali bent down for a few seconds and then straightened up and said something to the other man. Together they lifted the body and carried it into the courtyard from where the dead man had emerged with such angry energy only minutes before.

*

Wills brooded on the incident as the afternoon slipped into evening and the voice of the *muezzin* floated hauntingly from the mosque next door, a call to prayer but also a call to war, to the *jehad*, with all the mystical authority of the Prophet behind it.

'*Allahu akbar...*' The thought that God is great and only God is great seemed strangely comforting in the violent context of Kabul and the conflict that pounded on its outskirts, like surf on a shore. And not only its outskirts. Unexplained explosions, whether bombs or incoming rockets, punctuated the more normal sounds of city life and kept everyone on edge. That was one now, a low dull boom, then another, and possibly a third. They sounded a long way off, perhaps near the airport, but nowhere was safe. The mujahideen, who operated from the mountains which surround the city, were able to bombard it at will, thanks to their new 122-millimetre rockets with a range of more than twenty kilometres. Their favourite targets were the big Russian compound at Microrayon, the base at Darulaman and the Soviet Embassy itself. A number of staff had been killed or wounded in the past few months and the ambassador was said to spend most of his time in his blastproof bunker, dictating pessimistic telegrams to Moscow.

Wali reappeared at that moment carrying a Tilley pressure lamp and a big pot of tea in response to Gradinsky's apparently unslakeable thirst. The lamp's harsh white light banished the deep shadows in the corners of the room and jerked the men reclining on the floor out of their somnolence.

'You know what, Anatoly?' Wills said as he drank the hot sweet liquid gratefully. 'I've changed my mind.'

'About what?'

'About the Salang.'

'Oh yeah? Tell me.'

'You know what happened this afternoon, outside in the street. I've been thinking about it ever since. It made me feel physically sick. To see animals like that shoot down an innocent man as if he were a mad dog and snatch that girl off the street in broad daylight and know that we were powerless, absolutely powerless to do anything about it. It really makes me so bloody angry ... I could strangle them with my own hands.' He held out his big, square hands, dark with sun and dirt. 'When I think what those bastards are doing to her now ... No, I can't bear to think about it. But I tell you this, Anatoly. By Christ, I want that tunnel, I want the Salang and everybody in it, I want to see it go up like that.' He smacked his hands together with a crack like a pistol shot going off. 'What makes it all the worse is that they'll get away with it, won't they?'

'The soldiers? Of course. Nobody cares in the army. I told you that already. And if they're really leaving the damned place, there's no chance at all of any disciplinary action being taken against them.'

'Well,' Wills said, speaking very deliberately, 'I don't see why those bastards who just shot that bloke, whoever he was...'

'The girl's father.' Panna, who had been sitting quietly, interrupted. 'He was a very good man. He very much liked the mujahideen.'

'That makes it even worse. As I was saying, I don't see why those bastards should get off scot free...'

Gradinsky interrupted him. 'Here's Fatima. Sit down and listen to this, Fatima.' Wills thought she looked exhausted. 'Wills has seen the light. He's changed his mind about the Salang.'

'Really? That's wonderful news. I'm glad. What made you change?'

'That business this afternoon. The shooting.'

'Yes, I've been talking to the mother. As you'd imagine, she's beside herself with grief. I tried to comfort her.'

'Well, I've decided,' Wills said. 'Even if London did try to send us a message I don't see how we'd ever get it. And who knows, they might argue as you do. You can't trust the Russians when they say they're going to withdraw from Afghanistan, really to withdraw, until you've seen the last tank cross the border. And another thing. My guess is that this is an unpopular war. Young Russians must hate it. They must be as anti-draft as the American college kids were about Vietnam. If Gorbachev says he's willing to withdraw, it's because it suits him. He wants out for his own reasons, not because he's a nice guy.' He gave a bitter little laugh and Gradinsky joined him, his deep tones making the room reverberate. It was as if they were sealing a pact together.

A private pact to prosecute their own war to the bitter end.

'Can we go and see the tankers as soon as possible?' Wills asked Fatima.

'Yes, but Wali says we must be very careful. There are many, many spies in Kabul and a lot of security checks. So we will have to go in the night. But first he must see if everything is ready and when the next convoy is going. It may take a day or two.'

It was after one in the morning when they left the house and walked, silently and in single file, through the narrow streets of the old bazaar towards the garage about half a mile away. They had discarded their Russian uniforms and were now dressed as Afghans. No traffic moved but occasionally there was a burst of automatic fire and flares climbed lazily into the dark sky, burst and for a tense thirty seconds illuminated the skyline, making them feel suddenly naked and vulnerable. As they neared their destination they heard a couple of big explosions some distance away, followed quickly by two more. Wali turned and whispered cheerfully, '*Raket*. Mujahideen.'

Almost immediately, closer and louder, a battery of BM27 multi-barrel rocket launchers opened up in retaliation and they could clearly hear the swish of the rockets leaving the tubes. 'Always when mujahideen fire, they shoot back very much. I think they very nervous.' Wali sounded pleased. They stopped on the next corner and Wali whispered instructions. 'Here is more dangerous. Sometimes Russian or KHAD patrols. You wait until I give signal.'

He disappeared with Panna, while the others waited in the shadows. They could hear the noise of traffic some distance away but the gunfire had died down and the city slept fitfully.

'They don't like moving about at night, the Russians. Only if there is an emergency. After dark, the city really belongs to the mujahideen.' There was a faint whistle and Fatima raised her hand. 'That's Wali. Come, follow me.'

The garage was a modest establishment which boasted only one ancient pump and a small forecourt. There were no lights and the nearest street-lamp was fifty yards away. Wali stood in the shadow of the doorway, his face a pale blur, and they moved past him into the building without speaking. Inside it was pitch dark. They waited until Wali switched on his torch and followed him through to the back where there was another much bigger workshop. He fumbled with a key and unlocked the door. There, gleaming dully in the beam, were the two tankers, their military green paintwork scarred and travel-stained from the journey through the Khyber Pass. Wills and Gradinsky stepped forward to inspect the nearest vehicle. They knew, if Hashem had done what he had promised in Rawalpindi, that tanks two to six would be empty, but that tank number one should be full of liquid high explosive. To prove that, they would have to unlock the inspection cover on the top of each separate tank and look inside. Wills examined the gauges fitted to the side of each tank: all of them registered empty.

'We'd better have a look,' Wills said in an aside to Gradinsky. 'I just don't trust anyone.'

They climbed up a gantry and Wali opened each inspection cover in turn, flicking his torch inside to reveal an empty, hollow-sounding chamber until, finally, he came to tank number one. Then, with considerably more caution, Wali opened the last cover and flashed his torch inside. There was a pungent whiff of fumes and Wills and Gradinsky found themselves looking down on a still mass of almost colourless liquid. One thousand gallons of methyl nitrate. It looked infinitely evil in the beam of the torch.

'Jesus,' Wills said. 'That lot could blow us all, and half of Kabul, to kingdom come. Screw the cover on, Wali, as tight as you can, for God's sake.'

They climbed down the ladder and walked to the second tanker. It was exactly the same: tank number one was filled to the top with methyl nitrate; the rest were empty. Wills felt almost sick. Either fear or the fumes made him feel momentarily dizzy. Finally he took a deep breath and climbed up into the driver's seat of the first tanker. He ran his right hand along the dashboard until it touched a plastic cover. It needed quite a lot of strength to remove it. Underneath was a small black panel with two switches, one ringed in green, the other in red. Between them nestled a small red warning light.

He fingered the switches lightly. They were taped in the 'off' position, but if he moved the green switch to 'on' it would start the silent countdown of the carefully programmed delay: thirty minutes, one hour or whatever they chose. To arm the system, he would simply throw the red switch and that would bring the electric detonators into play. If the switches were turned off in the wrong sequence or the wrong wire was cut in the delay circuit, there would be strawberry jam for tea, as their explosives instructor at Asford had waggishly put it.

The one thousand gallons of methyl nitrate which filled the number one tank were fairly safe at the moment. It was less sensitive to impact than nitro-glycerine, but it would be highly dangerous if there were any leakage or vaporisation. The night before they reached the tunnel they would fix to the belly of each number one tank a small Soviet limpet mine, looted by the mujahideen from a consignment ambushed in the Salang. The irony was not lost on Wills. Running from the mine to the detonator under the dashboard would be a length of black electrical cable, or so it would seem. In fact it would be a plastic-coated detonating cord, as issued to the Spetsnaz. Wills guessed this must also have fallen off the back of a lorry on one of the remoter reaches of the Salang Highway. The cord would carry the detonating impulse at six thousand metres per second, faster than a rifle bullet travels, to the limpet mine which in turn would trigger the explosive with a force equal to six thousand kilograms of TNT.

Wills eased himself out of the seat and dropped to the ground. He found that he was determined that whatever happened he was not going to blow himself up with the tanker. Gradinsky could do as he liked. He seemed mad enough for anything. But Wills who, not very many months ago, had seen no future for himself and would not have minded very much if he had got himself killed fighting as a mercenary in some God-forsaken banana republic, suddenly felt an acute desire to make a success of this job and survive. Above all survive.

Despite the hardships of the present and those to come – perhaps because of them – life seemed suddenly sweet. He gave an involuntary glance in Fatima's direction. She was sitting in the corner of the garage cross-legged, head bowed, busily cleaning her Makarov pistol.

Eleven

It was almost light by the time they had walked back to the house and Wills and Gradinsky were still asleep when, several hours later, Fatima burst into the room.

'Quick, get up, the *Shurawi* are here.' Both men had slept in their clothes on the floor, mujahideen-style, and were immediately awake. They rolled out of their blankets, pulled on their boots and seized their rucksacks.

Wali appeared, gesturing frantically. 'Come quickly, *Shurawi* try to get inside.' As he spoke, they could hear shouting and banging on the gate with what sounded like rifle butts.

With Wali leading, Wills and Gradinsky ran up one flight of stairs, then a narrower and darker second flight and finally, very dark and rickety, a third flight. Here, on the top floor, a door opened on to the flat roof. Wali stepped out cautiously, peering over the edge. They could hear the banging more clearly now, not summoning attention but the more purposeful noise of someone trying to break down the gate. There was a splintering crash and the shouting stopped.

'They're in the house,' Wills whispered. 'Get a move on, Wali.'

The Afghan finally succeeded in locking the door from the outside and, moving quickly to the end of the flat roof, pushed aside the top branches of one of the trees growing up from the courtyard. 'Here.' He pointed through the branches at the next house, its flat roof exactly level with theirs, but a good eight feet away. The gap yawned uninvitingly; the ground seemed a long way beneath them. As they studied it they heard the sounds of movement below. The Russians would be searching the house; their voices were muffled but coming closer.

Wali was searching for something. 'What the hell are you looking for?' Wills's voice cracked with strain.

'Ladder. Usually, there ladder here.'

'Well, it isn't here now. We'll have to jump. Out of the way, let me go first.' Wills pushed through the branches to the edge of the roof. 'Here, hold the branch.' He retreated a couple of paces. 'Right back. Hold it right back.' Then, like a long jumper launching himself from the board, Wills took a short run and flung himself into space. Small branches whipped across his face, almost blinding him. He teetered on the edge of the other roof and for a panicky moment thought he was going to fall back. But then he was on his knees, sprawling forward. As he got up, his foot kicked something solid. It was the ladder, half hidden under a piece of sacking. He bent, lifted it with both hands and slid it across the gap to the far roof. Gradinsky gave a whoop of relief. 'I couldn't jump so far.' On hands and knees he started to crawl forward. There was a shout from the house. The search party was rattling the door on to the roof. Wali threw the rucksacks across the void.

'Hurry, for God's sake.'

Gradinsky half crawled and half jumped the last two feet, falling clumsily. Wali was so close behind that he tripped against Gradinsky and as both men fell, sprawling, the Russians fired a burst into the lock of the door behind them.

Wills pulled the ladder towards him and gave it a push that sent it spinning down to the courtyard below. Then he turned and ran after the others. There was another door leading off the roof but when Wali pushed against it it jammed, leaving them outside just as the Russians emerged behind them. Wali struggled desperately.

'Here,' Gradinsky shouted, 'let me have a go.' He stepped back and launched his formidable bulk against the door. It gave so suddenly that he went careering through the doorway on to the floor beyond.

One of the Russians fired a snapshooter burst at them although he barely had a target. Wali was leaping down the stairs, two at a time, Wills and Gradinsky hard on his heels. Reaching the ground floor, they made for the courtyard, well hidden from the next-door house, and ran to the far end where a small gate was set in the wall.

'This way leads to street. Walk close to me.'

Wali pushed the gate which opened with a loud squeak. They were in a street so narrow it could not have been more than three paces wide. It was also empty. They walked fast, without speaking, to the far end and turned into one of the main arteries of the bazaar. Wali slowed down.

'We all right now, I think. Walk quick and don't look at anyone.'

Wills craned round to see if they were visible from the roof of the house they had just left, but they were out of sight now, submerged in the busy traffic of the bazaar. A few months ago, they might easily have run into a group of Russian soldiers out shopping, prepared to run the risk of being shot by a mujahideen gunman for the sake of a Japanese radio or watch which they knew they would never be able to buy at home. But today no Russians were to be seen nor, for that matter, were any Afghan soldiers. The only person in uniform was a solitary policeman whose diffident manner suggested that the last thing he wanted to do was to make an arrest. All the same, Wills and Gradinsky walked in silence, gaze averted, willing themselves to be inconspicuous, grateful they were in Afghan dress. They knew that the real danger was not from the uniformed minions of the Communist regime, but from the faceless secret agents of the KHAD, that army of spies and watchers trained by the KGB, who, more than most, feared a Russian withdrawal and, in their fear, were all the more vicious.

Two or three hundred yards from the big house by the mosque, Wali turned into a side street and slipped through a broken-down archway leading into another courtyard. He tapped three times sharply on a door. It was quiet here, the sounds of the city muffled by the high walls. A man's head appeared from an upstairs window and, recognising Wali, grinned a greeting. A few seconds later the heavy door creaked open and, like foxes alert to danger, they slipped silently into the cool dimness. As they climbed the stairs the smell of cooking floated towards them and Wills realised they had had no breakfast and that he was hungry. There were other signs that a family lived in this house: the carpet in the guest room was clean, and the cushions had brightly coloured covers, unlike the dust and neglect of the safe house by the mosque. Wali's friend invited them to sit down and called to an unseen wife to make tea. The two men talked in whispers, an Afghan trait that Wills had come to recognise as a product not so much of a particularly secretive society as of one in which privacy was the exception. Finally Wali turned to the others.

'Jan Mohammed send his wife to find out what happen at the house.'

'And to Fatima and Panna?' Wills said.

'*Inshallah.*'

Jan Mohammed interrupted. His English was better than Wali's and, like himself, a bit flamboyant. 'You see, it is better for my wife to go than me. I am of military age and maybe they arrest me as mujahid or force me join army.'

Jan Mohammed smiled half apologetically as if to say he did not usually hide behind his wife's skirts and left the room to give her her instructions. When he came back he was carrying a pot of tea and some *nan*, which they fell on hungrily.

As they ate and drank Wills turned to Wali. 'Was that a routine raid this morning, or did they have information about us?'

Wali shrugged. 'I think KHAD watch the house and see you arrive.'

'It's unusual for the Russians to carry out a raid, isn't it?' Gradinsky grumbled.

'Do you think whoever saw us arrive identified us as foreigners, not mujahideen?' Wills asked. 'Is that why the Russians came themselves?'

Wali shifted uneasily. 'Usually it is KHAD who make search. Or *tsarandoy*, the special police.' He looked at Wills and Gradinsky as if seeing them for the first time. He coughed apologetically. 'It is true you do not look like Afghans. Even in our clothes.' He grinned slightly. 'Maybe if you had turbans. But, it depend on Russian commander. If he think mujahideen entering his area, and if he not trust the KHAD people, he come himself. More and more, they not trust the Afghans. More and more they think all Afghans are traitors and against them. So for last month, maybe two months, they search themselves. I think they do not know who you are. Just that you strangers in the district and strangers they not like.'

Wills stuffed a piece of *nan* into his mouth and chewed hard. 'But it means they'll be looking for us now, doesn't it? Even if they think we're Afghans. And the safe house is blown.'

'Please?' Wali screwed his face up in incomprehension.

'The house where we stayed, we can't stay there any more. Its cover, as we say, is blown. Even if Fatima and Panna are safe, we have to move. The longer we stay in Kabul, the more chance we have of being picked up. What do you think, Anatoly?'

'I agree.' Gradinsky's gravelly voice made even the simplest statement seem portentous. 'I would think the KGB is very nervous of foreign agents infiltrating the city at this time. They are convinced the CIA and MI6 will try and sabotage their final withdrawal. They'll be convinced Western agents are being sent in to coordinate the mujahideen operations. What was it that the major at Ashford said? Even if the CIA didn't exist, the Kremlin would have had to invent it. So, even if Wills and Gradinsky didn't exist, the KGB would have had to invent us.' He laughed triumphantly. 'So, my opinion, Mike, is let's get the hell out of here. Fast.'

They heard footsteps in the courtyard below. Wali looked out of the window and called a low greeting. 'Allah be praised, Fatima is coming.'

Footsteps climbed the stairs and Fatima appeared in the doorway, throwing back her veil. She removed her shoes and walked across the carpet towards them. Wills found himself unexpectedly moved at the sight of her: he examined her face, the high cheek bones, the skin faintly pink beneath the tan, the big, lustrous eyes, the thick dark hair. But she looked upset.

'What's wrong. Where's Panna?'

'They captured him. Not the Russians. It was the KHAD people they had with them. When the Russians broke down the door and entered the house, I was upstairs in the big room. I was wearing my veil, like this.' She pulled up her veil to leave only her eyes showing. 'Panna was hiding in the corner. They didn't see him. They pointed their guns at me and shouted, "Where are the men who came here last night?" I said in Farsi, "I don't know which men you mean. My husband is in the army. There are no men here." I thought they were going to shoot me. They shouted something in Russian and then ran up the stairs. Then a few moments later, when we heard the shooting upstairs...'

'It was only the door to the roof. They shot the lock off.'

'Well, when we heard the shooting, we ran down to the courtyard — Panna was in front — just as the KHAD people were coming in. Three or four of them. They immediately pointed their guns at him and called on him to stop. I was just behind, out of their sight. Immediately, I turned and ran through to the back of the house. I looked out very carefully. There was no one, so I just walked out into the street.'

'And what happened to Panna?'

'They took him away. After they left I went back and asked the old man who looks after the mosque what had happened. He said the *Shurawi* had tied him up and beaten him. Then they took him away.'

There was a silence in the room for a moment, until Wills spoke. 'Poor bugger. They'll be giving him a hard time, trying to find out who we are.' He looked at Fatima. 'We were just saying when you arrived that we should leave Kabul as soon as possible. Wali says the Russians are convinced Western agents are infiltrating the place. Once they've put the thumbscrews on Panna they'll know for sure. And if he tells them about Anatoly, they'll get quite excited. How soon do you think we can pick up the tankers and go?'

'There's a convoy leaving tomorrow,' Fatima said. 'We have told the headman to keep an eye on you. He is one of our people. Very reliable. Jan Mohammed and I will go instead of Panna. I think we should go to the garage tonight, but late when everyone is asleep.'

'The sooner the better,' Gradinsky grunted. 'I certainly don't want to run into any old comrades.'

Jan Mohammed's wife, still invisible as far as the men were concerned, produced a traditional dish of *q'abli palau* for their last meal, although apologising for its inferiority: the war made some ingredients impossible to obtain, Jan Mohammed explained.

'This not good rice. Vairy bad rice. And also *kishmish*, how do you say, raisins, vairy, vairy difficult. I am sorry.' He turned his palms upwards, in a gesture of emptiness, and gave his clown's smile, half joyful, half sad.

They slept for a few hours and left the house shortly after midnight, walking through the shadows of the deserted city, listening to the occasional burst of gunfire and the frenzied barking of dogs that always followed and which seemed to go on all night. Wali kept twenty or thirty yards ahead, pausing at each street corner to reconnoitre. They had to cross one main road, waiting for fifteen minutes while two Russian patrols, each of two armoured personnel carriers, stopped for a chat in the middle of the road, the drivers' faces in shadow under their steel helmets. As soon as the vehicles had rumbled off into the night, Wali waved them across the road and ten minutes later they reached the darkened garage. Here there was another delay, the four of them huddling in the deepest shadow they could find while Wali negotiated somewhere out of sight. When they were finally admitted, Wali explained.

'There was man from the government who want names of all drivers. So my friend, Anwar, who in charge of convoys, he give this man your names and show him your papers. First of all, the man, he want to see you. Then Anwar give him some money and the man say OK. So now you official convoy driver.' Wali laughed. 'Here, you take papers and keep safe. Every time you come to roadblock, maybe they ask you your papers.'

Wills nodded at Anwar and dropped his voice. 'Your friend. Is he OK? Can we trust him not to give us away?'

Wali looked pained. 'No, no. He is very good friend. He is mujahid. You can trust him very much.'

Wali now said goodbye, embracing Jan Mohammed and almost bowing to the ground in front of Fatima. With Wills and Gradinsky he was more formal, merely shaking their hands and wishing them a safe journey.

'No embrace for you,' Wills teased Gradinsky. 'He could tell you were a Russian a mile off.'

'You're a bastard, Wills. At least we have fought only one war against the Afghans. Not three, like you bloody British. I'm surprised this guy didn't spit in your face.'

Anwar beckoned to them to follow. They passed a room where a number of bearded men were stretched out asleep on the floor but with a wave of his hand to indicate this was not good enough for Wali's friends, he led them to another, smaller room. Here the four of them would at least have some privacy.

'If those were the other drivers, they looked a pretty rough bunch to me,' Wills said as he stepped out of his boots. 'But then I don't suppose it's the most sought-after job in the country at the moment.'

Well before dawn, Anwar shook them awake and told them to be ready to leave in ten minutes. If they hurried they could have a cup of tea in his office. Wills and Gradinsky both wore combat trousers, khaki shirts, flat Chitrali *pukuls* pulled well down over their ears and thick sheepskin jackets, a present from Wali. They carried old Afghan army rucksacks with a change of clothes and some food. Wills and Fatima, who was dressed as a man, climbed into the cab of the first vehicle, Gradinsky and Jan Mohammed into the second. Behind the front seat was a long bulkhead cupboard with space for a first-aid kit, bedding and personal odds and ends. Each cupboard had a false back, masking a space big enough to hide a couple of special-issue Kalashnikovs, ammunition, half a dozen grenades, torches, a block of Semtex, a box of detonators and a couple of limpet mines.

They left the garage before first light and drove to the assembly point, a square near the British Embassy where convoys for the Salang often gathered. There they joined about forty other tankers, lining up nose to tail in the chilly pre-dawn, all going north of the Salang to pick up fuel. Anwar parked at the rear of the convoy and got out. Then he and Jan Mohammed walked over to a checkpoint to have their papers stamped. A couple of Afghan army officers walked down the line, smoking and so deep in conversation that they had no time for anything more than a cursory glance at the line of tankers. After they had gone past, Wills leaned towards Fatima.

'They look as if it would be beneath their dignity to speak to anyone as lowly as a lorry driver.'

'You know, these Khalqi officers are very arrogant. It is a good thing for us, I think. It is better they do not come and ask too many questions.' Anwar and Jan Mohammed came back with the papers duly stamped. Jan Mohammed climbed up to the cab and grinned through the window.

'It's OK. No problems. Anwar arranged for our people to open door in Salang. Is good, yes? We start in five minutes. We are the last two tankers in the convoy. Remember that. First you, then we come behind. OK? We should be in Charikar in four hours, maybe, and in Jabal-es-Seraj two, three hours after that. You know Jabal-es-Seraj is near entrance to Panjsher Valley. Then we start climb, very much climb and reach Salang maybe three, four hours after that.'

Wills made a quick calculation. 'So nine or ten hours approximately to the tunnel. Say ten to be safe.' He looked at his watch. It was a quarter to six. 'Which means we'll be there at around four this afternoon.' He grinned. 'In time for tea.'

Anwar said something and Jan Mohammed translated. 'He say maybe mujahideen ambush convoy near Panjsher, near Gulbahar.'

'Durran knows what we're doing. I'm sure he's given orders not to attack us,' Wills said with more conviction than he really felt.

'Yes, but not Durran people. Other people. Bad people.'

'Which people?' Wills asked.

'People who belong to man we call the Butcher. He is very bad man. And he hate very much Durran. I tell you about this man, the Butcher. His people never fight Russians. Never fight *Shurawi*. They spend all time fighting other mujahideen. He very bad man.' Jan Mohammed clicked his tongue in disapproval.

There was a shout from the front of the convoy and a sudden surge of powerful engines revving up. Clouds of blue diesel smoke belched from exhausts into the clear morning air. Wills looked north across the lorry park to the mountains beyond. The early sun made them stand out sharply against the pale sky. It was going to be a lovely day, this day they had been planning for and working towards for so many weeks, the complex and dangerous possibilities of which they had discussed so minutely and so endlessly. He could see Gradinsky sitting in the cab of the other tanker, his *pukul* pulled hard down over his eyes. His usual cheerful expression had left him and he looked a rather diminished figure, hunched against the early morning chill, apprehensive perhaps for the first time in his life. Wills felt nervous too: there was a numb, hollow feeling in the pit of his stomach that he had almost forgotten, but which he remembered so vividly now as preceding every operation he had been involved in with the SAS. A feeling almost of nausea, the physical symptom, as he knew very well, of the old enemy, fear. But then without fear, man's animal reflexes would not be sufficiently sharpened and ready to respond instantly and efficiently to danger. So fear, he told himself, was an unpleasant but necessary evil.

Gradinsky's reflection in the wing mirror set Wills's mind worrying yet again at a riddle that had become depressingly familiar in the past few weeks: a riddle that he found himself unable to answer. Was Gradinsky in reality the rather mad, anti-establishment Russian he purported to be or was he someone much more sophisticated and sinister? If he was going to shop Wills, he would have to do it in the next few hours; preferably, from Gradinsky's point of view, just before they reached the tunnel. Maybe at Jabal-es-Seraj, the Soviet base for the Salang? There would be plenty of support for a KGB major there. Or maybe at the checkpoint just before they went into the tunnel. The incriminating evidence was all there in the shape of two thousand gallons of methyl nitrate. What a show they could put on blowing that little lot up in front of the cameras.

Well, the next few hours would finally show, one way or the other. Or would they? After all, and it was a thought that had occurred with increasing frequency to Wills recently, what if Gradinsky were an ultra-sophisticated long-term sleeper, who was prepared to go through with the Salang operation in order to establish cast-iron credentials with which he would be able to gain entry into British intelligence? How could you doubt a defector who was prepared to blow up one of his country's key strategic communications links? And possibly kill a lot of his fellow-countrymen in the process? It was a riddle like those oriental carvings which depict a snake swallowing its own tail. It had no beginning and no end.

The tanker in front jolted forward, its exhaust vomiting diesel fumes in a great blue cloud. Wills felt his own vehicle shudder as Fatima started up the engine and then lumber forward. They had started. There was no turning back now.

Twelve

General Orlov looked at the piece of paper on his desk with distaste. It was a report which, with mounting anger and frustration, he was reading for the second time. It reported that, in raiding a house suspected of harbouring *dushman* elements in the Bala Koh quarter, Russian troops aided by KHAD personnel had arrested the well-known bandit Panna, wanted for many criminal acts including the bombing of an important convoy in the Salang.

'Under routine interrogation by the KHAD,' the report went on — the standard euphemism for torture — 'the bandit Panna confessed to belonging to the band of the criminal Durran and to having accompanied two foreigners to Kabul. Presumably they were two of the three men who were observed escaping across the roof before the search party was able to apprehend them.'

Orlov grunted angrily to himself before reading on. 'The suspect insisted that he did not know the names of the foreigners, nor their nationalities, despite repeated periods of interrogation. But he finally admitted that they were on their way to the Salang to undertake some action (unspecified) there. Unfortunately, during our determined efforts to ascertain more details of the intended criminal action, the *dushman* collapsed and was found to be dead on admission to the KHAD hospital.'

'Fools, bungling fools.' Orlov threw down the report and strode furiously to the window. What the hell could these two foreigners be up to in the Salang? It must be the tunnel, he brooded. An ambush or an attack on the tunnel itself. An ambush seemed more likely, but why send in two foreigners to carry out an ambush? That was something the mujahideen could easily arrange by themselves – God knows they had done so often enough in the past nine years. It could be an attack on the tunnel, but what precisely?

Orlov stared out of the window at the mountains beyond but he did not see them. Were these two foreigners an advance party of some kind? Setting up a radio beacon to bring in American or Pakistani F16s to bomb the tunnel? If they precision-bombed the entrances they could collapse and block them, but even with Smart bombs it was a bit chancy. And would they go that far? Or was it some kind of sabotage operation, designed to have the same effect? But what and how?

And the bloody clumsy fools had gone and tortured the only source of information to death. They didn't deserve to survive, those fools in the KHAD and the PDPA. And why hadn't they arrested the accursed foreigners?

Orlov pressed the buzzer on his desk. Almost immediately the door opened and his ADC came in, a smart-looking KGB captain. 'Yes, Comrade General?'

Orlov tapped the report on his desk. 'Do we have no description at all of these foreigners?'

'Apparently not, sir. It's a typical KHAD balls-up, if you don't mind me saying so, sir.'

'Say anything you like. You couldn't be half as rude about them as I am. So we don't know who these bastards are, eh? I'd take a bet they're Americans or British. CIA most likely, or MI6 acting for the CIA. Have you seen anything at all that ties in with this?'

'Can't think of anything, Comrade General. But I'll have Records make a thorough check.'

'Not just thorough. Tell them I want the most exhaustive check they've ever made. Comb through every blasted computer tape. Check every agent who has operated in this area. From every country. Tell them to make every cross-check they can think of: under Salang, sabotage, infiltration, *dushman*, Durran ... Don't forget that bastard.' Orlov's voice was bitter. The rebel leader had slipped through his fingers so many times that he had come close to despairing of ever catching him. But like the good policeman he was he told himself to be patient. In the end, he would get him. Even if it was the last thing he did.

His ADC, who was standing expectantly by the door, gave a cough. 'Anything else, Comrade General?'

'No. Let me know immediately if they turn anything up. Oh, and get Colonel Shahnawaz on the phone, would you?'

The ADC noticed that, untypically, General Orlov was frowning. Usually the mere mention of the delicious KHAD colonel was enough to put him in a good mood for the rest of the day. Something must be wrong, he told himself as he closed the door.

Thirty seconds later, one of the five phones on the General's desk purred. It was a direct line to KHAD headquarters. The others connected General Orlov to KGB internal, KGB Headquarters in Moscow, the Commander-in-Chief's office and the Russian military net for the whole of Afghanistan. 'Colonel Shahnawaz speaking,' a soft feminine voice said.

General Orlov stopped frowning and smiled. 'Ah, Zarina, how nice to hear your voice, even down a telephone. I wonder if you would make me the happiest man in Kabul, no, in Afghanistan, by letting me see you tonight?'

There was a slight pause on the other end of the line and then Zarina laughed. 'That would be very nice,' she said primly. 'What time?'

'I'll send the car for you at the usual time, about eight. Is that convenient?'

'Yes, that's fine. Until tonight, then.'

'And wear some of that perfume you had on the last time, will you, my darling?'

She laughed again. 'Of course. You gave it to me. I like it very much.' Her voice changed. 'Someone is here. I must go. Goodbye.'

Orlov put down the phone and the frown returned. Not because of the change in Zarina's voice, but of what he would have to say to her tonight. Zarina was back in Kabul, her transponder mission against Durran having failed. Either she had bungled it or – and this was the unpleasant thought which he kept rejecting but which kept forcing itself back into his mind – she had fooled him, him of all people, and was secretly working for Durran.

*

The dust from the convoy rose into the still air above the plain north of Kabul like smoke from a fire. The long line of tankers and their escorting Afghan Army APCs ground along at a slow pace, the drivers apparently oblivious to the wrecks that lay scattered along the route, the victims of previous mujahideen ambushes or simply discarded breakdowns, their hulls stripped clean of every removable part. It occurred to Wills that the local Afghans were every bit as ingenious and quick-fingered as the Egyptian wide boys who, in the Canal Zone in his father's day, had removed the tyres from British lorries while the drivers were in the nearest café having a beer. The Afghans could clean the corpse of a Russian APC quicker than a vulture could devour the flesh of a dead donkey, but the *pièce de resistance*, the liver and heart, so to speak, was the big DShK machine gun mounted on the hull of the vehicle. In good condition, that would fetch 20,000 Afghanis in the bazaar.

They passed Charikar and the big Soviet base at Jabal-es-Seraj which was responsible for the security of the Salang Tunnel and the area round it. Apart from the usual infantry and armoured units, a battalion of Spetsnaz were based here, ready to be helicoptered out to deal with any emergency. They reached Gulbahar at the mouth of the Panjsher Valley without incident, but now began the slow climb up to the Salang Pass and Tunnel and that was where an ambush would most probably come, if come it did.

Fatima drove with an assurance that impressed Wills. When he complimented her, she said she had often driven one of Durran's captured Russian staff cars, as well as lorries. A tanker was not very different. She changed down, double declutching expertly, as they came to the first bend in the long series of zigzags that led eventually to the tunnel.

At first Wills did not hear it above the roar of the engine as they laboured up the gradient. Fatima did. 'Someone's shooting up ahead. It must be mujahideen.'

Then Wills did hear it. A rattle of machinegun fire and one or two heavier explosions, either mortars or rockets.

'Sounds like an ambush. Yes, look, something's been hit up front.'

A thin column of black smoke rose into the air some-where near the front of the convoy which immediately began to slow down and then stopped. Somewhere ahead of them, an APC opened up with its heavy machinegun, the blast amplified by the mountains on either side of the road so that sound and echo became blurred in one long drum roll. The smoke was thicker and blacker now, and the crackle of automatic weapons noisier.

Wills found the sweat running down his face and wiped it away impatiently. 'Jesus, if we get hit the whole bloody lot will go up, us included.'

'If the shooting comes closer, we'll have to get out.' Fatima's voice was calm, but her face was pale. The tanker ahead of them suddenly jerked into motion. 'Allah be praised! If we can keep moving we may be all right.'

Fatima let in the clutch and they ground forward in bottom gear, slowly creeping round the long bend until suddenly, they came on the APC, firing long bursts of heavy 50-millimetre rounds at the hillside from where the ambush had apparently come.

'Reinforcements,' Wills shouted, pointing upwards. Fatima peered through the windscreen and then ducked as the roar of an Mi24 gunship filled the cabin, the down-draught from the rotors sending a cloud of brown dust and grass spinning into the air in a mad dervish dance.

A hundred yards further on there was another hold-up. A Soviet tank was bulldozing a still-burning tanker off the road. They waited, engine running, while the wind drove the smoke across the road. A motorcycle siren keened behind them high above the sound of engines and small-arms fire and a Soviet military police patrol shot past. A few minutes later, the convoy started forward again.

When they came level with the smouldering tanker, Fatima slowed down to inspect the damage. A Russian MP stepped forward and blew his whistle at them, making urgent signs that they should drive on.

'Go on,' Wills said. 'We don't want to argue with this bloke.' The MP was striding towards them menacingly, looking like a man from space in his heavy white plastic jacket and thick trousers. He shouted incomprehensibly, but the hand signals were unmistakable. Fatima let in the clutch and the tanker jerked forward, leaving the MP still mouthing angrily behind them.

'Fuck you, Jack, we're fireproof.' Wills laughed.

Fatima spoke without turning her head. 'What do you say, Mike? Something's on fire?'

'No, no. It's British army slang. It means I don't care about you. I'm all right.'

'It sounds very selfish. And uncivilised.'

'It is. But I suppose that's what war does to you.'

'Maybe. I don't think the war has made Afghans more selfish. But it probably has made them less civilised, more brutal. And it has brought some of the worst elements to the top.'

'Like your friend the Butcher?'

'He's no friend of mine.' She spat out of the window in contempt. 'This man is the worst sort of Afghan leader. He gives all mujahideen a bad name.'

'I'm sorry. It was a joke.' Wills knew it sounded lame. Then she surprised him. She gave him a brief smile. 'I know. It's the British sense of humour.'

As they pulled away, out of the smoke, a high-pitched scream invaded the cab, followed a split second later by a succession of tremendously loud bangs, like giant firecrackers at Chinese New Year. 'Bang-bang-bang-bang-bang-baaang.'

'Jesus.' Wills craned round in his seat to see what was happening. 'It was just behind us. There's a hell of a lot of smoke and dust. Must have been rockets — 122s, probably.'

Fatima, eyes on the road, face tense under her hat, had her foot hard down. The tanker lurched from side to side, the bodywork groaning with the strains of the bumpy surface.

Wills was still peering into his wing mirror. 'I can't see the others ... yes, there they are now. Thank God, I thought they might have copped one of those rockets. Who the hell's firing at us? If it's your people, they ought to be shot.'

'It's not our people. They had strict instructions. It must be people belonging to the Butcher. He's always making trouble, as you know. This is exactly his kind of operation. Against a soft target.' The tanker crawled down a slight hill before starting to climb again.

Two miles further on, the convoy stopped. One of the tankers had broken down. Repairs took several hours and by the time they had it going again, it was almost dark.

'How much further?' Wills asked.

'An hour perhaps. Maybe longer.'

The long line of vehicles, their headlights making it look like some phosphorescent snake, began the long haul to the tunnel. Eventually, after an interminable series of sharp zigzags, Fatima said, 'There it is. The Salang.'

Excited despite himself, Wills leaned forward and peered through the dirty windscreen. Ahead of them, in the darkness, he could see what looked like a semi-circle of yellow lights.

'It looks like the mouth of an illuminated whale. And we're Jonah, about to be swallowed up.'

'Please?'

'Nothing. A story from the Bible. Jonah was swallowed by a whale and spent a long time in its belly before being spewed out safe and sound. God saved him.'

'I hope Allah saves us.'

Wills shouted above the roar of the labouring engine, 'What will happen when we get to the checkpoint? Do they search every vehicle?'

'No. The head of the convoy stops to show his papers and then they usually let you drive straight through. After paying a bribe, of course.'

'They always have to pay a bribe?'

'Of course. The Russians always want money, or hashish. He will give them both today, as well as telling the Russians we are forty vehicles instead of forty-two.'

'And if the guard counts them and finds the figure's wrong?'

Fatima shrugged. 'The chief of convoy will just say he made a mistake. And give the guard some more money. Don't worry.' She gave a good imitation of a laugh. It was a brave effort. He could hear from her voice how nervous she was.

Wills glanced in his wing mirror at the tanker behind. All he could see were its headlights, moving up and down with the vagaries of the road, but he could visualise Gradinsky, one elbow thrust aggressively out of the window, watching their tail-lights and, like himself, thinking anxiously about the mission ahead.

'Do you trust him?' Fatima's question surprised Wills.

'Who, Gradinsky? It's a bit late to start distrusting him, isn't it?'

'I suppose so. Perhaps it's because we are nearly there now and the question that's been in my mind for so long, like a seed, is suddenly growing.' She was silent for a moment, as she wrestled the wheel round the last bend before the approach to the tunnel. There were only a few hundred yards to go now. 'Isn't it strange that a Russian, for whatever reason, should want to blow up his own people?'

'Not so strange if you think of the things that have happened to Gradinsky. They killed his brother, after all, in a particularly sadistic way. I don't think he'll ever forgive them. I was suspicious, too, at the beginning, you know. I thought he was almost certainly a KGB agent. God knows, he still may be. But I doubt it. And in any case, when we get to the tunnel, I'll be watching him. And if he steps out of line, there is always this.' Wills patted his left armpit. Fatima knew he carried a Makarov pistol, the standard personal weapon for a Soviet paratroop officer on active service.

'Well, we'll see very soon now. But I'm surprised to hear you defending him. Perhaps you are trying to convince yourself too!'

The gaping black mouth of the tunnel was only two hundred yards away, and the crags of the Salang mountain were a dark mass, rising almost sheer to the summit of the pass at 13,350 feet, 2,000 feet higher than the tunnel itself. The head of the convoy must have reached the checkpoint and stopped, because the rest of the tankers began to slow down and bunch together.

The brake lights of the tanker in front glowed red. Fatima braked and stopped, too, but kept the engine running. As the minutes crawled past, Wills patted the pistol in its shoulder holster again, to reassure himself, and rehearsed in his mind the exact sequence of things he had to do to start the count-down. Whatever was happening at the front of the convoy, it took an agonisingly long time. They sat in tense silence, expecting a guard to materialise and demand to see their papers.

But no one appeared and eventually the convoy started to move forward again. As they trundled towards the checkpoint, Wills examined it: brightly lit, strong enough to withstand a direct hit by a 122-millimetre rocket or an 82-millimetre recoilless rifle. In the middle a window, heavily sandbagged. Wills could see a soldier, staring straight at them, but busy talking into a handset.

'He's on the telephone,' he told Fatima.

'Yes, he's reporting to the checkpoint at the other end how many vehicles in the convoy and when the last vehicle has gone through.'

The tunnel entrance yawned huge and black above them and suddenly, with a roar and stink of diesel, they were inside.

Thirteen

General Orlov's car was waved through the gate of the old palace compound and swept up to the dimly lit lower house front door, guarded by two KGB sentries with walkie-talkies. As the car approached, one of them spoke into his radio and a brighter light went on above the door.

Colonel Zarina Shahnawaz, wearing a long black dress and high heels, got out and walked slowly towards it. When she reached the doorway she turned and looked back, as if at the lights of the city below. The door was open behind her, and for a second or two her silhouette was framed against the light.

'Come in quickly, Comrade Colonel.' The voice of the orderly in a white mess jacket who was holding the door betrayed his anxiety. Zarina understood perfectly why he was nervous. The lighted open door would be a tempting target for any sniper hiding in the hills round the palace. But she was all innocence as she turned to greet the man.

'Hello, Mikhail, sorry to keep you waiting.' She spoke almost perfect, unaccented Russian and her warm husky voice was so attractive that the man immediately forgave her and smiled.

'Don't worry, Comrade Colonel. It's just that since those bastards of *dushman* shot us up a few weeks ago, we try to give them as little opportunity as possible. The Comrade General has ordered a semi-blackout. Come with me, please.'

He led the way across the hall, the once elegant parquet floor loose and broken now, to a big room at the back of the house. The door was open and the orderly tapped on it and announced the visitor.

Orlov, who was sitting reading official papers in a comfortable armchair by the empty fireplace, made a show of getting to his feet in a hurry. 'My dear Colonel, how exceptionally nice to see you.'

As the door closed he put his arms round Zarina, kissing her full on the mouth. He sniffed appreciatively. 'You smell delicious.' He stepped back slightly to study her, almost as if she were a picture he was thinking of buying. Her long thick hair, jet black with the faintest sheen of mahogany, the dark, almond eyes, skin the colour of a ripening peach and wide, inviting mouth made her the most beautiful woman Orlov had ever seen.

'Come and sit down, my darling, over here. I have of course read your report but I want to hear about it from your own lips.' He laughed. 'But this is supposed to be a celebration.' He rang a bell beside the fireplace. 'I have a little surprise for you.'

The orderly appeared in the doorway. 'Mikhail, bring in the caviar and the champagne. Is it chilled? Don't take all night.' He turned to Zarina. 'With all the damned power cuts we have these days, you never know if the fridge is going to be working. If ever we arrange a party in the mess, you can bet your last rouble that the *dushman* will choose that night to blow up the power lines.'

Orlov laughed, a slight edge to his voice, as if she were somehow to blame.

He pulled her down on the sofa beside him, turning his blue eyes and all his charm on her. 'Zarina, my darling, I need your help.'

'Of course, Sergei. But how can a KHAD colonel help the head of the KGB in Afghanistan?'

Orlov, sitting facing her on the sofa, looked at her directly, his blue eyes ice-cold despite the warmth of his manner. 'I'll tell you how.' He smiled. 'By letting me make love to you after dinner.' As he moved towards her, there was a knock on the door and the orderly came in, poker-faced, wheeling a trolley. On it stood a bottle of Dom Perignon, a plateful of blinis and a big bowl of caviar.

'This is the best — both the champagne and the Beluga. Look how big the grains are, and the colour. Almost like pearls, aren't they? And all for love of you, my darling.'

'Sergei, you are too kind and I don't deserve it.'

'Don't you? Why not? You are not up to something behind my back that I don't know about, are you? A secret lover somewhere. A *dushman*, maybe?' He laughed and Zarina blushed.

'Of course not, Sergei, why do you say such things? I had no lover at all until I met you. You know that.'

'I was only teasing you, my dear.' He patted her hand and poured her a glass of champagne. 'Here, drink this, it's delicious. Like you. Your good health, my darling, and a speedy end to this bloody war.'

'*Inshallah*.'

Orlov took a mouthful of champagne. 'You must eat some of this caviar. It really is very special and I don't know when we'll get anything as good again.' He loaded a blini with caviar, and stuffed it into his mouth. He took a mouthful of champagne, leaned over and pulled Zarina towards him, his face close to hers.

'I said I needed your help. I meant that. Shall I tell you why? It is not only I who have read your report about your trip to see your sister in the Panjsher. Several of my officers have also read it and I must confess, my dear Zarina, that they have raised some awkward questions.' Orlov took her soft chin in his fingers and twisted her head round so that she had to look straight at him. 'For example, they seem to think that the foreigners we nearly arrested in Kabul may have been in the Panjsher some time ago, possibly about the same time as yourself.'

There was silence as his fingers dug into Zarina's soft flesh. She twisted away suddenly, her strength and speed throwing Orlov off balance so that he slipped off the edge of the sofa and fell fowards, banging his knee painfully on the parquet floor. He was up immediately, cursing angrily, his blue eyes ablaze.

Zarina shrank back into the corner of the sofa, two red marks showing on her chin where Orlov had gripped her so savagely. 'I'm sorry, Sergei, I didn't mean you to fall, but you were hurting me.'

The Russian sat down, rubbing his knee, and forced a smile. 'It is I who am sorry. I did not mean to hurt you, my darling, but my anxiety got the better of me. Let me explain.

But just have some more of this delicious caviar, it would be a crime to waste it.'

Zarina tried to refuse, but Orlov insisted, his eyes glittering as he helped her. He downed his glass of champagne and refilled it. 'Let me tell you why I'm anxious. These officers of mine, men who have been in the KGB for many years and whom I trust implicitly, are saying that – forgive me for even repeating such a thing – are saying that perhaps you have tricked us. They are suggesting, that instead of working for us, you are really working for the *dushman*. That you are, not to play with words, a traitor in the ranks of KHAD and therefore a traitor to the KGB.'

'Sergei, this is not true. Why do these people say such things? I have been a member of the PDPA all my adult life. I have worked for KHAD for five years. I have been trained in the Soviet Union, by your own KGB. I have been promoted repeatedly until I am now the only woman to hold the rank of colonel in the KHAD. My work has been commended by the Interior Minister himself. Why now should I suddenly be a traitor?'

Her dark eyes flashed and she looked more beautiful than ever, something that was not lost on Orlov.

He tried to calm her. 'I didn't say I believed them. I simply said these people had read your report and this was what they were saying.'

'Why didn't you stop them? Why didn't you defend me?'

With an angry gesture, Zarina stood up and made for the door. But Orlov was quicker and caught her half way across the parquet, gripping her arm and swinging her round to face him.

'Where are you going? Are you trying to run away?'

'I'm not running away. But I'm not going to stay here and be told I'm a traitor. Do you think I have no pride?' She twisted free. 'And you're hurting me.'

Orlov let go of her arm. 'My darling, let us discuss this thing rationally. I am sure you can put all our minds at rest. For myself I would ask for nothing better. Please, come and sit down. I promise I won't hurt you again.'

He forced her to swallow a further mouthful of blini heaped with caviar. 'Let me ask you a few questions. When

157

you arrived in the Panjsher, you say that your sister Fatima was not there but that she arrived later?'

'Yes, she was away on a brief mission, but they sent her a message saying that I had arrived and she came the next day to see me.'

'And then you saw Durran? You said in your report, I think, that he was in the Parende Valley, one of his favourite hiding places, and you went there to see him?'

'Yes, my sister and I went together to meet him in Parende, in one of the caves he uses from time to time. You know he moves about a lot to avoid capture.'

'I know all about the slippery bastard, you don't have to remind me.' Orlov's expression was sour. 'And the transponder?'

'I told you in the report. I switched it on as soon as we arrived in Parende. We were there for two days and a night. Did you not pick up the signal?'

'Nothing!' Orlov's eyes were hard. There was a long pause. 'And you gave him our message that we would like to talk to him seriously about taking part in a new transitional government? That we might have a very important post to offer him?'

'Yes, I told him everything you had said, exactly. He asked many questions and I answered them as you had told me to. That he would be offered safe conduct to Kabul, that he would be allowed to bring his own bodyguards, that he would be treated as a VIP and that he would have talks with you, General Ustinov and the Russian Ambassador. We had a very long talk and then he said he would think about it and discuss it with his top people and that he would give me his answer in a couple of days' time. Meanwhile he said my sister, Fatima, would look after me and would tell me how they, the mujahideen, the *dushman*, saw the future.'

'And what did she tell you, remind me, my darling?' Orlov was almost purring.

'She said they wanted peace, too, but that they would never accept a PDPA government in Kabul. However, she said, Durran saw the need for a compromise to stop the killing and the suffering and that was why they were interested in the message I brought from you.'

'So what did Durran have to say, tell me again in your own words.'

'Well, next day, he came back to Parende...'

'Where had he been?'

'I don't know, they never say where he has been or where he is going. But he was very friendly and said he had discussed your proposal at great length with his senior commanders and the elders of the valley and they had come to a unanimous decision: they wanted to end the war which had killed and maimed so many Afghans and destroyed so much of the country, but not at any price. There must be a government in power which reflected the true wishes of the people.'

'Meaning?'

'Meaning a government acceptable to Durran, his commanders, the elders, the *mullahs* and, of course, the people of the country. But no PDPA.'

'He must know that's not acceptable to us.'

'Yes, of course, but he is prepared to talk in order to see if a compromise is possible.'

'But not to come to Kabul?'

'Not yet. He wants talks first in what he called a neutral spot. Under four eyes. You and him.'

'A bandit demanding to talk to the general commanding the KGB in Afghanistan, as if he were an equal!'

'He thinks he is.'

Orlov kept control of himself with difficulty. 'Well, he'll soon find out he's making a big mistake. A very big mistake. So when did he ask you to spy for him?' Orlov's voice was suddenly sharp-edged.

'Spy for him? Sergei, why do you ask a ... crazy question like that?'

'Crazy? We too have our people, one of them very close to Durran. He has told us that he asked you to spy for him and you accepted. I have his report on my desk.'

There was a moment of absolute silence in the room, accentuated by a distant explosion which made the glass in the big windows rattle.

Zarina had gone pale, but her eyes flashed with anger. 'I don't know who your spy is, Sergei, maybe he only exists in your imagination, but Durran did not ask me to spy for him and I never accepted any such offer.'

Such was her emotion that he could see her breasts rising and falling. Orlov found her maddeningly attractive. He took her hand impulsively.

'I believe you, Zarina, of course I believe you.'

There was a discreet tap on the door and Mikhail appeared with another bottle of cold Dom Perignon. 'That's the last one, sir. There are some fresh mulberries and cream, if you'd like me to bring them in.'

Orlov smiled indulgently. 'Bring them in, Mikhail, and then you can go to bed.' He filled their glasses from the fresh bottle and raised his glass. 'Here's to you, my darling, I never doubted you personally, but I wanted to hear it from your own very beautiful lips. My mind is now at peace and we can enjoy the rest of the evening together.' Orlov clinked glasses and watched until Zarina took a sip.

Mikhail returned and set down two plates of purple mulberries. They were as big as loganberries and had a delicate, slightly watery taste. Zarina ate a few and then pushed the plate away. 'I love them more than anything else in the world, but I am not hungry.'

'More than you love me?'

'That is different, Sergei. My love for *tut* is to do with my childhood, our old house in the country and its lovely garden. There used to be lots of *tut* trees in that garden.'

'Where was your house?'

'Near Jalalabad. Have you been there? It is very beautiful?'

'A couple of times, but I did not have time to appreciate its charms.' He reached out his hand and stroked her cheek. 'I am much more interested in your charms, Zarina.' His hand dropped to her breasts. 'I want you desperately.'

He pinned her against the cushions and kissed her with such passion she had to twist her head away to breathe. 'Sergei, you are so strong, and so passionate.'

His voice was thick with ardour and champagne. 'Come, my darling, let me take you upstairs.'

Orlov had just unbuttoned Zarina's dress and was running his hand over her gently curving belly when three or four sharp explosions shattered the relative calm of the night.

'Damn those *dushman*. Don't they ever get some sleep?'

'Don't worry, Sergei, what are a few more rockets?' Her small, soft hand began to unzip his trousers and to fondle him at the same time. 'Come, lie down on the bed and let me undress you.' So subtle were her attentions that Orlov hardly heard the next salvo of rockets, and even the throb of helicopter gunships scrambling to try to find the mujahideen gunners was not enough to distract him from the pleasure Zarina was bringing to a head so skilfully. The climax, when it came, was long and violent and left Orlov panting.

'Zarina, promise me one thing?'

'Anything you want, Sergei.'

'Promise me you will never do that for any other man. Promise.'

'Of course I promise, Sergei. Never.' She kissed him gently and, with a contented sigh, he rolled to one side, turned on his back and was soon asleep. Zarina climbed softly out of the bed and walked to the window. The night was still again and beautiful, a half moon spreading silver across the lawn and edging the shadows which lay like black pools beneath the trees. She leaned half way out of the open window and breathed in the fragrance of the night, the smell of moist earth and a sudden sweetness, perhaps of jasmine. After a few minutes, she tiptoed back to the bed where Orlov was asleep.

She started to dress and in the darkness, fumbling for her earrings, knocked a bottle off the table beside the bed. It crashed on the floor and bounced away across the room, bringing Orlov awake with a start. 'Zarina, is that you? What's happening?'

'Shhh. It's me, Sergei. I knocked something off the table. I'm just getting dressed.'

'Why are you getting dressed? Come back to bed.'

'I have to go home. The driver will still be waiting. Please, Sergei.'

'Let him wait. I want to make love to you again.'

Orlov lunged forward and caught Zarina by the arm, dragging her on to the bed.

She struggled. 'Please, Sergei, let go. You're hurting me again and you're ruining my dress.' Orlov ignored her pleas and tried to unzip her dress.

161

'Sergei, stop it.' She twisted away from him, her elbow catching him painfully in the eye.

'You bitch, that hurt.' He slapped her savagely across the face and then, as she ducked, he seized her by the neck and started to shake her. Zarina thrashed from side to side in an effort to throw him off, but Orlov was so strong that she could not break his grip. Her breath whistled in her throat. She began to panic and, as her arms flailed wildly, one hand struck a metal object on the bedside table. It was a statuette in bronze which Orlov had won at some stage in his military career and which always stood beside his bed. Her fingers closed round the base and, with a desperate strength, she swung it straight-armed at him. The bronze made a rubbery crunch as it met Orlov's skull and immediately the terrible grip on her neck slackened.

For a few moments she could only lie panting, trying not to vomit. Her neck felt as if it were burning, her head throbbed. She thought she would pass out, but after several minutes she was able to sit up and with a shaky hand switch on the bedside light.

Orlov lay sprawled on his back, quite still, a huge red mark above his left eye. She bent closer. He did not seem to be breathing. She shook the still figure.

'Sergei, Sergei, wake up, wake up.' The round blond head fell sideways, like a doll's. 'Oh, my God.'

For a moment Zarina stood as if transfixed and then, trembling with the effort, she dragged the body into a sleeping position, pulled up the sheet and smoothed away the signs of the struggle. If they did not discover the body until morning, it would give her a few valuable hours.

Then, hands still shaking, she zipped up her dress, tidied her hair and walked swiftly and quietly downstairs. Mikhail had disappeared, but the guard on the front door, half asleep, roused himself grumpily and rang for the General's driver. He let Zarina out but did not respond to her good night.

The driver was even less enthusiastic. He dropped Zarina with a curtness that fell only just short of downright rudeness, spinning his wheel and racing off up the empty street.

She let herself into the dark, silent house she shared with

her mother and ran up the stairs and into her bathroom, snapping on the light. The face she saw in the mirror gave her a profound shock. Haggard, black-circled eyes stared wildly back at her, but it was her neck which caught and held her horrified gaze. Orlov's fingermarks were imprinted there in angry red weals, like a disfiguring birthmark.

She turned away and, resisting the impulse to burst into tears, began to change into a long black *chador* that covered her whole body from head to foot. She took nothing except a small pistol, slipping it into an inside pocket, scribbled a note to her mother and tiptoed down the stairs.

Outside, it was still dark, the streets deserted. She closed the door behind her and started to walk in the direction of the Bala Koh. There she would find one of Durran's men and he, she hoped, would hide her.

Fourteen

As Wills and Fatima plunged into the tunnel, they were immediately swallowed up in a swirling blue cloud of exhaust fumes. The headlights picked out the reflectors of the lorry in front which glowed at them like the eyes of a predator. Wills knew he had only a few minutes before they reached a point roughly one kilometre from the southern entrance and seventeen hundred metres from the northern end, where they planned to stage their breakdown.

He flicked on the torch and looked at his watch. Three minutes to eight. He took a small object out of his top left-hand tunic pocket. It was made of black plastic and was the size of a matchbox. The voice of the jovial instructor from the safe house at Hidbrook, explaining to Gradinsky and himself the black arts of bomb-making, came back with amazing vividness.

'This is the timing device, known in the trade as the E cell and used by Black September – that's Fatah's old battle name – since about 1972 and also, more recently, by gentlemen like Abu Ibrahim of the 15th of May Group which specialises in aircraft bombings.

'The E cell is a miniature electroplating device no larger than the filter tip of a cigarette. A few tiny transistors convert it into a timing device which will fit easily into a matchbox. It is silent, shockproof and highly accurate.

'Now, to set the cell, you pass a known current through it for the desired delay time. Remove the battery and you leave the delay permanently imprinted in the cell's "memory". Pass the same value current through the cell in reverse and when the exact period of time programmed into the cell has elapsed, its resistance changes, and that triggers the detonator firing circuit.'

The instructor, a cheerful giant of a man, had grinned. 'A handy chap with rudimentary knowledge of electronics could easily tune a pair of E cells to give the same delay times. That's you two beauties,' he had added, nodding at Wills and Gradinsky. 'Since you won't know until you're virtually in the tunnel when you want to set off your charges — after all, there might be a traffic jam or some other kind of hold-up — it's really much more sophisticated than you need. But we're going to give you the E cell all the same because it's so reliable.'

Wills peered out at the crudely hewn rock walls of the tunnel. Occasionally there was a gleam of silver as the headlights caught a trickle of water from the roof.

The instructor had then gone into a long rigmarole about how the thing worked, which Wills had barely understood at the time. Curiously, most of the words were still sharply imprinted on his memory, perhaps because they were so strange.

'For those of you who are technically minded, the E cell operates in the following manner. It measures the flow of electrons between a silver case and a gold electrode at its centre. During the setting or programming phase the electrons flow to the silver case and silver ions plate on to the gold electrode. The rate is a function of current and time.'

'Whatever that means,' Wills had whispered to Gradinsky.

'To act as a timing device, the same current is passed through in reverse and the silver deplates over the same period of time, ending with a voltage rise. That's to say the E cell can be programmed with a specific battery current for a specific period of time... It is highly accurate,' the instructor had concluded, 'to .9995 of a second.'

Wills's digital watch started to bleep. It was ten o'clock. He knew that behind him Gradinsky's watch, synchronised precisely, would also be bleeping. In his wing mirror, Wills could see the dipped headlights of the second tanker following about fifty metres behind. He reached forward for the convoy light switch — Gradinsky would be watching their tail-lights — and flicked the switch off and on: one, two, three times. Then quickly he removed the black panel on the dashboard and snapped the green timing switch firmly down. Behind them, his whole body tense, Gradinsky would have waited for the lights to come on for the third time and immediately snapped his own switch down.

'How far are we now, Fatima?'

'Five hundred metres from the entrance of the tunnel.'

Wills's heart was thumping from the realisation that he had started an irreversible process, a process that would blow two enormous holes in the living rock of the Salang mountain, as well as atomising whoever else happened to be in the vicinity at the time. He was also acutely conscious that if anything went wrong with their own escape, they would all be blown to kingdom come themselves.

'The others should be stopping now.' Wills kept his eye on the lights behind. They started to drop back. 'They've stopped. Right on target. Only five hundred metres more for us.'

In precisely thirty minutes the timing circuits in each tanker would start the detonating train to the deadly cargo in the number one tanks, each carrying one thousand gallons of methyl nitrate. 'Like the E cell, methyl nitrate is favoured by Middle East terrorist groups. and has 32 per cent more kick, or *brissance* as they call it in the trade, than nitro-glycerine.' Wills remembered the jolly instructor promising, with an anticipatory smile, that it would be 'an almighty great mother and father of a bang.'

'Two hundred metres to go.' Fatima's eyes kept jumping from the road to the brightly lit speedometer in front of her. 'God give me strength.' It was a cry of anxiety as well as of supplication.

Wills reached across and put his hand on her arm. 'Don't worry. Everything's going to be all right. We'll have plenty of time to get away.' He looked at his watch. Twenty-eight minutes precisely. Not much room for error.

Fatima kept her eyes on the road. 'It's not myself I'm worried about. The breakdown people will be Afghans. Maybe Russians too. I don't care about them. But the Afghans will come first, to tow us away. It's them I'm thinking about. They're going to be blown to bits by us, by me, another Afghan. For you it is nothing. Another job, another mission. But these are my people, my flesh and blood.' Her voice was shrill above the noise in the cab.

'Take it easy. It's bloody, I know. But we have to do it.' You shit, he told himself. It's all very well for you. They're not your people, you don't give a damn, only about your own rotten skin.

'One hundred metres to go.' Wills wiped the sweat from his face with his sleeve. Despite the cold at 11,000 feet, it was like an oven in the tanker. The red lights of the vehicle in front danced like a will o' the wisp in the haze of diesel fumes. The walls of the tunnel were a brown blur.

'Fifty metres ... Get ready.'

Wills reached into the rucksack between his feet and brought out a small hacksaw. Fatima took her foot off the accelerator and let the tanker coast for twenty yards. As they rolled to a halt Wills bent forward, checked the safe arming light on the timer was off and snapped the red arming switch on. Then he opened his door and jumped down on to the road, hacksaw in hand, as the red tail-lights of the tanker in front disappeared into the darkness.

A few seconds later he had the bonnet open and was feeling for the metal pipe which ran from the diesel fuel tank to the engine. It worked on a suction basis so all he needed to do was to cut a thin slit in the pipe. He started to saw. The metal was hard, possibly steel, and it took Wills nearly a minute to make a cut deep enough to make sure the engine could not be started. That should slow the recovery team down a bit.

Five hundred metres behind them he could just see the dipped headlights of the other tanker, but it was too far to detect any movement beside it. Apart from the four of them, the tunnel was empty, the wind whistling disconsolately; the cold, even in early summer, beginning to bite. The weak overhead strip-lighting only emphasised the gloom, and where the neon tubes had burnt out, pools of shadow lay in the roadway.

Wills remembered the briefing about the mass suffocation of 1982; of how, it was said, seven hundred people had been trapped in the tunnel and had been gassed by their own exhaust fumes, unable to get out. At least that could not happen to them, whatever else might.

Fatima had pulled their rucksacks out of the cab and placed them against the side of the tunnel. Wills took out the two Kalashnikovs with folding stocks and snapped on the magazines. He glanced towards the northern entrance, in the direction of the Soviet Union: the tanker that had been immediately in front of them would be well out of the tunnel by now. If the driver reported that there was a breakdown behind him, the recovery team could be on its way in a matter of minutes. On the other hand, if he did not, the fact that two more tankers had gone into the tunnel than had come out might go unnoticed for some time. It depended too, as Wills knew, on the flow of traffic, generally light at this time of night, and on whether that traffic was Russian or Afghan. Wills looked at his watch. 22.06.

He had one more thing to do. Slinging the rucksack over his shoulder, he ran thirty yards beyond the tanker, dumped the rucksack on the ground and pulled out what looked like a small black box. It contained about a quarter of a pound of Semtex. Wills knew all about its lethal properties from his Special Forces training. Quarter of a pound was more than enough to cause a nasty surprise to any recovery vehicle coming to tow away the broken-down tanker. Wills taped the small black package to the side of the roadway. Finally, to activate it, he turned on a small clockwork timer and connected the detonator. Then he shouldered the rucksack and trotted quickly back to where Fatima was waiting.

'Twenty-one minutes to go. Time we were moving.' Torch in one hand, Kalashnikov in the other, Wills set off at a fast trot south down the tunnel towards the second tanker. Fatima ran with an easy, athletic stride close behind him, the thud of their feet echoing off the rock walls. When they were about half way, a torch started to flash on and off in the half darkness ahead.

'That must be Gradinsky and Jan Mohammed.' Wills stopped and returned the signal, pressing down the button on the top of his torch and releasing it three times in quick succession. Then they started running again, faster now, the air cold in their lungs, towards the solitary tanker.

'Come on, you're three minutes behind schedule.' Gradinsky's voice was gruff and it was too dark to see his face. Wills did not answer directly.

'Did you throw the arming switch?'

'Right.'

'Disable your vehicle and set the delaying charge?'

'Sure, what the hell do you think we were doing?'

'I make it exactly 22.13. Seventeen minutes to go.'

'Check. Let's get out of here.' Wills could not help smiling to himself. If he had not known Gradinsky was Russian, he would have sworn that the voice belonged to an American. 'OK, Major, lead the way, you're pointman.'

'I already checked the door. Durran's men have done their stuff. It's open. This way, and mind you don't step on the delaying charge.' Gradinsky followed the rock face for a few yards, to where, half hidden in a slight recess, the solid steel door Gradinsky had described was let in to the outer wall of the tunnel.

'Here's the door. I remembered it pretty well, although it's easy to miss in the dark.' Gradinsky started to pull the door open, swearing in Russian when it jammed.

Outside, the air was cold and the wind whistled unwelcomingly. Gradinsky shone his torch carefully downwards to a small ledge below the door. Beneath that the mountain seemed to drop sheer away in the dark.

'Come on, there's some sort of step here, but watch how you go. We don't want anyone breaking a leg.' Finding a handhold on the rock beside the door, Gradinsky swung himself down, dropping the last couple of feet to the ledge. 'Here, Fatima give me your hand. OK? Right, Mike? Now Jan Mohammed. You don't need a hand. OK everybody? Let's go.'

Moving cautiously at first, until their eyes became accustomed to the starshine, Gradinsky led the way down and across the steep south-east slope of the Salang mountain, picking his way between enormous boulders which over the centuries had come crashing down from the ridge above. Some were the size of a small house, perched crazily above the void which they could only dimly discern below them.

'We'll head towards the road, but about half way down before we get to it there's a donkey track that takes you

169

along the north slope of the Panjsher and eventually to the Anjuman Pass. Jan Mohammed has been telling me all about it.'

'We have thirteen minutes before the Big Bang,' Wills said.

'*Inshallah.*' To everyone's surprise, including her own, Fatima managed a chuckle.

They climbed down the rest of the way in laboured silence, even the Afghans occasionally slipping and stumbling, Wills and Gradinsky swearing when they missed their footing or banged into a rock. Below them the road was a dark blur, without traffic or movement. They used their torches sparingly, pointing them only at the ground or when Wills and Gradinsky consulted their watches.

Three or four hundred yards below the tunnel, Gradinsky, trying to see the time while on the move, tripped and fell heavily with a smothered curse. He stood up rubbing his knee and swearing quietly to himself. 'I thought I'd broken my goddamn leg.'

They all stopped while Gradinsky tested his leg, hobbling awkwardly. Wills peered at his wrist. '22.26. Four minutes to go. How far from the track?'

'It's hard to know exactly. I'd say another few hundred metres.'

Wills took charge. 'Then I think we should get behind a big rock and wait for the bang. Afterwards we hit the path and make our getaway in the confusion.'

'I think this is the best plan,' Fatima agreed. 'Jan Mohammed says there is a big rock here where we can shelter...' She broke off. 'Listen, something is happening on the mountain.'

They all looked up. Torches were flashing near the tunnel, and they could hear shouts.

'Sounds like a patrol. Are they Russians or Afghans?' Wills demanded.

'Russians,' Fatima said after a pause. 'I think they have discovered the door and are looking for us. Did we leave it open?'

'I think we did. It's too late now to worry about it.' Wills's voice was abrupt. 'Let's get behind the rock. I make it two minutes to go. No one's going to find us in that time.'

Gradinsky was staring up at the darkened mountain. 'If

they try to turn off the arming switch, they'll blow themselves to hell and back. Anyway, let's take cover. Jan Mohammed, lead the way.' Gradinsky limped after him.

'Are you going to be all right?' Fatima asked.

'Sure, it's nothing. Be OK in a minute.' The rock had a slight overhang towards the road and they crawled under its broad canopy, squeezing their bodies as close to the mountain as they could. Wills kept up a running commentary, his torch making a tiny red glow inside his jacket in the darkness. 'One minute to go...'

The pause seemed endless. The wind blew in chilly gusts, swishing through the grass. That and the huge bulk of the rock between them and the tunnel made it impossible to hear what was going on above them.

Jan Mohammed, who had been keeping a watch, reappeared. '*Shurawi* soldiers still outside tunnel. I see their torches flashing.'

'They coming this way?'

'No, they stay beside the tunnel.'

'Thirty seconds...'

Gradinsky cleared his throat. 'After the explosion, stay where you are until I tell you. There'll be a helluva lot of stuff raining down on top of us.'

'Ten seconds...'

The wind dropped. Silence.

'Five, four, three, two, one...'

Wills stopped counting and for a split second he thought he had made a mistake. The silence seemed to expand, grow, and finally burst.

Like a volcano erupting, a huge reverberation gathered deep inside the mountain, as if the world were coming to an end. Fatima gave a low cry. Wills felt his mouth dry with fear. An enormous pressure squeezed his head, and then a great rumbling explosion shook the ground like an earthquake. He felt dizzy and disorientated as the echoes swelled across the valley. It started to rain debris; at first small stones and lumps of earth, then big rocks and finally huge boulders went spinning past. One landed on top of their rock with a crack like a bursting mortar; two more just missed and went crashing down the hill in front of them.

For a terrifying moment when the whole mountain seemed to be on the move they thought that their own huge rock was going to keel over and crush them to death. But it stayed firm, sheltering them from the rain of shattered fragments. Finally there was silence.

Wills, who was the first to emerge, looked up at the mountain. To his amazement, it looked just the same, dark and forbidding and without visible signs of the chaos that must have been wreaked within.

'We'd better be moving.' Wills found himself speaking unintentionally in a stage whisper. The others stood staring in silence up at the tunnel. It was Jan Mohammed who broke the spell in matter-of-fact Farsi.

'He says we must go quickly, before the helicopters come looking for us.'

As they started down the mountain, a siren started wailing at the southern end of the tunnel.

'I wonder what's happened? Must be serious,' Gradinsky said. They all laughed, the sudden relief of tension making the joke seem twice as hilarious.

Fifteen

Once they reached the track, rough as it was, they began to make better time. Jan Mohammed, cat-like in his ability to see in the dark, led the way, striding out with a sureness of foot that Wills, who had fought with and against many mountain men in his SAS days, could only admire but not emulate. Gradinsky walked behind Wills, still limping slightly, and last came Fatima, her slimness and stamina suggesting a hard-as-nails boy rather than a woman. They were heading almost due east and they had, they knew, most of the night in front of them. It would be first light at about five-thirty, and half an hour after that the sun would climb above the mountains into a clear sky banishing concealment.

Wills waited for Gradinsky to catch up. 'When can we expect the first choppers?'

'Any moment now.' Gradinsky panted as they went fast up a sudden rise in the track. 'They'll scramble from Bagram and be here in five minutes. No sweat about flying at night now. Not like the old days.' He stubbed his boot against a rock. 'God-damn this country.'

'And foot patrols?' Wills asked.

'They'll have every man out on the mountain who can walk. Hey, Jan Mohammed, keep your eyes and ears open in case of an ambush. Understand? *Shurawi*. OK?'

Jan Mohammed, a shadowy figure in front, slowed down and waited until they were all together. 'All the time, I am watching for an ambush. If it happens, defend yourselves and then, when you can, go to the top of the ridge, above us. Wait for half an hour without moving and then listen for the cry of a little animal, like this.' He gave a sharp whistle.

173

'Marmot,' Wills said. 'Little orange-coloured animal. Sits up and stares at you among the rocks.'

'Yes. Just like this. Marmot, you say? I will make that call. Then you come to me. Now, we should all keep silent.'

Jan Mohammed disappeared into the darkness, walking fast. The moon had just risen and they could see its radiance lighting the sky above the ridge, although they were in deep shadow. Wills and Gradinsky occasionally tripped or stumbled, their eyes unable to tell the difference between a patch of sand and a small bush or a rock.

'Damn and blast.' Wills's boot caught in a tuft of grass and he went sprawling painfully on his face among the stones. As he got to his feet, he felt Fatima's hand on his arm steadying him, a delicately feminine gesture and strangely comforting on that bleak mountainside.

'Thanks, clumsy of me. I just can't see in the dark like you and Jan Mohammed.'

'We are brought up on the mountains. It's our country, you know.'

It was Fatima who heard the helicopters first, a second before Jan Mohammed and several seconds before Wills and Gradinsky were able to pick up the staccato beat. Once you had it, it was unmistakable, even at a distance, the hurrying sound full of menace.

They stopped and listened, trying to gauge the position of the two Mi24s flying without navigation lights. All they could tell was that they were approaching from the south, probably from the big base at Bagram, north-east of Kabul, and heading north. As they passed almost directly overhead, the engine note began to recede slightly.

'They're circling, heading west. Lucky for us.' Gradinsky gave a short laugh. 'We might as well keep going while we can. You know, they have night-sights. That is, if they're the Mi24Ds, which I guess they will be.'

'Can you tell by the engine sound?' Wills was rubbing his shin which he had banged against a rock in his fall.

'Don't think so. Not me, anyway. But only the Russians fly Ds, we don't give 'em to the Afghans.'

'We? I thought you were on our side?' It was impossible to tell if Wills was joking.

'Hell, you know what I mean. The Communists. Anyway, even with the night-sight they'll have a job spotting us. But we don't want to take any chances. If they come close, take cover right away. OK?'

'Yes. These image intensifiers work on body heat, and there isn't too much of it around up here.'

Jan Mohammed spoke urgently in Farsi to Fatima. 'He says he knows a cave on the way to Panjsher. He wants to get there before it is light. We can hide there during the day and continue when it is dark.'

'How far?'

Fatima shrugged. 'You Westerners always ask this question. Maybe four hours. It depends on how fast you walk. Listen.' The helicopters sounded a long way away. 'We should move while they are still above the tunnel.'

'*Birra*,' Jan Mohammed urged. '*Birra*.'

'Know what "*birra*" means, Mike? It's one of the few Farsi words I picked up in the army. It means, "move your ass".' Gradinsky laughed, pleased with the Americanism, and started after Jan Mohammed.

As they strode on fast on a gradual down slope, the rotor beat of the Mi24s, which had been barely audible, grew louder with disconcerting suddenness. The helicopters were heading towards them, following the contours of the ridge and not very high. 'Down, everybody!' Wills shouted and ran towards the only rock he could see near the path, just big enough to hide behind. As he crouched down a shadowy figure came running towards him.

'Fatima? Over here.'

'I don't know if he saw us, he came so quick.' They had to squeeze together to conceal themselves. The unseen lead Mi24 advanced along the ridge, the swish of its rotor blades like some grim scythe, the infra-red night-sight searching for its prey. Wills and Fatima flattened themselves behind the rock which now seemed pitifully small. They could feel the down draught from the rotors as the big gunship slowed down and went into a semi-hover, like some overweight kestrel. Wills guessed what was coming and reached out a protective arm towards Fatima, his hand brushing her cheek. She caught it in her fingers and clung to it.

There was a sharp sound like a whiplash and an ear-splitting report. The sky burst into flame above their heads and two rockets, one from each pod, struck the ground on the far side of the rock with colossal force. They could feel the shock of the impact as they pressed themselves flat on the hard, cold earth, hearing the whine of shattered fragments of rock flying past their heads like shrapnel. In a moment of aberration Wills thought he was back in Oman, pinned down by tribesmen in a blazing hot *wadi*. He had lost three friends that day, and very nearly his own life as well.

He came back to the present with a start as the first gunship wheeled away, raising himself on one knee to listen for the second Mi24. Suddenly he saw it, briefly silhouetted against the moonlit sky, a dark predatory shape, its ugly snout poking forward in their direction.

'Here comes the second bastard.'

Wills pulled Fatima towards him, trying to shield her. As the beat of the rotors approached, deafeningly close now, they both pressed themselves flat, careless of the hardness of the ground, trying to make themselves as small as possible, fragile bundles of flesh and blood at the mercy of this all-seeing monster in the sky.

Wills's ear told him the Mi24 was slowing down, going into the hover and lining up the target. There was a *whoosh*, a vicious crack and the rockets raced over their heads and smashed into the hillside behind them. Twice more the Mi24s circled and struck, some of the rockets ricocheting off the ground and describing wild arcs in the night sky. They made one last circle without firing and then headed for home, the thud of the rotor blades becoming almost innocuous as it dwindled into the distance.

Wills stood up and pulled Fatima to her feet. To his surprise, she was crying. He put his arm round her shoulders and held her tightly.

'You'll be all right in a minute. It's the shock.'

'It's silly of me. I have been bombed many times, but never like that, so close and so loud.'

'It terrified me, too.' He disengaged his arm gently. 'We'd better get moving, before they change their minds and come back for another try.'

Jan Mohammed and Gradinsky appeared round the side of the rock. Gradinsky brushed bits of earth and rock dust from his hair. 'Hell. That was too bloody close for my liking. You all right, you two?'

'Fine now, thanks. Do you think they spotted us?'

'Not sure. I think they saw something down there, but didn't know what it was. So they just hosed the mountain, in case.'

'What they used to call prophylactic action in my days in the army. Come on, Jan Mohammed, lead us out of this damned place. I don't think it's too healthy.'

The next few hours became for Wills and, he guessed, for Gradinsky too, a purgatory which seemed as if it would never end. It reduced all of them to stoic silence, the only sound now the occasional clink of Kalashnikov against rock, the thud of a tripping boot and always, like a perpetual refrain, the harsh breathing of people whose physical endurance was being tested to just short of breaking point.

The path, a pale, narrow blur in the moon's reflected radiance, wound up and down and across the steep southern flank of the Salang ridge at a height of about 12,000 feet, sometimes perilously near the edge of a sheer drop, with a river cascading noisily but unseen at the bottom.

Wills had learned in the army that long drawn-out physical effort, like the forced march which this was, became more manageable if he could switch his mind off the tortures of the present and in the direction of almost any fantasy, preferably gastronomic or sexual. This he did now, with some success. At least it made the pain tolerable. Shortly after the moon had set, Jan Mohammed lost the way and as they cast about in the dark, they heard a dog barking. Wills's immediate thought was of a Russian patrol. But Jan Mohammed, after listening for a few seconds, said, '*Shurawi ne, Kuchi.*' Not Russians, but Kuchi nomads.

They walked in the direction of the barking dog, Kalashnikovs at the ready, for the big mastiffs could be savage. The barking grew more and more hysterical as they drew closer and then, in the dim light of the stars, they could just make out the dark shape of a tent pitched on a patch of grass above a stream. Jan Mohammed called out in Farsi, '*Dost, dost*. We're friends. Is anyone at home?'

A man's voice replied and a figure emerged from the tent, shouting at the dog to be quiet. When it still went on barking he picked up a stone and flung it: the dog gave a yelp, and reduced its protests to deep growls.

Although it was now nearly four in the morning, the Kuchi approached and engaged Jan Mohammed in friendly conversation. 'He says we missed the path about half an hour back and we now have to climb higher to find it again,' Fatima explained.

Wills and Gradinsky protested in unison. 'Not up again. Why is it always up and never down in your country, Fatima?'

'It is better to be up.' Fatima did not realise the question was facetious. 'The Kuchi is telling Jan that the cave is about one hour from here and that we will be safe there.'

The nomad led them uphill for about ten minutes until they were on the path again and sent them off with loud prayers for their safety. Despite his fatigue, which made even speech an effort, Wills wondered aloud at the helpfulness of a total stranger. 'There can't be many places in the world where, if you wake a man up in the middle of the night, get him out of bed and ask him the way, he not only tells you without complaining but gives you his blessing as well.'

'I think it's bloody marvellous. And yet we have the gall to call these people underdeveloped. Underdeveloped! Someone's crazy and it's not them.' Gradinsky made a rude noise.

They toiled on, the path winding in an apparently endless zigzag up the mountain, no sound now except the scrape of their boots on the stones, the painful intake of breath and the blood pumping in their ears. At about five, Jan Mohammed stopped and pointed at something ahead. As they stood, straining their eyes, the faintest tremor of light began to lighten the sky to the east.

Fatima's voice was excited. 'You see there, straight ahead? That big rock? The cave is there, at the foot.'

'God be praised. I've never wanted to sit down as much in all my life.' Gradinsky gave a groan.

They climbed the last quarter of a mile at a quickened

pace, despite their tiredness, the sky growing brighter with each passing minute. Jan Mohammed, who had been made responsible for their safety by Durran, wanted to reach the cave before the sun was above the mountain rim.

'He is worried that some spy will see you and report your presence to the Russians,' Fatima explained.

'Spies, why should there be spies on the top of this God-forsaken bloody mountain?' Exhaustion was getting the better of Wills's patience.

'Why? Because there are spies everywhere. You should know that.'

Jan Mohammed reached the cave well ahead of the others and stood just outside the entrance, peering in, torch in hand. When Gradinsky arrived and made as if to go in, Jan Mohammed held out his hand. 'Wait, one minute, please.' He inspected the interior by torchlight for several more seconds and then took a cautious pace forward. 'You see? Here. Tripwire.' It was invisible except when the light caught it. Jan Mohammed disconnected it with great care. 'Over there. You see those stones? Under the stones, there is mine. You walk into cave, so, then ... Boom!' He threw his hands in the air and mimicked the sound of an explosion.

'Thanks for stopping me. Let me know when I can do you a favour, too.' Gradinsky, for once, was serious.

They advanced into the cave rather tentatively, until Jan Mohammed said something. 'He says you don't have to worry any more. You are quite safe now. Come to the back of the cave. You can rest here.'

Someone had collected a pile of wild rhubarb and spread the big flat leaves on the floor at the back of the cave. They crackled noisily when they sat on them but made a very adequate bed.

'My God, it's good to sit down. I don't think I've walked so far and so fast since I completed my Spetsnaz training. Now I can have a little rest.' Gradinsky rolled on his side and was asleep within seconds.

Outside the cave, a little before six, the golden rim of the sun rose tentatively above the jagged edge of the eastern mountains, paused as if to catch its breath and then climbed the sky with the swiftness and splendour of a god.

It was out of the sun, at five minutes past six, that the two SU25 jets came in a silent rush, flying at one and a half times the speed of sound. The sudden roar of a jet engine and the blast of the bombs as they dropped a hundred yards from the mouth of the cave came almost together and then the first SU25 was gone, climbing steeply to avoid the ridge. The second jet followed hard behind, the 500-kilogram bombs dropping even closer and hurling rocks and earth high in the air. It too climbed steeply away above the mountain and into the cloudless blue of the morning sky.

The first bombs shattered the slumbers of Gradinsky and Wills and sent them scrambling forward to join Jan Mohammed who was standing outside the entrance of the cave.

'Where's Fatima, Jan Mohammed?'

He pointed down the hillside in the direction of the Kuchi tent.

'God, I hope she's all right.'

'Probably safer than being here in this goddamn cave,' Gradinsky growled.

'Maybe. But how the hell did they come to bomb the cave? Did the bastards know we were here? Or is it just guesswork?'

Before Gradinsky could reply, Jan Mohammed pointed down the valley. 'Look, they're coming again. Quick.'

Wills shaded his eyes and peered into the sun. 'I can see them, coming straight for us.' They were travelling at enormous speed, and in silence, two black specks against the pure blue of the sky, rapidly becoming recognisable as SU25s, their wingtip fuel tanks clearly visible. As they came on, still uncannily silent, two small roundish objects detached themselves from the belly of the first jet and started to fall in a precise arc.

Jan Mohammed had already disappeared inside the cave but, with the coolness of men who have been shot at many times, Gradinsky and Wills watched professionally as the two bombs, their fins sharply etched in the pristine air, came racing towards them. The scream of the jet and the crash of the bombs, the two explosions so close together as to become one, made them duck involuntarily as stones, rocks and debris flew towards them. Wills's attention was caught by a rock the size of an armchair describing a lazy parabola high in the air. Mesmerised, he watched as it came straight towards them, his mind frantically trying to calculate if it had the velocity to reach the cave.

'Look out, for Chrissake,' Gradinsky shouted. 'It's going to hit us.'

They started to scramble backwards towards the mouth of the cave but the big rock dropped thirty yards short with a thump that made the ground tremble. Smaller stones and earth rained down all round them.

The jets made one more run and then they heard them climbing away into the blue and silence descended again on the valley. Wills looked into the sun half way up the sky now in unruffled majesty, but it was innocent of any threat.

Jan Mohammed pointed. Two tiny figures were coming up the ridge, about a quarter of a mile below them. One was clearly Fatima, the other looked like the Kuchi from the previous night. Seeing them standing outside the cave unharmed, one of the figures started to wave.

'Thank God, she's safe,' Wills said unsteadily.

'Thank God we're all safe, you mean.' Gradinsky laughed and then put his hand on Wills's shoulder. It was the first time that he had done such a thing and Wills, also for the first time, felt real warmth for the man. After all his doubts about Gradinsky, he now felt he could trust him. Irrational, maybe, but being bombed together did generate a certain cameraderie.

'Yes, thank God we're all safe. But when Fatima arrives and we've had breakfast, and I must say I'm absolutely famished, I think we should push on, don't you? Maybe they were just bombing on spec, but this cave doesn't seem all that safe, any more.'

Gradinsky shrugged. 'They must know the muj use this cave from time to time. After all, they mined the place, so they certainly knew it existed. They probably thought, what the hell, let's give it a go.'

Sixteen

The staff cars started arriving at Soviet military headquarters at Darulaman, in south-west Kabul, shortly after
two in the morning. General Orlov, his head heavily
bandaged, sat hunched in the back seat of his camouflage-
green, bullet-proof staff car, staring bleakly out of the
window at the sleeping city. In these declining days of the
Soviet occupation the population, once cowed and sullen,
had become overtly and actively hostile. As in Saigon in
1975, which Orlov had monitored from Hanoi, no matter
how many roadblocks you erected, you could never keep all
the guerrillas out. How could you tell who was a guerrilla
and who was not, anyway? They did not wear uniforms and
they came in all shapes and sizes: old men, boys, and of
course women. When a woman was veiled from head to toe,
you could not tell what she was carrying under her *chador*:
it might be a Kalashnikov or a Koran. And if you were an
Afghan, you would not think of searching her, in any case.
It was a sure way to start a riot. There had been a number
of ugly incidents when Soviet troops had made the mistake
of trying to search Afghan women in the street. On one
occasion it had led to a pitched battle between Afghan and
Soviet troops in the middle of Chicken Street.

Orlov had telephoned General Ustinov half an hour ago.
'Bad news, I'm afraid, sir. The *dushman* have attacked the
Salang Tunnel. I've just had a call from the night-duty
officer. First reports say two very big explosions. Very
extensive damage and the tunnel blocked.'

'What the devil's going on? How did the *dushman* get
into the blasted tunnel, let alone blow it up? Who's
supposed to be in charge of security there?'

It was a rhetorical question and Orlov sidestepped it. 'I've ordered a full alert. Roadblocks in the whole area. Patrols everywhere and the air force mobilised. We have a report the criminals have been seen.'

'Seen? I want them hung, drawn and quartered, but only after I've personally cut their livers out. Get over here right away. I want all senior commanders in my office in half an hour.'

'Very good, sir.' Orlov had put the phone down and rung his ADC on a house line. 'Get dressed quickly. The old man's hopping mad and wants us there in half an hour.'

By 2.30, General Ustinov was facing his senior commanders across the table.

'There's going to be hell to pay for this, I can tell you, comrades. But before we go into all that, we'd better hear the latest details. General Orlov, what have you got to tell us?'

Orlov cleared his throat. As a result of Zarina's blow, his head was throbbing painfully, but he was too old a soldier to let himself be rattled. He smoothed a piece of paper on the table in front of him. 'I spoke to the desk officer in KGB headquarters from the car, just before I got here. He confirms two very big explosions inside the tunnel, quite a long way apart, more or less at either end. A tanker convoy had just gone through. We don't know for sure yet but one possibility is that a couple of the tankers were rigged as lorry bombs and deliberately halted in the tunnel. It's also possible of course that the bandits got the stuff into the tunnel by some other means. The quite exceptional size of the explosions, however, inclines us to believe they were lorry or tanker bombs.'

'Could it have been a tanker, or two tankers, blowing up from what you might call natural causes?' General Ustinov glowered across the table, jaw jutting aggressively. 'I mean do we definitely know it was sabotage?'

Orlov took his time about replying and then spoke with measured emphasis. 'You mean an accident?'

'We've had one before,' Ustinov snapped.

'Out of the question, sir, in my opinion. It was sabotage, and no *dushman* hit or miss job, either. This was a thoroughly competent piece of work, cleverly conceived,

183

carefully planned and expertly executed. A first-class sabotage operation carried out by professionals. Real professionals.'

Orlov paused and looked round the table. Ustinov sat stony-faced, as well he might: his job was on the line and the rest of them knew it. Grishin, the air-force commander, who was wearing a flying jacket as if he had just come back from a sortie, looked smug: he and his were clearly blameless. Fodorovich, the armoured-corps commander, looked half awake and bad-tempered at being disturbed in the middle of the night; and finally there was the new infantry commander, Brodsky. Orlov did not like him, and referred to him as one of the jumped-up generals brought in by the Gorbachev regime.

'To me the whole thing smells like a CIA or SAS job, or maybe both. In the last couple of months we've had reports of foreign agents crossing the border, being seen near the Panjsher and so on, and then we captured one of Durran's people, you may recall, who told us that at least two foreign agents were actually in Kabul and on their way to carry out some operation in the Salang area. You may remember, sir, the army got the tip-off and without informing the KGB, who as everyone knows, are in overall charge of security in general, and of measures against foreign agents in particular, went ahead and raided the house in the old part of the city where these people were staying. And what happens?' Orlov spread his hands as if to emphasise the magnitude of what was to follow. 'The bloody fools let them escape.' He glared at Brodsky. As infantry commander, the riflemen concerned were technically under his control.

Orlov turned back to Ustinov. 'I must stress they were not my people, Comrade General. We in the KGB had nothing whatever to do with that abortive operation. And if you want my opinion, sir, the people the army let escape from that safe house in Kabul are the people we are looking for now.'

Ustinov saw Brodsky bridling and cut Orlov short. 'Let's keep this as factual as possible, gentlemen. Anyone else got anything to say? No? Right.' He pressed a buzzer on his desk and his ADC, a brigadier, came in.

'Boris, take a note and then do an Order of the Day to all

184

units. Operation Clean Sweep to find the foreign agents who carried out acts of sabotage against the Salang Tunnel and Soviet and Afghan army forces on duty there has absolute priority. General Grishin, I want you to make a helicopter force available to search the whole area. Do that right away.'

'We've already scrambled two Mi24s from Bagram, Comrade General. And when it's light we'll start scouring the whole area.'

'Right. I want them alive, if possible. Understood, everybody? Brodsky, I want the Spetsnaz put on immediate alert and standing by to jump on these bastards when we find them. Where's the standby battalion?'

'In Bagram, sir.'

'Right. Put one company on alert for a dawn take-off, Fodorovich. I want all roads in the area patrolled with immediate effect. Especially the road into the Panjsher. Send a strong column right up to Rokha and beyond, if necessary.'

'I'll have to take them from the Kabul reserve, sir. There's no one else. The Fiftieth went home last weekend, on normal rotation, as you know.'

'Yes, yes, I'm not senile, yet. Although I may be by the end of this charade.' He turned to Orlov last. 'General Orlov. I'm putting you in charge of Operation Clean Sweep. You will be responsible directly to me.

'Now, comrades, the general plan is this. Sooner or later, these people will be sighted, either from the air or by a foot patrol. As soon as they're spotted, it's imperative that headquarters is informed as rapidly as possible. That's number one. Number two is speed of reaction. I want a Spetsnaz team in the air within minutes. Their job is to find the saboteurs, do a snatch job and bring them back alive. I want to know everything about these people: who they are, what they are, where they come from, who sent them, which bandit groups they're connected with, the routes they used and, don't forget everyone, I want them alive.'

General Ustinov pushed his chair back noisily and stood up. The meeting was over. 'Sergei, wait a second, would you?'

Orlov gathered his papers slowly while the others filed out of the room.

185

'Feeling better?'

'Thank you, sir. Much better. The doctor said I've got a thick skull.'

'Lucky for you. But for God's sake, watch your step, Sergei. Any more slip-ups and Moscow will start asking awkward questions. And neither of us wants that, do we?'

'No, sir.' Orlov had gone pale, the sweat beading his forehead.

'Caught the girl yet?'

'Last night, sir.'

'That's something. She said who she's working for?'

'Not yet, sir, but she will.' Orlov spoke through clenched teeth.

'Right. You better get on with it, then. And let's have some results this time.'

Seventy miles to the north, as the crow flies, Jan Mohammed was leading his three companions at a fast pace to the east, towards the Panjsher. They kept high on the side of the ridge, sometimes following goat trails but, where they petered out, scrambling across the screes. It was hard going and Jan Mohammed drove on ruthlessly. Three times they heard the sound of helicopter gunships and knew that they were being hunted. They took no chances, going to ground when the gunships were still a long way off, lying hidden among the rocks with their *pattus* covering them until the beat of the rotors faded into the distance. At midday, when they stopped to drink from an ice-cold stream and to chew a few bits of *nan*, they caught their first glimpse of the Panjsher Valley, a narrow green and gold furrow between two sharp-peaked mountain ranges, the southern one a distant blue wall.

Gradinsky sat resting his back against a rock, looking out over this scene of beauty and apparent tranquillity. 'Our main danger is going to come from a Spetsnaz patrol. And we probably won't see them until we're right on top of them.'

'If you were calling the shots, how would you use them?'

'Well, I'd have some out between where we are now and the Panjsher, on the basis that we might easily be headed that way. The only problem they'll have now is that with no bases left in the Panjsher, it's not so easy for them to operate

186

there any more. They're probably nervous of dropping in a company of men and having them cut to pieces by Durran and his boys. They'll be anxious to avoid casualties at this stage in the game. That might just work to our advantage.'

Jan Mohammed, who had been studying the mountains ahead through binoculars, said something to Fatima. 'He thinks we will be safest if we go down the valley of Parende which is over on our right. It is very narrow and there are some caves there where we can spend the night, if necessary. From there we should be able to make contact with the local mujahideen and get a message to Durran.'

'Maybe they'll give us some food as well. I'm starving.' Wills patted his stomach. 'Listen. It's completely empty. Any more *nan*?'

Fatima shook her head. 'All finished. But we will get something in an hour or two. *Inshallah.*'

Wills managed some sort of laugh. 'Of course, *inshallah*. Let's go on then in the hope of reaching human habitation before it gets dark. Having got this far, it would be a pity to break a leg pretending to be a mountain goat.'

They walked fast, thankfully downhill now, across a bleak field of bare rock and stony earth. The wind whistled in the crags, whipping the grass almost flat. It was like being on the edge of the world. The short rest had revived them and Wills found his spirits lifted by a carpet of tiny blue flowers – a kind of gentian – flourishing on a south-facing slope. They rounded a patch of rocks and surprised a family of snow buntings, buxom and unafraid, as if there were no enemies at this altitude, their streaky brown and white camouflage blending perfectly with the background.

'These birds are very tame. And you only find them up here, in the mountains.'

A shadow touched them briefly and Wills looked up to see a lammergeier vulture sweep past on great, black wings. They watched as it circled and came gliding past them again, the cruel beak and expressionless yellow eye watching them speculatively above the handsome yellow beard and breast. It kept them company for half an hour, soaring high above a ridge and then sweeping down behind them as if investigating their suitability for the next meal. Disappointed, perhaps, it veered away and began to rise on outstretched wings, riding the thermal currents until eventually it was only a speck against the blue sky.

'They do not kill like other birds of prey,' Fatima explained to Wills. 'They eat only dead things. Horse, donkey, anything that dies on the mountain. In that way they are very useful, as well as beautiful.'

'He looked as if he would have been very happy to have eaten us as well, if only we'd been dead.'

They crossed a high meadow. On the far side, half a mile away, stood a small *banda* and, as they passed, two men appeared at the doorway and gazed in their direction.

'Who are those people?' Wills asked.

'Kuchis,' Fatima said. 'Nomads, or maybe refugees.' At the lower end of the meadow, a stream cascaded through a thicket of silver birches and plunged into a ravine where they could hear it rushing and roaring far below them. Jan Mohammed was on home ground now, making very fast time downhill, with the others following at fifty-yard intervals. They crossed the river, a raging torrent, by leaping from rock to rock, the path taking them past a handful of ruined houses, destroyed by the Russians in the days when they still thought they could bomb the Afghans into submission.

A few miles further on the valley narrowed, squeezing the path between the river and the limestone cliff. Jan Mohammed signalled to them to halt and went ahead to reconnoitre. It was cool and damp under the trees, the air filled with the steady roar of the river as it poured in a crystal flood over a huge boulder in midstream. Grey wagtails flitted from rock to rock, their melancholy calls like the voices of drowned souls, and occasionally a dipper, like a black bullet, went shooting past.

After a quarter of an hour Jan Mohammed reappeared and, beckoning them to follow, began the steep climb up the cliff. Half way up, on a hairpin bend, a couple of trees had been felled, blocking the path and forming a natural checkpoint. Pointing at them through the leaves was a Russian DShK heavy machinegun. A fiercely bearded face under a flat Chitrali cap appeared beside it and shouted at them to stop. There was a loud click which sounded like the safety catch being moved to 'off' and the wild-looking mujahid shouted at them to identify themselves.

'*Dost*,' Jan Mohammed replied, adding a rapid explanation of who they were and mentioning the magic name of Durran. This seemed to satisfy the guard, who beckoned them round the end of the barrier, embraced Jan Mohammed and shook hands with the rest of them.

'He wants us to go up to the *qarargah*, the headquarters,' Fatima explained, 'to meet the commander.'

They climbed another few hundred feet to where, near the top of the cliff, the rock jutted out to form a narrow ledge, with a cave behind it. Most of the entrance had been walled up with big stones, leaving only a narrow gap at one side. Trees clung to the face of the cliff, half concealing the cave, and under them an old UNRWA tent had been adapted to make an awning. On the outer rim of the ledge, the mujahideen had built a solid-looking, breast-high *sangar* or wall made of big rocks. In the middle, where the ledge stuck out several feet, they had installed another DShK.

Wills inspected the position with a critical eye. 'They seem to have done their homework, what do you think, Anatoly?'

Gradinsky craned his neck to look upwards. The cliff went up another one hundred and fifty feet, with a pronounced overhang at the top. 'I wouldn't want to be the one who had to abseil down. Not if I wasn't invited. I don't suppose they have an alarm system up there, but I would want one if I lived here.'

The commander now appeared, a large, bushy-bearded man with an engaging smile and a crushing handshake. 'This is Abdul Wahid,' Fatima explained. 'He is a very famous commander and has killed many Russians. He tells you welcome and hopes you will be his guests.'

'*Bishi, bishi*.' The commander's large hand indicated they should sit on the rather tattered carpets which covered the rock ledge. At another word from him, a mujahid brought cushions and thrust them behind the guests' backs.

'Please sit down and rest.'

Wills and Gradinsky sank gratefully on to the carpets and stretched out their exhausted limbs. An attentive mujahid brought hot sweet tea and *nan* while Abdul Wahid apologised for the inadequacy of his fare.

'Tell him not to apologise,' Gradinsky said. 'We know there's a bloody war on. I don't know about anyone else, but I'm so hungry I could eat a horse.'

'*Amerika, Amerika*?' the commander asked, much impressed.

'Yes, *Amerika*,' Gradinsky said. 'From New York.'

The commander turned to Wills. '*Amerika* too?'

'No, English. From London.

'Ah, *Angrezi*, Lon-don.' The commander gave the two syllables their full weight, gazing at his guests with almost embarrassing attentiveness.

Fatima distracted him by launching into a long explanation of their importance, but without going into details of the Salang operation, explaining to Wills and Gradinsky in an aside that if she told the commander everything, the knowledge that he was harbouring such important criminals might have alarmed him unnecessarily. As the shadows deepened, the commander's men brought out a Tilly lamp which they pumped vigorously until it threw enough light for them to see one another, as well as the plates of rice and goat meat which the younger mujahideen carried out and set in front of them. There was little talk as the rice was devoured, but over the tea afterwards the conversation revived.

'How many men does the commander have here?' Gradinsky wanted to know.

'Twenty-five, but they are not all here today. Some have gone down to the Panjsher on a mission and so there are only eight here now. One guard you saw when we arrived. Another is on top.' Fatima pointed to the top of the cliff behind them. 'And the rest are here.'

'Has there been much fighting here, in this valley?' Wills asked.

'He says yes, a lot before. When the Russians were trying to smash Durran's organisation, they made all those offensives against the Panjsher. They used to give them numbers. In 1982 it was Panjsher Five and Six. They got up to Ten eventually. Maybe it was more, I can't remember exactly. Several times they sent commandos up this side valley, the Parende. Durran comes up here sometimes and they were always trying to catch him. You saw those houses which were bombed, on our way down? But they have not been here for a long time.'

Gradinsky gave a prodigious yawn. 'I think I'll turn in.'

'Me too, I can hardly keep my eyes open.' Wills got up and walked over to the *sangar*, leaning his elbows on it and looking out through the trees. The sound of the river rose to meet him, filling the darkness with a comforting roar.

It occurred to Wills that it was also loud enough to mask all the other noises of an Afghan night.

Seventeen

For a second Wills thought it was thunder. There had been some earlier on, just before they went to sleep. But now there were too many crashes in quick succession.

He was half out of his sleeping bag when a bullet ricocheted off the rock outside the cave. As he tried to find his boots, he bumped into Gradinsky who swore at him in Russian.

'I think your friends have arrived, Anatoly. Someone who hasn't been invited, anyway.'

The commander burst out of the cave, shouting orders to his bewildered mujahideen.

Fatima's voice rose above the din. 'Mike, Anatoly, over here. I have your spare ammunition.' She was standing by the entrance to the cave, a faint silhouette against the starry sky. They stepped outside warily, ducking down to reach the *sangar*. The machinegunner was firing short bursts into the trees below, the sound that originally woke Wills. Spurts of flame stabbed the darkness as the attackers fired back. Wills, his eyes just above the *sangar*, watched the course of the battle for a few minutes. 'Fatima, tell the commander to save their ammunition. Fire only when they see a flash.'

A bullet struck the *sangar* beside them and whined off into the trees. Crouching, Fatima moved down the ledge to talk to Abdul Wahid. He shouted orders to his mujahideen and then took over the machinegun himself. Wills wondered how much ammunition they had.

During a lull in the attack, there was a loud hiss and a rocket shot high above the trees. 'Flare,' Gradinsky said before it exploded high above them and started to drift down, casting a harsh white light on the trees and rocks around them. As it drifted lower and the outline of the cave came into view, an intense burst of fire made the defenders duck below the shielding breastwork. Something swished just over their heads and exploded against the rock face with a colossal bang.

'RPG.' Gradinsky's voice was matter-of-fact. 'Here comes another goddamn flare.'

The rocket went shooting up into the night sky and, almost lazily, burst above them. Only Gradinsky and Wills kept their eyes on the darkness in front as another RPG thumped against the rock, below them this time. Gradinsky pushed his Kalashnikov over the edge of the *sangar* and fired a couple of bursts at the place where he had seen the muzzle-flash from the RPG. There was a shout of pain in the darkness below. Gradinsky's cry of triumph was greeted by another heavy burst of firing, this time closer and from a different angle.

Wills turned urgently to Fatima. 'I think they are trying to outflank us. Ask the commander if they can get as high as us on either side.' After a few moments of rapid talk and pointing, she turned back to Wills. 'Yes, on this side, the right, they can. But not the other one.'

'Right, ask him to send a couple of men to the right, to stop them getting above us. And to fire only when they have a target.'

'He says he is sending two men right away. They know exactly where to go.'

Two men started to dodge along the *sangar* and disappeared into the darkness. Almost immediately there was a heavy burst of firing from the trees thirty yards away, on a level with the ledge.

'Just in time, Mike, well spotted. Those bastards were trying to creep up on us.'

As the shooting died away a loud electronic squawk broke the silence and a voice, amplified by loudhailer, echoed through the trees. The English was heavily accented but unmistakable. 'We know who is there. We know there is a group of *dushman* living in this cave. But we also know there are two or three foreign agents of the CIA in the cave as well. We have no quarrel with the *dushman*. If you surrender, you will go free. I promise that on my honour as a Russian officer.' The loudhailer gave a tinny shriek and there was a pause while the speaker tried to adjust it.

'Spetsnaz,' Gradinsky said.

'How do they know we are here?' Fatima's voice was tense.

'Maybe the two shepherds. They would shoot one of the poor guys and the other would tell 'em. Simple. Standard Spetsnaz stuff.'

The loudhailer squawked again and the voice boomed through the trees, the words distorted but the message clear. This time it was in Farsi, for the benefit of the Afghans.

'*Dushman*, lay down your arms and you go free. When we shoot the next flare, drop your weapons, raise your hands above your heads and walk down the mountain. You have two minutes to decide and then I fire the flare.' The Russian paused to let his message sink in. On the ledge there was no response. They all waited, the sound of the river suddenly louder in their ears.

The electronic voice boomed out again. 'When you see the flare, drop your weapons and start walking. If you don't, you will all be killed. You understand? All of you. More troops are on their way by helicopter now. You have no chance. Why should you die for the CIA? I repeat, you have two minutes only.' The voice echoed round the cliff and died. The silence was profound, even the roar of the river seemed muted.

Wills and Gradinsky turned to one another in the darkness. 'Clever bastards...' Gradinsky hissed but, before he could finish, the commander spoke in urgent Farsi.

'What does he say?'

'He says they will never surrender and the mujahideen will never betray a friend. When the flare goes up he will start shooting.'

'And the others?'

'They will follow their commander.'

Wills hoped privately that they were all as brave as Abdul Wahid.

The loudhailer squawked. 'One minute.'

The seconds ticked away. No one spoke; the only sounds the clink of metal as the mujahideen reloaded magazines and readied themselves for the coming battle. Abdul Wahid fed a new belt of the heavy steel-tipped bullets into the breech of the machinegun and patted his captured weapon affectionately, making what sounded like a joke in Farsi. Jan Mohammed translated, 'Commander say this Dashaka good gun. Vairy good gun. He himself take it from the Russians after big fight.' Abdul Wahid gave a chuckle.

'He's a brave man.' Gradinsky's voice was full of admiration. 'Fatima, tell him when the flare goes off to start firing straight away. And traverse the gun, from side to side. OK?'

The last few seconds ticked away. Gradinsky was reading off the stopwatch timer on his digital. 'About ten seconds to go.'

There was a noise like a sharp intake of breath. The flare hissed into the sky, burst and opened like a white poppy, flooding the scene with a garish brilliance. The commander leaned forward, depressing the muzzle, and started to fire, swinging the long barrel in a slow traverse from right to left. For a moment, as the tracer cut a swathe through the trees, the Russians seemed to have been taken by surprise. He had completed the traverse and was swinging back again by the time they recovered, opening fire from all sides, the bullets and RPG rounds smashing against the *sangar* and the rock face and ricocheting off into the darkness like angry bees.

There was a cry of pain from the far end of the ledge and Fatima vanished, clutching the first-aid kit. She was back five minutes later, out of breath. 'One man badly wounded. Another dead. Very heavy firing that end.'

Wills and Gradinsky had been taking it in turns to try to pick off anyone who tried to get too close, waiting for a flash and then shooting straight at it. The other meanwhile had been making a pile of hand grenades on each side of the machinegun, ready to repel a frontal assault.

In one brief lull, they heard cries and shouts from the trees below them. Gradinsky poked his head over the *sangar* to listen. 'They have some wounded. Two or three, I guess. Someone, probably the officer, says to call up the Medevac choppers. And I think I heard him say Bagram.' There was more shouting, some of it from a distance. 'I think they're waiting for daylight and reinforcements before hitting us.'

Abdul Wahid was having an urgent conversation with

Fatima. 'He says he doesn't think he can hold out much longer. At least one man is dead, maybe two, and one badly wounded. He does not know what has happened to the guard on the barrier below us. He has not been shooting for quite a long time. That leaves only four mujahideen up here, the commander and us. He says the enemy will wait for more people now and for the daylight.'

Gradinsky grunted. 'I think he's right. If I was the Spetsnaz commander, I would do exactly that. Why lose good men in the dark when time is on your side?'

The loudhailer gave a preliminary shriek and the voice of the Spetsnaz commander echoed up to them. 'Listen carefully, *dushman*. This is your last chance. Very soon now our reinforcements will arrive. You have until daybreak to decide. Surrender or we will attack your positions with helicopters. We will blow you to pieces. Your lives are in your own hands. Think about your families. Do all of you want to die?' There was a screech and a click and silence returned to the cliff.

The wind must have changed because they could hardly hear the river now. Abdul Wahid had a long whispered coversation with Fatima.

'He says he thinks the Russians will not attack again until dawn but we cannot be sure. So he will keep watch. He says you must be very tired and that you should get some rest. They are making tea and there is some *nan*. When we have eaten we should sleep. The commander will stay on guard.'

'Has he got any Stingers?' Wills asked.

Fatima shook her head. 'He says Durran has a supply but not here. But he has sent one mujahid to get two RPGs from another cave.'

'Better than nothing,' Gradinsky commented. 'You can shoot down a chopper with an RPG if it's low enough. And if you're a good enough shot.'

A few minutes later a smiling mujahid brought a pot of tea and bits of *nan* wrapped in a cloth.

'My God, that's the most refreshing drink I've ever had.' Wills held out his glass for more.

'I agree. I think it even beats champagne. But I never did like this *nan* stuff very much.'

196

Five minutes later, they were asleep, huddled against the *sangar*.

Wills woke in the night to hear a mujahid groaning in pain in the cave. He heard Fatima get up. 'Can I do anything?'

'No, sleep. You will have to fight later. I will go.'

Wills drifted off to sleep again, jerking awake when she reappeared. 'How is he?'

'He just died, poor boy. He was so young. Not even eighteen.' He knew she was crying although she made no sound.

Gradinsky rolled on to his back and his snores reverberated off the rock face. Wills kicked him and the snores stopped.

Shortly after dawn, a mujahid shook Wills by the shoulder, his voice agitated. '*Birra, birra*, allicoptair, allicoptair ...' They had slept with their boots on, wrapped in their *pattus*. On the opposite side of the river, the tops of the mountains glowed in the early sunlight: the river itself and the trees below were still in deep shadow. The beat of the rotor blades grew louder.

'*Do!*' An excited mujahid pointed. Two sand-brown Mi24s were flying along the crest of the mountain opposite. For a moment it looked as if they were going to continue up the valley. Gradinsky spotted the change of direction first.

'They're turning this way, and I think they mean business.'

Abdul Wahid gave urgent orders to his three remaining mujahideen and stationed himself behind the machinegun, Fatima next to him. Overnight, the mujahid despatched by the commander had retrieved the two RPGs and a supply of rockets. The first Mi24 was less than a quarter of a mile away, its predatory snout sharply etched by the low sun, the rocket pods on either side of the fuselage bulging ominously. It came on with surprising speed for such an unwieldy-looking ship.

'As soon as you see it hover, look out. That means he's getting ready to rocket us.' Fatima translated and Abdul Wahid nodded vigorously. 'He says he knows. He has been fired on many times by these.'

Wills prayed that the *sangar* would not receive a direct

hit. He and Gradinsky had an RPG each, with half a dozen rounds apiece, and Fatima and Jan Mohammed to help them reload.

'I'll try to take him when he hovers, Mike. You take him if he comes over us after firing.'

The fear of a possible Stinger attack had undoubtedly communicated itself to the pilot of the first Mi24, judging by the steady stream of flares he threw out as he manoeuvred himself into position. The big gunship slowed down and hovered in the firing position; there was a tense pause, then a flash and two rockets streaked towards them, roared overhead and exploded with a vicious CRAAACK against the top of the cliff one hundred and fifty feet above the cave.

Gradinsky did not open fire. 'I think he's checking to see if we have Stinger. He'll probably come lower next time.'

The second Mi24 pilot was equally nervous, staying high, firing wide and then turning tightly and scooting away. The *whoosh* of the rockets as they streaked overhead was intimidating, even to men who had been in battle many times.

The next time the big helicopters came in lower, although still too high for accurate shooting, and the rockets were still well wide of their target. As he watched the first Mi24 start its third run in, Gradinsky became excited. 'This time he means business. Wait for it, this is it.' Gradinsky shouldered his RPG and tracked the big machine as it came in only a few hundred feet above the river and barely above the top of the cliff. Abdul Wahid started firing bursts with the heavy machinegun but, although they could see the rounds striking the nose, the heavy titanium armour and bullet-proof plexiglass simply deflected them. The pilot steadied the gunship, lining up his sights on the mouth of the cave. Two rockets, trailing a slim wake of smoke, hurtled overhead and smashed into the top of the cave, scattering stones and jagged pieces of rock over the ledge. A split second later, Gradinsky fired. It looked for a moment as if the rocket was on target then it suddenly dived and dipped under the belly of the Mi24, exploding seconds later on the side of the mountain opposite.

The gunship was now almost overhead, turning away and climbing to avoid the top of the cliff behind them. For a moment, the vulnerable flank was in Wills's sights and he pressed the trigger.

A terrific white flash filled the sky, immediately followed by an enormous orange and black fireball. The deafening explosion knocked Wills and Gradinsky off their feet. The whole horizon seemed to be on fire and bits of burning wreckage were landing in the trees all round them. One piece fell on the carpet in front of Wills and he watched, half bemused, while a mujahid stamped it out with his boot.

As the mujahideen cheered and embraced one another, Abdul Wahid threw his arms round Wills and lifted him off his feet.

'Bravo, bravo.' Gradinsky clapped him on the back as though he were trying to dislocate Wills's spine. 'What a fantastic shot. Fantastic!'

Fatima was almost crying. '*Allahu akbar.* Allah be praised. You didn't need a Stinger...' The admiration in her eyes completed the sentence wordlessly. Wills squeezed her arm and then anxiously scanned the sky for the second Mi24. He could see no sign of it.

'I think he chickened out. Didn't fancy having an RPG up his ass.' Gradinsky's laugh was interrupted by a burst of firing from the trees in front which made them all duck hastily. For the next half hour the Spetsnaz patrol unleashed a barrage of intensive fire – small arms, RPGs and light machineguns. A mujahid beside Abdul Wahid gave a cry and fell back from the *sangar*, shot through the chest. Fatima dropped on her knees beside him to cradle his head as his life ebbed in agonising gasps.

Wills heard an RPG whistle over his head. In the split second it smashed into the rockface behind him, something struck him with terrific force on the right shoulder, spinning him round and flinging him full length on the rocky ground.

The force of the blow knocked him out for a moment and when he came to, someone was bending over him, but he could not understand what he was saying. Strangely, he could feel no pain. As his eyes focused, he saw that it was Gradinsky, though he still could not make out his words. Then another face appeared and gentle hands started to unbutton his shirt. Wills could still feel nothing, only a spreading numbness. Then, he realised what had happened and struggled to sit up. 'Christ, I've been hit. Some bastard's just shot me.'

'Don't try to get up. Please lie still.' Fatima held him down gently. 'Just let me see how bad it is.' Her face went out of focus again and Wills felt himself drifting out to sea, he could hear the waves, a roaring sound and then silence. And pain.

Fatima worked quickly although she looked exhausted, her face smudged with dirt and blood. She bent over Wills, carefully cutting his shirt away so that the wound was exposed. 'Allah be praised, it doesn't look too bad.' She examined the small hole in the fleshy part of the shoulder.

'That's the entry wound,' Gradinsky said. 'What about the exit wound, though? If it's bad, then it was a Kalashnikov. The bullets tumble, you know, and make a hell of a mess.'

'I know,' Fatima said tersely. 'I have seen it many times.'

Gradinsky did not seem to notice the rebuke. 'Before we move him, you'd better give him a shot.'

'Yes, I have some morphine ready.' Fatima pulled up Wills's sleeve and pushed the needle in. Then, with Gradinsky holding him up, Fatima examined the back of Wills's shoulder. 'It's quite a big exit wound, and bleeding a lot.'

'As long as it missed the bone.' Gradinsky craned his neck to see. 'Yeah, right through the shoulder. You won't be able to play cricket for a bit.'

Wills's voice was weak but clear. 'Go fuck yourself, Gradinsky.'

'That's enough, you two. Here, can you hold him for a minute while I put on a field dressing? It's the last one.'

Fatima had just finished bandaging him when Wills tried to stand up.

'What's happened, where am I?'

'You've had a little accident but you're OK.' Gradinsky's big round face swam into view. 'Just lie still and have a nice sleep.'

But Wills was wide awake now. 'What happened exactly?'

'You stopped a bullet with your right shoulder. But the wound looks good and clean and you should be on your feet again in a few days.'

'A few days! God almighty, I can't lie on my back for a few days...'

Wills struggled to get up but Fatima held him, stroking his forehead. Eventually, his eyelids drooped as the morphine took effect. In five seconds he was unconscious, breathing peacefully.

'He'll be all right now,' Fatima said pulling a *pattu* over him.

Gradinsky picked Wills's Kalashnikov off the ground. 'Hey, what the hell's going on?' Heavy firing was coming from the direction of the river.

Fatima listened anxiously. 'Is that more Spetsnaz arriving?'

Gradinsky, only his eyes above the *sangar*, was listening intently. There was a lot of confused shouting below. Then more shooting, this time not in their direction but aimed at the river. The firing by the river became more intense. Gradinsky spoke over his shoulder. 'It's either Spetsnaz reinforcements, and they're fighting one another. Or it's your people.'

One of the mujahideen came running up the path, shouting excitedly. Fatima's face broke into a smile. 'Allah be praised! One of Durran's mobile groups has just arrived to save us. The Spetsnaz are withdrawing up the river.'

Gradinsky was on his feet, his right hand gripping his Kalashnikov, a big grin on his face. 'The US Cavalry, that's who it is. Come to rescue us in the goddamn nick of time.'

The battle was moving away and after half an hour it petered out. Then there were shouts from below, this time in Farsi. It was Abdul Wahid's turn to give a victory whoop.

Fatima was crying with joy. 'It is our people. They heard we were under attack and came to help us. Allah be praised.'

'It's too much. I'll have to sit down.' Gradinsky squatted down, his back against the *sangar*, suddenly realising how exhausted he was. 'What wouldn't I give for a glass of vodka now, eh, Mike? Wake up! I never thought we would come out of that one alive.'

Wills slept on, the morphine dulling the pain as his body started the slow work of healing. Fatima passed a blood-stained but comforting hand across his brow. 'We'd never have got him out if we'd had to retreat.'

'Retreat? Where would we have retreated to?' Gradinsky's voice was mocking. 'If your friends hadn't come when they did, we'd all have been killed or captured.' He looked hard at Fatima. 'And I for one would not have waited to be captured.'

'What would you have done? Jumped off the rock?'

'No. Better this way.' Gradinsky half opened his jacket and patted the Makarov in its shoulder holster. 'In the Spetsnaz, they taught you one thing about fighting the Afghans. Always keep the last one for yourself.'

Eighteen

It was some days later and evening by the time they reached Durran's base, a network of caves high above the valley floor. The sky was a washed-out blue, as if the heat of the day had drained it of colour, and in the fading light the short-stemmed wheat made pale green whorls as the breeze touched it.

Abdul Wahid had managed to commandeer a horse to get Wills, who was in considerable pain, up the last few miles of stony track, too steep even for a jeep. They were put in a house near one of the caves and half an hour after they had eaten and drunk tea Durran came to see them, bounding up the steps and into the upstairs room like a boy home from school. With him were only Azim, the big quartermaster, Abdul, his former agent in Kabul, and a young bodyguard. They sat in a semi-circle, Durran with his back to the window, facing the half-open door. The bodyguard sat on the steps with his back to them, out of earshot. Fatima translated, sitting beside Durran, her slim legs encased in Russian combat trousers, her hair tied severely back.

Durran was solicitous about Wills's wound, recalling how he had been wounded himself at the very start of the war. 'It was right at the beginning. I was in Pakistan when the coup took place against Daoud in 1978. So I gathered a few friends, a handful of weapons — we only had about half a dozen, I remember, a couple of old Sten guns and a few Kalashnikovs — and what money we had and started for the Panjsher. We began by attacking government outposts and did well for a time. But we became too ambitious and they suddenly counter-attacked us with overwhelming force. They took us by surprise, surrounded us and we just managed to escape. But I was wounded, in the leg, here.' Durran pointed to the top of his thigh.

'I could not walk, they had to carry me. It was a bad time. Our organisation was virtually wiped out. But it taught me one thing: the value of training. So we started again from the bottom, with only thirty people. Many of them are still with me. And we trained; and trained; and trained.' Durran grinned. 'That's what has got us to where we are today.'

He put his hand on Wills's good arm. 'So I know how it feels, my friend. You will get the very best treatment we can give you, although as you know we are still very short of drugs and medical supplies. And I have asked one of the French doctors to come and see you as soon as possible. I hope today or tomorrow, *inshallah*.

'And then I thank you from the bottom of my heart, both of you.' His intelligent eyes embraced Gradinsky as well. 'For your heroic and skilful operation in the Salang. We will honour you later, but for the moment let me tell you you have changed the whole situation. The Russians are desperately trying to reopen the tunnel but it may take them several months. All their convoys are having to go via Kandahar and the west. This takes much more time and makes them more vulnerable to attack. Also, to keep pace with their withdrawal timetable, they have had to mount a big airlift and this is expensive. Most important of all, they now have much more difficulty supplying the puppet regime.'

Durran looked round the room and smiled. 'Thanks to you, my friends, the Russians are very, very angry. In fact, they say they will feed you to the vultures if they catch you, and we expect them to attack the Panjsher at any moment, in revenge.' He grinned at Gradinsky and Wills. 'So, to discourage them, we have put out the word that you brave men are, alas, dead, killed by the Spetsnaz patrol in Parende, just before we were able to rescue you.'

A murmur went round the room. Fatima abandoned her translator's role for a moment. 'What about Jan Mohammed and me? Are we dead too?'

'I hope not. We need your support for many years yet, both of you.' The others laughed. 'No, we have said nothing about you. The Russians spoke only of CIA agents and in our communique we said that you were foreign friends, who to strike a blow for the cause of Afghan independence offered your skills to blow up the Salang Tunnel. We did not say if you were British or American, CIA or not CIA. But we did say that most unfortunately, and to our deepest regret, the two heroes who blew up the Salang Tunnel were themselves martyred shortly afterwards, honourable *shaheed* who gave their lives in the holy cause of Afghan freedom.'

'Do you really expect them to withdraw?' Wills asked.

'Yes, *inshallah*. Although the blocking of the tunnel has made things more difficult for them, we think they will still go. We hear that half their troops have been told to be ready to leave. Quite soon, only the Kabul garrison will be left.'

'And after they have gone?'

'Ah, you always ask such difficult questions.' The other Afghans laughed. Durran, sitting cross-legged, rocked himself forward. Lowering his voice, he talked quietly but with great conviction. 'We will begin to move from here in a few months' time. We are gradually bringing in mujahideen units from all over the north-east. From Takhar, Kunduz, Mazar, Badakhshan. They will take up position, according to a prearranged plan, round Kabul. On a given signal, whenever it comes, we will move forward and take the city.'

'You make it sound very easy.' Gradinsky, for once, did not laugh.

'I do not say it will be easy. There will be fighting, of course. But we have made our preparations over many months and years, as you know, and we still have a little longer to go. I tell you now something that is very secret. Some of the biggest commanders in the Afghan army in Kabul have been on our side for a long time. When the time is right, they will make a *coup d'état* against the government and take power in the city. At that moment, and on a signal from them, we will move forward and together we will liberate Kabul. *Inshallah*.'

The others repeated the word and the sound of it ran round the room like a small wind. Was it a wind that would grow into a gale, Wills wondered?

He had a last question for Durran. 'Can we come with

you, Anatoly and I? We might be of some help and we would very much like to see what happens.'

Durran gave his slightly wolfish grin. 'Yes, you have deserved it.' He said something to the others, then, with that characteristically swift movement, was on his feet and shaking hands in farewell.

Fatima rose too. 'He wants me and Jan Mohammad to go with him now. But he wants you to rest here, where it is safe, until your wounds have healed. He has given orders that you are to be given fresh clothes and the best food we have. Nothing is too good for the heroes of the Salang.'

'I think you're pulling my leg, aren't you, honey?' Gradinsky had recovered a flash of his old humour.

'Please? You want to eat honey?'

Gradinsky burst out laughing and it took Wills a little time to explain the joke. When she understood, Fatima gave a giggle.

The doctor, who arrived the next day on horseback, was small, bushy-bearded and very French. His examination of Wills's shoulder was meticulous and punctuated with little 'tssks' of annoyance.

Finally, his eyes bright and earnest behind their lenses, Jean-Louis pronounced his verdict. 'My friend, you are a lucky man. I cannot be quite sure, because we do not have the possibility of an X-ray, but I think...' He laid his finger on the side of his nose with deliberation. 'I think the bullet has not damaged the bone or any of the important muscles or ligaments.' He raised Wills's arms a few inches. 'You see, if there was serious damage, I would not be able to do that. I think the bullet has gone through the soft fleshy bit of the shoulder and although the exit wound is a little bit nasty, I think we can tidy that up for you. *Bon*. Now I give you a small injection and bandage you up properly. I will come and see you in a few days' time, *inshallah*, or send one of my colleagues.'

The next few days followed an almost identical pattern of cloudless perfection. They had an eagle's-eye view of the valley, its narrow patchwork of fields threaded by the silver flash of the Panjsher river as it wound its way through tree-lined narrows and across broad bands of shingle to the end of the valley and eventual union with the brown waters of the Kabul river. Sitting outside the house, Wills with his arm in a sling, they looked out at the distant south wall of the Panjsher, where pockets of snow still lay in the north-facing corries and the blue haze of autumn softened the sharpness of the skyline.

In those slow days of healing and resting and waiting, Wills asked Gradinsky about his future. 'What will you do when we get home?'

'You mean when we get out of jail for disobeying orders? Well, I suppose Durran might offer us a job in his army. There's a lot of precedent for foreigners fighting in other people's armies. But I suspect the fact that I'm a Russian wouldn't be too popular with a lot of people. So I suppose I'll head for California in the end. I have some cousins there. White Russians, I suppose you'd call them. Been outside Russia for a long time. First they lived in Paris, where my grandfather, Prince Gradinsky, was so poor he had to make his own vodka. He and his wife, a princess in her own right, lived in this little apartment in a poor quarter of Paris, with all the down and outs. He nearly died of cold sitting at the open window in the middle of winter putting a kind of plastic covering on metal hooks.'

'Couldn't he have shut the window?'

'No, the window had to be open. He had to soften the plastic with some kind of chemical which gave off poison-ous fumes. So the window had to be open, winter and summer, otherwise the fumes would have killed him. It just about killed him anyway, poor old buzzard. My mother told me about him. She said he was a wonderful old man. He's long dead but his son emigrated to the States, and he and his family live in Santa Monica. They run a dry-cleaning store. So that's a bit of the Gradinsky family history, Mike. How about you?'

'Well, I don't have any princes in my family tree, as far as I know. But I may have to come with you to California. The Brits are far more likely to throw me into jail for going ahead with the Salang operation than anything else.'

'Hell, if Durran takes over and peace breaks out in this part of the world, they should be mighty grateful.

They ought to make you a Sir or a Lord. Maybe even a Prince!'

'More likely to end up in the Tower of London charged with treason. But if I can avoid that, I suppose they might offer me a job.'

'What sort of job?'

'Well, a job doing things like this. You know, cloak and dagger. It's about the only thing I know about. That and the army, and I'm finished as far as the army's concerned. Or set up my own business. A lot of ex-special forces people do it, these days. But it helps if you're on the old-boy net and a bit respectable. We could always go into partnership, Anatoly. Offices in London and the West Coast. What about that?'

'That's a great idea. We could call ourselves Salang Partners Inc.'

'Shouldn't think anyone's registered that name, would you?'

The sound of jets high above the valley interrupted their day-dreaming.

'There they are.' Gradinsky spotted them first, silver specks against the deep blue of the noonday sky. 'One ... two ... three ... four. SU25s.' As they watched, the jets made a wide circle and then disappeared into the sun. When they picked the first jet up again, it was diving very fast.

'Christ, they're coming this way.' Gradinsky was quickly on his feet watching the speck hurtle towards them down the valley.

Two elliptical black shapes detached themselves from the SU25's belly and swooped like twin peregrines on their prey, a small village of honey-coloured mud houses framed among fields of wheat and barley directly below them. One house burst silently in a cloud of dust and smoke which billowed slowly into the still air. Seconds later the rumble of the explosion floated up to them as the jet pulled out of its dive and went screaming away over the southern rim of the valley. The others followed in rapid succession, the black bombs which looked so small and harmless at this distance smashing the toy houses in a slow-motion dance of dust and death. As the last SU25 began its steep climb to avoid the

208

fangs of the mountain wall, a streak of white smoke rose from the valley floor at phenomenal speed.

'Stinger!' Gradinsky shouted, as if urging the missile on.

The SU25 was well above the mountains now, the Stinger trail a white squiggle against the cobalt blue, closing fast. There was a single bright flash, then a fireball, an orange inferno framed in black like a funeral notice, and pieces of SU25 began to fall out of the sky.

'Son of a bitch! He never knew what hit him.'

'Those decoy flares didn't do him much good, poor bastard.' They watched one large piece of debris, possibly the engine, fall in lazy spirals to vanish in a field of wheat as the sound of the explosion still reverberated off the valley walls. Wills shaded his eyes with his good arm and peered into the sun. The other three SU25s had disappeared, leaving their downed comrade to his fate. 'No sign of the pilot. Not that he'd have had much chance to eject. My God, if that's Stinger, it's bloody impressive.'

'Tell you one thing.' For once Gradinsky looked deadly serious. 'I wouldn't want to be the last Russian pilot to be shot down in Afghanistan. That's an honour I could well do without. Eh, Mike?'

'Do you think they were looking for Durran? Or us?'

'Hard to know. They weren't too far out. I suspect they're bombing anything that might be on our route. Or his.'

The energetic Jean-Louis came again three days later and pronounced that Wills was healing well. After his third visit two weeks later, he said that Gradinsky could change the dressing and make sure the patient took his pills. After that it was a matter of letting the slow process of healing take its course.

The days turned slowly to autumn and then to winter and one bitterly cold night they had their first heavy snow fall. The affable old man in whose house they were staying arrived next morning with their breakfast of oiled *nan* and fresh butter and in a comical pantomime, accompanied by endless repetition and dramatic gestures, indicated they must leave immediately for more sheltered pastures.

Wills found the walk down the mountain exhilarating. He was much stronger than he had dared hope and the exercises Jean-Louis had prescribed had given him back most of the movement in his shoulder. The wound had healed completely, leaving only an angry red scar. But it was still sore and the only way he could use his Kalashnikov was from the hip.

In a half deserted village at the bottom of a valley they celebrated a spartan Christmas, although Gradinsky went to great lengths to procure a token Christmas tree which he decorated with scraps of silver foil and spent cartridge cases. He gave Wills a Penguin paperback on Islam which he had acquired from the French doctor, and Wills presented Gradinsky with a small bottle of vodka, carefully wrapped, which a friendly mujahid had found in a government post at the mouth of the Panjsher when the garrison withdrew. Gradinsky cooled it in the snow for an hour and they drank it before their Christmas lunch of chicken *palau*, cooked specially by their host's wife.

They chopped and carried wood and went for walks along the road, discussing politics, war, love and poetry until even Heraclitus, as Gradinsky said, would have been weary. Finally, out of boredom and frustration, they began to get on one another's nerves, arguing constantly and pointlessly.

Then one morning, after breakfast, they saw two mujahideen climbing the narrow path that zigzagged up to the house, obviously in a hurry.

Wills shaded his eyes. The second figure looked familiar. 'Hey, it's Fatima. Fatima and Jan Mohammed. It must be important. They're climbing at a hell of a pace.'

When she was within hailing distance, Fatima stopped and shouted up at them. 'Collect your things! Durran wants you to come quickly. He is ready to go to Kabul.'

One of Durran's captured Russian jeeps, its windscreen neatly punctured by a bullet, was waiting for them a mile or two down the valley, parked under some trees to avoid detection from the air. The driver was a taciturn man with a spade beard and a rugged countenance which reminded Wills of someone he knew. It puzzled him for several minutes and then he suddenly got it.

'Asterix the Gaul!' he cried to an astonished Gradinsky. 'To a T. The likeness is amazing.'

They climbed into the jeep; in front the driver, a mujahid

who Jan Mohammed assured them was an expert mechanic, a *mullah* who wanted a lift and Jan Mohammad; in the back Fatima had to squeeze in between Gradinsky and Wills. Although it had clearly seen better days, the jeep was remarkably comfortable, riding the potholes and bumps in the road with well-sprung ease.

'I didn't know they could build this kind of thing in the Soviet Union. It's as smooth as a Rolls.'

'Sure, if it's for the army. Not so good if it's for the ordinary people, though. What the hell, Mike, you know how a popular democracy works, don't you?'

'Doesn't work, you mean.'

The road to the end of the valley was deserted, apart from a couple of farmers driving half a dozen donkeys heavily laden with sacks of flour and once a herd of goats and fat-tailed sheep which held them up for several minutes, the goats glancing at them disdainfully with their clear amber eyes before scrambling out of the way. They passed several old Russian outposts which had been evacuated in the early days of the withdrawal, despite the strategic importance of the Panjsher. The fortifications looked dilapidated, the mujahideen having removed anything of any practical value and blown up the rest.

'Did the Afghan army not take over any of these places?' Wills asked.

'There is one further down, at Anawa, but the garrison will do nothing if we don't attack them. We will drive right in front and you will see.'

The valley broadened out now, the mountains lower and further back, the river lost in a waste of shingle. They rounded a bend and there in front of them was the outpost, an unimposing collection of sand-coloured mud forts, a flag hanging limply in the still air above the main building. In methodical Russian style, the base was ringed by machine-gun positions, rolls of barbed wire and minefields. As they drove past, Jan Mohammed waved at the sentries on the gate only fifty yards away and, casually, as if he knew the jeep well, one of them raised a hand and gave a cursory wave back.

'My God, you're right, Fatima. These guys really are spaced out, even by Californian standards.'

A few miles beyond Anawa they came to the end of the valley and joined the main Kabul-Salang road. Normally this was the busiest road in the country, carrying a constant stream of tankers going north to pick up fuel and an even heavier flow of big Russian Kamaz lorries heading south with tons of arms, ammunition and food for the Soviet and Afghan armies: today it was uncannily empty. Wills looked across at Gradinsky.

'Well, that's good news for us. They must still be having a problem with the tunnel.'

Gradinsky squinted into the sun. As far as he could see, the road to the Salang was deserted. 'You remember the last time we came along this road, Mike? We could hardly breathe, let alone see with all that dust from the convoys. Hey, look out, here's some really heavy traffic coming now.'

Approaching them was a solitary Afghan, the end of his turban half covering his face, driving in front of him three very small, heavily loaded donkeys. They all laughed, even Asterix. His beard jerking, he launched into an excited monologue.

'He says in the many years he has been driving this road, even before the *jehad*, he has never seen so little traffic, until now. But wait, something really is coming now.' Without warning, Asterix pulled off the road and drew up beside a solitary clump of trees. Across the snow-covered plain of Jabal-es-Seraj which stretched away in front of them advanced an ominous-looking sight. The light-hearted chatter died away and they all sat silent.

Asterix produced a battered pair of binoculars and studied the approaching column for a few seconds. He spoke and Fatima translated. 'He says this is a very big convoy. He can see tanks. He thinks they are Russians, although maybe there are Afghans as well.'

'Shouldn't we get a bit further off the road?' Untypically, Gradinsky's voice sounded slightly nervous.

'The driver often comes this way. He says the *Shurawi* convoys drive past without looking or doing anything as long as the mujahideen don't shoot at them. You don't plan to blow them up, do you?' Fatima giggled.

Gradinsky was silent, his eyes on the road. A huge T62, its flail sweeping the road for mines, came lumbering towards them like a prehistoric monster. Two more T62s followed, their tracks churning up the slush, then a string of armoured personnel carriers, the soldiers tense and ready for action, then fuel tankers, ammunition lorries and, near the end of the column, a ludicrously ungainly-looking field kitchen. Finally, a couple more T62s brought up the rear, the tank commanders standing upright in their open turrets, staring straight ahead.

'You know what?' Gradinsky broke his silence.

'What?'

'I don't think they've heard the news.'

'What news?'

'The news that the Salang Tunnel is blocked.'

'You must be joking.'

'Well, what the hell are they doing on the Salang road, looking like it's Termez next stop? I mean these guys have got everything with them except their mothers-in-law.'

The convoy took a good five minutes to go past and as the roar of the last T62 died away Gradinsky wiped the back of his hand across his mouth and spat towards the road. 'Those guys are going on what the Americans in Vietnam used to call a search and destroy operation. Tank commanders at battle stations, with machineguns at the ready. That's no home-bound convoy. Those boys are out to get somebody. Could be us.' He gave his *basso profundo* belly laugh.

Asterix was pointing excitedly. 'He says they are turning off the main road, towards the Panjsher. Look, you can see now.' Like a battle pennant, the thin plume of diesel smoke which trailed behind the armoured column was now moving almost due east, towards the mouth of the Panjsher Valley.

'I think you're right, Anatoly. They look to me very like a heavily-armed column engaged on what the British used to call a punitive raid. Teaching the natives a lesson. In the old days of the Frontier, we used to warn them in advance that we were going to blow up their villages. Gave them time to get the women and children to safety. But no one fights wars like that any more.'

'Certainly not my fellow countrymen.'

Two hours later, a mile or two short of the first roadblock on the outskirts of Kabul, the driver turned off on to a side road and they began to climb to the west. A bumpy hour later they came to a ruined village. Asterix drew up and made a sign indicating that they had arrived.

'We stop now. This is Paghman where Durran has his headquarters. Take your things. We leave the jeep here.'

Fatima led the way to the far end of the village to a house on its own surrounded by a high wall and a thick screen of trees. Half the roof had been shot away, exposing one of the upstairs rooms, but down below the walls seemed solid and there was even a dusty carpet on the floor of the 'guest' room. Durran was not there but Fatima said he would arrive later.

'Now we will drink tea and eat some rice and have a rest. When he comes, I think we will go quickly.'

'You mean tonight?'

'I think so. Night-time is best for entering Kabul.'

Nineteen

It looked and sounded like summer lightning, a continuous series of flashes, some bright and relatively close, some feeble with distance, and always the rumble and crash of thunder.

'We call it mujahideen thunder.' Fatima sounded excited.

They were last in the little convoy of three jeeps: Durran was in the first and a full load of heavily armed men packed the second. They had driven straight into the city, pausing only briefly at one checkpoint where they were clearly expected and quickly waved through by men in Afghan army uniform. Soldiers who had defected to Durran, or mujahideen masquerading as government troops? Impossible to say, Wills reflected, but probably the former.

Flares rose unceasingly into the sky, their arcs intersecting above the nerve centres of the city: the big base at Khair Khana, Soviet headquarters at Darulaman, the Soviet Embassy compound, the presidential palace. A number of loud bangs suddenly sounded close.

Jan Mohammed twisted in his seat and, although they could not see his face in the dark, they knew he was grinning. 'This mujahideen racket. Big racket. Very good.'

'One-twenty-twos. Range twenty clicks. From Beijing with love,' Gradinsky explained.

The 122-millimetre rocket, a long thin tube packed with high explosive, was a Chinese copy of a Russian original. The Russians had started the modern Chinese armaments industry in the late Forties and when the two Communist superpowers fell out in the Fifties, the Chinese simply carried on, copying the Russian originals and in some cases improving on them. The 122's range of twenty kilometres

215

made it an ideal weapon for bombarding a city from a safe distance.

Wills had studied the Vietnam war in the SAS at Hereford and knew that the Vietcong had fired hundreds of Chinese-made 122-millimetre rockets into Saigon, in one instance starting a fire which burned down a whole refugee shanty town. On another occasion they had hit the Majestic Hotel beside the river and nearly put paid to the distinguished career of the *Observer* correspondent, Mark Frankland.

A battle broke out ahead of them, the tracers zipping up the night with perforated red weals. Simultaneously, a Soviet battery went into action about one hundred yards away, the multi-barrelled rocket launchers sending a stream of incandescent rounds raging into the sky towards the 122 launch sites in the distant mountains.

'I'd forgotten just how terrifying those goddamn Stalin organs are,' Gradinsky remarked.

The jeep jerked forward, following the vehicle in front, and they started to zigzag through the deserted, potholed streets, making for the Bala Koh area where the houses climb higgledy-piggledy up the side of the mountain and the shifting population makes government control almost impossible. They drove without lights, relying on the flares which rose spasmodically into the sky, and came eventually to a wide, dimly lit street which the jeeps crossed one at a time, after making sure no patrols were in sight. Wills thought the place looked vaguely familiar.

'Yes, this is the street we crossed before when we went to the garage to pick up the tankers,' Gradinsky said. 'You remember?'

'Of course.'

They crept down the narrow side streets but this time they approached the front of the garage where, in the darkness of the forecourt, a torch flashed on and off three times. There was a brief pause while someone spoke to the occupants of the first jeep and then the double doors of the workshop, where the tankers had been made ready, were opened from the inside. They drove in, the doors closed and a weak overhead bulb was switched on.

The man with the torch came forward, shaking hands

with each of the new arrivals and whispering instructions. When he reached Wills and Gradinsky, they recognised him as Anwar, the mujahid who had organised the convoy to the Salang. He recognised them, too, and embraced them silently before speaking urgently to Fatima.

'He says it is too dangerous to stay here. He will take us to a house a short distance from here.'

'You mean an Afghan short distance? Five miles?' Wills smiled at Fatima.

'Not five miles. Just a few minutes from here, you bloody Englishman.'

They walked up the hill, the track twisting and turning between the houses which were built against the mountain in tiers, separated from one another by narrow passageways. They crossed a dark courtyard, climbed steps and found themselves on a flat roof that looked out over the city. In daytime, it would have commanded a spectacular view. Now, whole areas were blacked out, especially the Russian enclaves and government buildings, in an attempt to offer as few targets as possible to the mujahideen gunners. They were ushered into a big room where Durran and his immediate entourage were already installed.

Fatima explained apologetically, 'This room is too small for everyone so our host will give us another room shortly, just for ourselves. He has to send his family away first.'

'Poor family. Pushed out of their own home by these bloody foreigners.' Wills meant it as a joke, but when their host reappeared, Fatima told him what Wills had said.

'He is shocked. He says you are friends and guests, not foreigners, and you honour him by coming to his house. He is only sorry he has nothing better to offer you.'

Two young sons of the house appeared with trays of rice and vegetables, placing the dishes on a cloth spread out on the carpet. They were still eating when several men arrived and were shown in. Durran immediately got to his feet, embracing them warmly and making them sit next to him. More men who looked like bodyguards were dimly discernible on the balcony outside.

Fatima leaned over and whispered. 'These three men are very powerful army officers who have come to see the Commander.' At that moment the newcomers looked over at

Wills and Gradinsky with what seemed to be intense approval, nodding their heads as Durran apparently explained who they were and how they had carried out the attack on the Salang.

One of them asked a terse question in Farsi. 'He asks how you blew up the tunnel?'

'We used two thousand gallons of methyl nitrate and that would have made a pretty big hole in it. What we can only guess at is whether the explosions caused a heavy rockfall. They were deliberately designed to go off five hundred metres apart and with any luck would have brought down a big chunk of the tunnel in between. But we simply don't know.'

One officer, a tall man with a shock of black hair, leaned forward and spoke animatedly. 'He says he has seen Russian signals saying their engineers are making very slow progress. Half the tunnel is blocked. Their convoys have had to be re-routed via Kandahar and Herat. It is a very long journey and they keep losing men and vehicles. But now they are virtually all out except for the headquarters' staff, a Spetsnaz battalion and the advisers.'

'How many advisers do they think they'll leave behind?'

'They say a few hundred, most of them in Kabul, the others in the big bases like Bagram and Shindand which are now under the puppet government's control.'

Tea was brought in by one of the host's sons. Durran and the officers withdrew to a corner and, dropping their voices to a whisper, held a long, animated conversation, inaudible to everyone else in the room. Ten minutes later the visitors rose to their feet and departed, accompanied by their bodyguards. Soon afterwards Durran left as well. 'They go to get some sleep,' Fatima told them. 'It is a good idea for us too. Tomorrow Durran will tell you his plans.'

Their host appeared with a bundle of bedding and led them to their room. A few minutes later silence descended, interrupted only by the powerful snores of Gradinsky. Outside, the flares still criss-crossed the night. A sharp rattle of small-arms fire drifted downwind and was followed by about a dozen distant explosions: probably incoming 122-millimetre rockets, Wills thought sleepily. About thirty seconds later, the reply came in a series of rapid explosions, much louder, from an Afghan army multi-barrelled rocket launcher. A dog howled in the distance and was answered by a chorus of barking, echoing off the mountains which surround Kabul. Finally, towards morning, the city slept uneasily.

Durran was fond of coffee and, while they breakfasted, his young bodyguard, Musa, prepared a cup for each of them. Durran seemed untroubled by lack of sleep, his eyes clear and his khaki shirt remarkably clean and crisp. Fatima sat beside him. 'He says things are moving very fast and the situation is quite confused. The officers he saw last night want to make a coup against the PDPA and they say they have much of the army behind them.'

'Why do they want to make a coup? Aren't they members of the PDPA too?' asked Gradinsky.

'Once, but no more. They say they were Communists once because they thought that was best for our country. Commander Durran says he respects their, how do you say, integ. . . ?'

'Integrity?'

'Yes, integrity. He respects them for honestly believing in what they did although he doesn't agree with them. But what the officers said last night to the Commander was that after all the things, the terrible things, the Russians have done to our country, they no longer believe in the Soviet Union, Communism or the PDPA. They are on the side of the mujahideen because they know the mujahideen are on the side of the people. So they want to join hands with us to overthrow the PDPA government.'

'*Inshallah*.' Wills hoped he sounded suitably reverent. 'How do they plan to make this coup? Is it top secret?'

'Yes, of course. But Durran will tell you. Last night he and the officers discussed this plan and he has told me to pass on the message to you. First he asks for your promise that you will not reveal the details of the plan to anyone, even under torture, should you be captured. You give this promise?'

'Yes,' Wills said, looking at Durran. 'I give my promise, except that under extreme torture I might betray the plan, despite my intention not to.'

'We understand. If we think that has happened Durran

will change the plan. You do not know the names of the officers and you will forget you saw them.'

'Understood.'

'You have my promise too,' Gradinsky rumbled.

'Good. Now listen carefully. In the next week or so, our people will be entering the city secretly, in twos and threes, some dressed as farmers, driving donkeys and bringing food to the city. Among the wheat or the barley or the vegetables, they will hide their Kalashnikovs. Some will come in as refugees, with nothing ...'

'How will they conceal their shooters?'

'They will not be carrying their weapons, these people. But we have big stocks here, hidden all over the city, in the Bala Koh, in the Karte Parwan and lots of other places. They will get them after they have arrived. Others will drive in lorries, even buses. We also have a good underground network, our own people, many of whom have lived in Kabul for many years. They are divided up into different units, in the cell system, and all have weapons. The new people will work closely with the underground. We even have some mujahideen coming as *mullahs*, and a few young boys will be dressed as women, in long *chadors*.' Fatima smiled briefly, but her voice was serious.

'When all these people have arrived secretly and are ready, Commander Durran will give the signal and the plan will go into action. The army will secure the military targets like the Khair Khana barracks and, most important of all, the airport — that is the first priority in case the Russians try to fly troops back in. The mujahideen will attack the political targets like the PDPA headquarters and the Pul-i-Charki prison.

'What about the Russian Embassy?' Gradinsky growled.

'We will surround it so no one can get in or out but we will not attack it. The ambassador and his staff will be treated correctly, as diplomats.'

Durran, who had been sitting quietly, drinking his coffee, leaned forward and spoke to Fatima.

'The Commander says we have no quarrel with the Soviet Union now that they have almost withdrawn their forces from our country. We will not attack them as long as they do not attack us.'

'Who do you expect will give you the stiffest opposition?' Wills asked.

'The KHAD will undoubtedly fight hard. They always do, because they know everybody hates them, and they also know that the bad ones, most of their officers and others too, will be tried as war criminals — the ones who have done all the killing and torturing under Russian orders. Then there are some special army units, which contain many butchers with blood on their hands. They will fight to the last, but others will come over to us. We have had secret talks with a number of them and they say they want to join us. Of course, they see what is going to happen and they want to save their skins.'

'And will you accept them?'

'First, they must lay down their arms and co-operate with us. But if they have committed atrocities, they will be tried like the others. We accept their surrender but we make no promises. But these are only small groups, the Commander says. Most soldiers hate the government because they were forced to join up. Many, you know, have been arrested in the bazaar or in the fields and dragged into the army. Why should they want to fight the mujahideen?'

'Where will we be while all this is going on?'

Fatima turned and spoke to Durran. 'You can go to your embassy if you feel it would be safer. Or you can stay with the Commander. He invites you to join him but only if you wish.'

'Frankly, that's exactly what I would like to do, stay with the Commander,' Wills said, looking hard at Fatima.

'It's all very well for Mike here, but what the hell's going to happen to me? I don't have an embassy to go to. That's to say, I can't go to the Russian Embassy and I'm not sure the Brits would have me. No, I would like to see the last act in the company of the Commander and, of course, our charming escort and interpreter.' Gradinsky bowed to Fatima.

Durran got ready to leave but had a last warning. 'He says he has to go now to attend to many things. But he wants you to stay quietly here, where you will be safe. He asks you, please, not to go outside and show yourselves, as there are still many spies in the city. They will be on the lookout for any mujahideen and especially for foreigners, so he asks you to be patient. Your food will be brought by the man of the house and his family. They are very old friends, and very trustworthy. He is the head of our organisation in Bala Koh, so he will look after you. If you need anything — food, clothes, anything — tell him and he will get it for you. He can speak a little English, he is only a bit shy.'

'You're not staying with us, then?'

'The Commander wants me to go with him for a few days. But I will come back after that.'

'*Inshallah*.' Gradinsky raised his eyes in mock appeal. Durran rose to his feet, shook hands and was gone, followed by Fatima and the young bodyguard. Only Fatima looked back, turning at the door to smile.

As they listened to the departing footsteps going down the wooden stairs, Gradinsky looked at Wills. 'It's going to be dull without our girlfriend. The thought of having to spend my time talking to you, you boring sonofabitch, is almost enough to make me want to defect back to the Sovs. Nearly, but not quite.' Gradinsky gave a bellow of laughter and sat down heavily on the carpet.

'Mike, ring the bell and ask the help to bring some tea, would you?'

They spent much of the next day sitting looking out of the window at the panorama of the city spread out below them. There were a number of unidentified explosions early in the morning, probably incoming rockets, and one big bang which might have been a bomb. But it was all much less spectacular than at night and somehow seemed less dangerous. However, there was plenty of activity of another kind. All day long, helicopter gunships criss-crossed the sky and, although they could not see the airport, they could hear the distant roar of jet engines as a steady stream of aircraft landed and took off.

'Seems like the withdrawal is going full blast.' Gradinsky's blue eyes had a wicked glint. 'I wonder if the whole of the Central Committee of the PDPA is on the evacuation list, or only the Politburo.'

'Sounds more like the whole of the PDPA being airlifted out,' Wills said. 'Plus the KHAD. Where do you think

222

they'll take 'em? Somewhere nice and warm, like the Crimea, or a punishment station, like Siberia?'

'Siberia?' Gradinsky gave a shiver. 'Don't mention that place to me. That was where my brother Boris died, in the Gulag. Shot full of dope, insane, out of his mind ...'

Wills coughed. He had to ask the question that had troubled him for so long. 'How do you know he was out of his mind?'

Gradinsky shivered again; his eyes were haunted. 'What do they say in the States? Someone walked over your grave?' There was a pause, while he seemed to search for the right words, clasping his big hands.

'One of the men who was in his ward told me after he was released. He came to see me in Leningrad when I was home on leave. Boris had given him our address. They were friends, you see . . . Well, he said the end was terrible, terrible. Boris was fastened down to his bed, you know, strapped down, like in a strait-jacket. And they kept increasing the doses, of the drugs, you know, and Boris was fighting like a maniac against the shots. He knew they were trying to kill him. The man, his friend, who told me all this, he was weeping, sobbing, he could hardly get the words out. Christ, it was terrible. In the end, he said, Boris just lay there screaming, screaming until they forced a gag into his mouth. This man said he tried to stop his ears. He lay facing the wall, he couldn't bear to watch it. And then that night, after the orderlies had gone, this man got up and went over to my brother. There was a little light in the ward, not much, but he could see my brother was awake and that he wanted him to take the gag out of his mouth. So the man did, although he said he was frightened that Boris would start screaming again and that he would get into trouble.

'But as soon as he took the gag out of Boris's mouth, he realised he was ...' Gradinsky choked, unable to go on. He blew his nose very hard and wiped his eyes with the back of his hand. '... He realised he was dying. He could barely speak and the friend had to put his ear right down to his mouth. Boris spoke very quietly, matter-of-factly, the man said, and asked him to come and tell me the whole story and to give me his blessing ... The man said he had become a very strong believer, there, in the hospital. And then he just closed his eyes and ...' Gradinsky's voice broke on a sob.

Wills stared out at the view of the city. Finally, he cleared his throat.

'What had he done to make them treat him like that?'

'You remember the poem about Stalin that Mandelstam wrote? When he called Stalin the peasant slayer? Boris was the same sort of man. He wrote some very sharp, critical things about our leaders, the Communist Party. And ironically, the poem that got him into trouble, real trouble, was called "Afghanistan". In it he said our invasion was totally wrong, immoral, and would turn out to be a disaster. And then when he was called up, he refused to go on the grounds of conscience. So they said he must be ill and put him in the psychiatric hospital. And murdered him, the bastards, as deliberately and systematically as Hitler murdered the Jews. At first I couldn't believe it, you know. I was one of the blue-eyed boys of the system. Military Academy, high pass-out mark, asked to volunteer for the Spetsnaz, decorated for service in Angola. Assistant Military Attaché in Washington. Then Afghanistan. And while I was here, the news of Boris's death. It hit me like a bullet. For three days I could not think of anything else. Then I went on leave and met his friend. After I came back here I wanted to kill the bastards who had murdered him. I would have strangled them myself, with pleasure, slowly, and watched their eyes come out of their heads. And then I thought, fuck this rotten system, the whole lousy stinking system. One night, I was duty officer. After I had done my rounds at midnight, I let myself out of the camp by a back gate and started walking.'

Gradinsky shrugged. 'I don't regret it. This way I can avenge, in my own way, Boris's death. I feel happy now, after the Salang. And I'll feel even happier when I see the last of my fellow-countrymen get the hell out of Afghanistan and watch the mujahideen take over. That's the day I'm waiting for.

'Me too. And I don't think it's far away.'

'*Inshallah.*'

Twenty

In the days that followed, the mujahideen tightened the noose round Kabul. To the north, the Salang Highway was still out of action because of the closing of the tunnel. The other main supply lines, to Kandahar and Herat in the south and west and more importantly to Jalalabad and Pakistan in the east, were constantly cut, with convoys harassed and held up. There were more mujahideen checkpoints than government ones now and each extorted its toll in sacks of wheat, drums of cooking oil, fresh meat or anything else that the guerrillas needed. The tanker drivers had the worst time, their cargoes being either confiscated or blown up. The capital's stocks of food and fuel began to run dangerously low. In Kabul, the poor virtually live on *nan* and as the bread queues grew steadily longer the people were becoming desperate. One day, when a long line of hungry citizens who had been waiting for an hour or more in the freezing cold for their meagre ration saw an army lorry load up with fresh bread, the women at the front of the queue started to shout and wave their fists, trying to stop it from leaving.

'Why does all our *nan* go to these lazy cowards?' shouted one old woman with a face like a squashed melon.

'Go and get your *nan* from the *Shurawi* dogs,' another screamed, her nose bright red from the cold.

Petrol was now desperately short, even for party workers. The black market flourished, but the prices had soared far beyond the reach of the majority of the population. Only the rich could afford to buy luxuries like meat and sugar, and most of them had already gone. As food became scarcer and more expensive, many of the refugees who had flocked to Kabul to escape the fighting and the bombing began to think of leaving the city and trekking back to their homes in the mountain valleys outside the capital. But for the moment there was too much snow on the ground: the exodus would have to wait until the spring.

Wills sat up with a jerk, instantly awake. The sky was not completely dark and he saw something move against it. 'That you, Anatoly?'

Gradinsky grunted. 'Yeah, who do you think it was? Your mother-in-law?'

The tension dissolved. 'I don't even have a girlfriend, let alone a mother-in-law. Why are you prowling around waking people up at this ungodly hour?'

'I couldn't sleep. The jets kept me awake. Taking off and landing all bloody night. The Russians are flying a hell of lot of sorties, Mike. Non-stop. It sounds as if they're trying to grind the opposition into little pieces before the final pull-out. In fact, from the sound of it, we're not too far from D-Day, departure day.'

Wills got up and walked over to the window in his bare feet. Two flares rose with almost perfect timing from opposite corners of the city, their arcs intersecting in front of them. 'What makes you think so?'

'Well, you may not have noticed, but in the last few days they've been flying strike sorties at all hours of the day and night. The tempo is a lot hotter than when we were here last spring, before the Salang job. A lot hotter. I'm not talking about the transport flights, the Antonovs. I'm talking about the SU25s and MiG27s.'

'Aren't they flying cross-border, too, didn't Durran say?'

'Oh, sure. The heavy bomber bit. But these are local ground attack sorties. You can tell by the engine sound. Listen...' The faint but unmistakable roar of a jet fighter-bomber taking off floated across the city on the night breeze. They heard it four times in rapid succession and then it faded into nothingness.

Wills spoke into the darkness. 'They must be desperate to keep the mujahideen off their backs until they've got the last convoy safely across the border.'

'They are. I know my Sovs. There's only the top brass and the Spetsnaz guys left. What do you think, Mike, will the muj have a go at the last *Shurawi* out? For old times' sake?'

Wills laughed. 'Like Vietnam, you mean. If I were a muj, I'd have a go. The last chopper with the Russian Commander-in-Chief on board, eh? What a kill that would be!'

'Sonofabitch, you wouldn't need a Stinger, any old RPG is good enough for you.' Gradinsky's laugh was warm with admiration. 'But old Ustinov won't go by chopper. This is a little bit different from Vietnam, you know. He'll go out by road. Slower, but safer. If I know our generals, that's the way the bastard will make his exit. There'll be no time for hugs and kisses and garlands of flowers, that's for sure, but he'll keep his feet on the ground. The last thing he wants is a Stinger up his ass.' Gradinsky gave a huge laugh which turned into a gargantuan yawn. 'C'mon, I need some sleep.'

The final stage of the Russian withdrawal, the 'great defeat', as Gradinsky called it, continued for the rest of the week. They could see the big Antonov transports climbing ponderously into the sky, their kerosene trails hanging heavy behind them, escorted by clusters of decoy flares, as bright as diamonds against the deep blue of the winter sky. Behind the roar of the jets, they could hear sporadic shooting, some of it heavy.

'Hear those big thumps?' Gradinsky asked. 'Sounds like their new toy, the BM27. Packs a hell of a punch. The rounds weigh 150 kilos and have a range of about 40 clicks. You get a couple of salvos from those and you know about it!'

'Plenty of outgoing, precious little incoming,' Wills observed. 'The muj seem to be holding their fire.'

It was around five o'clock one afternoon, just as it was beginning to get dark, when they heard voices in the bottom part of the house and shortly afterwards footsteps on the stairs. A slight, uniformed figure appeared in the doorway.

'*Salaam Aleikum.*'

'Fatima. Good to see you.' Wills was quickly on his feet.

'Hi, stranger.' Gradinsky was more laconic.

'Durran sent me to fetch you. He wants you to come now, right away.'

Wills grinned. This was how things always happened in

227

Afghanistan. You could sit around, waiting, for days and even weeks. Then when the summons came, you were expected to rise to your feet and depart without more ado. They had anticipated this and knew reaction time would be short. Both men had their rucksacks standing packed in a corner of the room. They slipped on their boots, picked up their weapons and were ready to go.

At the bottom of the steep, narrow street a jeep was waiting with Durran's spade-bearded driver behind the wheel. He waved a hand to the two foreigners and indicated the back seat. Fatima got in the front beside him, her Kalakov across her knees, and they set off into the gathering darkness. The streets were suddenly empty, hushed, ominous even — like the room at the court martial, Wills remembered, just before they brought in the verdict against him.

They drove for twenty minutes into the heart of the old city, stopping finally beside a mosque pockmarked from stray rocket and small-arms fire, the outline of its minaret lit by a few coloured bulbs. Fatima put her finger to her lips and led the way to the back. As they approached a doorway, a mujahid stepped out of the darkness, blocking their way until he recognised Fatima and waved them through. The interior of the mosque was dark and cold, smelling faintly of hay, and their feet rang hollowly on the stone floor. They walked to the far corner where a few chinks of light seeped from behind a curtain. Another guard made Wills and Gradinsky leave their weapons on the floor and then, after a brief whispered conversation with Fatima, pulled the curtain aside.

For a moment they stood in the entrance, half dazzled by the sudden brightness of the lights, until a big man, who had been sitting on the floor cleaning his weapon, sprang to his feet and crushed each of them in turn against his chest, muttering gruff welcomes in Farsi. It was Azim.

'He says the Commander will be with us in a moment.' Fatima nodded past his shoulder.

Wills became aware that Durran was at the far side of the room with two or three other men, standing in front of a big map of the city. A radio crackled suddenly and the operator advanced towards Durran, holding out the receiver. Durran listened and then spoke with great deliberation for about a minute, as if he did not want to miss or misunderstand a single word. He handed the receiver back and turned to greet the new arrivals, Fatima translating.

'I asked you to come because the Russian withdrawal is now almost complete. General Ustinov left early this morning and the Spetsnaz have been flying out all day. There are only advisers left and, of course, the puppet government.' Durran smiled, 'We will deal with them soon, *inshallah.*'

'May I ask how, sir?' Wills asked formally.

'Yes. We have had to change our plans a little, but at midnight tonight our friends in the armoured division of the Afghan army which is responsible for the security of the city, will leave its barracks and move to prearranged positions: the airport, the radio station, the ministries of defence and interior and so on.' Durran broke off to take another call on the radio. He gave a curt reply and then resumed his briefing. 'Their job will be to secure all these key points and prevent anyone else taking illegal action.'

Gradinsky coughed. 'Do you have anyone particular in mind?'

Durran grinned. 'Yes, there are a few people we can think of. One is the man they call the Butcher — you may have heard of him. His real name is Habibullah. He is ruthless and well-organised, but he has no wide support in the army, except among a group of extremist Khalqi officers who are based in PDPA headquarters. His only chance is to make a surprise move and seize control of the city quickly before anyone else realises what he is doing.'

'Do you think you can stop him?'

'Well, we have the men and the firepower.' Durran was suddenly serious. 'We cannot allow this man, who is a fanatic and moved only by his own ambition, to take over Kabul. Some Afghans say he is worse than the Communists. I don't say that, but in some ways he is just as bad. Tonight our friends in the army will forestall his coup and we must destroy PDPA headquarters here. If more sections of the army join us, it could be the beginning of the end for the Communists in the city.'

The radio erupted into life again and Durran turned away to deal with it. The briefing was over. Fatima took charge.

'Come, we will drink tea and then later we will eat something and the Commander will rest. Afterwards, we will go with him.'

Outside, the city lay silent at last, no flares lighting the darkness, no jets making distant thunder, no helicopters criss-crossing the sky in pursuit of the ever-present but elusive mujahideen. They were here now, ensconced in the heart of the capital, ready to strike. Beyond the city, to the north, after frantic efforts by a team of engineers specially brought in from the Soviet Union, the Salang Tunnel was open again and the last Russian convoy was making its final, painful ascent of the snowy pass. Amon, Durran's local commander, and his men watched it go from a ruined village near the road — with hate in their hearts but with empty hands, in strict obedience to Durran's orders not to attack under any circumstances or to interfere with the convoy in any way.

'The Russians are leaving,' Durran had written in a message brought by courier the day before. 'The victory is already ours. Do not risk the life of a single Afghan, mujahid or civilian, in empty gestures. We need all our strength for the next stage of the struggle, the battle against the puppet regime in Kabul. With the help of Allah, we will soon achieve that victory too.'

At midnight in Kabul, Durran climbed into the turret of a new T62, captured a few days before from the Afghan garrison at Paghman, on the outskirts of the capital. Headlights blazing, the huge tank, escorted by two equally new armoured personnel carriers, also recently handed over to the Afghan army by a departing but distrustful ally, ground its way across the city, heading for the barracks at Khair Khana. One APC, flying the green flag of the Resistance, led the little convoy, followed by the T62, then came a new Russian jeep with Fatima, Wills, Gradinsky, Azim and two of Durran's mujahideen aboard and, lastly, the second APC. Durran ordered his radio operator to make contact with Khair Khana. 'Tell them we're on our way and will stop opposite the main gate. We will identify ourselves immediately. Ask them to confirm and to keep their fingers off the trigger.'

The guardroom at the main gate was floodlit, but no sentries moved. The T62 ground to a halt, flanked by the APCs, with the jeep behind. Wills and Gradinsky could hear the tank's radio crackling and Durran's voice carried clearly.

'He is talking to the General,' Fatima whispered. 'He will come now to speak to us.'

They waited. This was the moment of decision, Wills thought, when the plans to which Durran and his army friends had agreed weeks and maybe months ago would be put to the test; when the possibility of a double cross, so remote-seeming in daylight, suddenly loomed very real. He could hear the sound of a car approaching fast, saw it shoot through the gate and brake sharply in front of the T62. A man got out, in uniform, bare-headed, unarmed, and walked over to where Durran waited for him, also alone and unarmed.

'That is General Mohammed.' Fatima spoke in a whisper. 'He is the senior Afghan general in Kabul and commands the armoured division here. He and Durran went to school together and have been friends ever since, although on different sides in the war.'

'But they're on the same side now?' Wills watched the two men, facing one another, close together in the cold and dark as they talked.

'They both hate the Russians for what they have done to Afghanistan. They both despise the Afghan dogs who have wagged their tails every time their Russian masters have kicked them. They both want to stop the Butcher from seizing power and put a genuine Afghan government in the place of the puppet regime. So, yes, they are on the same side now, thank God.'

The General was saluting. He shook hands with Durran as if sealing a bargain, stepped into his car and drove off. Durran walked quickly back to the small group waiting for him beside the T62. His voice was tense with excitement. Fatima translated. 'He says the General is ready. His men will start to move immediately. We go now to carry out our part of the plan.' The tank crew were at battle stations, the engine running. The tracks squealed on the tarmac and the huge vehicle shuddered as it moved forward, the snout of its gun poking out into the darkness, ready to demolish anything that stood in their way.

They drove for perhaps a mile across the deserted city, making for the rendezvous with Durran's main battle group, his best, most experienced troops. They were waiting round the edge of what looked like a school sports ground. In the darkness, Wills could only guess at their numbers but they were certainly in the high hundreds. A cheer went up when Durran and Azim climbed down from the T62 and stood silhouetted for a moment in the headlights, before disappearing into a building which looked as if had once been the pavilion. Waiting for Durran inside, Wills could see about twenty men. According to Fatima they were his senior commanders, most of whom had been with him since the very early days. They stood up when he entered, Azim close behind, his bulk making Durran seem almost puny.

The door closed behind them, on what Wills guessed was Durran's final briefing for the coming battle.

Twenty-one

At three a.m. Durran's T62, positioned under a tree at one side of the square, fired the first shell at PDPA headquarters. Three more followed in quick succession, smashing the main gate and bursting in orange fireballs against the darkened building behind. The T62 broke cover and drove at top speed towards the gateway, followed by the two escort APCs and a couple of T52s. Smashing its way through the gates, the lead tank made straight for the building, ignoring the tracer which ricocheted off its armour like a *feu de joie*. The speed of the attack caught the defenders by surprise and by the time they got their heavy weapons into action, Durran's T62 was parked in front of the entrance, shelling it at point-blank range. The turret opened and, apparently oblivious to the gunfire raging round him, Durran emerged to select targets for the gunners.

First, he pinpointed the anti-tank gun dug-in on a corner at the far side of the building. Two rounds knocked that out. Then he switched his attention to a persistent BM27 multi-barrelled rocket launcher, mounted on the back of a lorry, which was firing horizontally with devastating effect. One of the APCs had been hit and started to burn. The second shell from the T62, a solid-cored projectile that delivered a fearsome punch, tore the MBRL apart, scattering the fragments like gruesome confetti.

Through the smoke from the tank cannon which filled the square, small groups of mujahideen started to run forward, stopping to take cover when the firing got heavier, waiting for a lull and then moving on again. The lead section reached the building and two of them ran up the steps, bending double to present as small a target as possible. It took them only a few seconds to place a charge at the foot of the big metal door, while the T62 and the APCs sprayed the area with covering fire from their heavy machineguns. Ten seconds later, the whole of the door disintegrated in a sheet of flame, bricks and debris raining down and bouncing off the armour of the T62. Durran swung his gun turret round to face the doorway and ordered his gunners to pump shells through it. After the third round, the whole front section of the building collapsed with a roar.

As the dust cleared, a few dazed and frightened soldiers started to emerge. Half an hour later, the demoralised remnants came out waving a white flag and bringing with them the civilian staff. Durran took off his headset, his face grimed with the heat of battle, and led the way into the shattered building.

The T62's headlights blazed behind them, illuminating them clearly and making Durran and his party an easy target. As they began to walk up the wide stairs, someone hiding in the shadows behind the banisters at the top opened fire without warning. The leading mujahid collapsed, hit by the first burst, but it was Gradinsky's quick reaction which saved Durran's life. His snap shot from the hip found its mark, spinning the shadowy figure of the attacker round, his rifle crashing to the floor below. For a moment the dim shape teetered at the top of the stairs, clinging desperately to the banister and then, overbalancing, fell forward, the body somersaulting down the steps to land at the bottom, narrowly missing Durran. Gradinsky turned him over with his foot and examined the uniform. 'A major. Judging from the blood on his tunic, he must have been wounded already. Maybe that explains why he didn't shoot so well.'

Durran placed his hands on the Russian's shoulders and embraced him — a rare gesture, Wills thought, from such a controlled person. Then, releasing him, he stood back and made a short speech in Farsi, which Fatima translated. 'He thanks you from the bottom of his heart for saving his life. He is in your debt and you can ask anything of him that you like. Whatever he has is yours.'

Uncharacteristically, Gradinsky looked embarrassed. Then he grinned. 'Ask him if he has any sisters. No, hell, that's a joke, don't say that.'

Fatima was not amused. 'You'd better say something polite quickly or you may not live very long.'

'I know. Please tell the Commander I was glad to be of service and that he does not owe me anything. My reward is to be here, now, at this historic moment, to witness the triumph of your cause.'

'That is better.' A grim little smile curled Fatima's lips as she translated.

While the prisoners were herded into lorries, Durran interrogated a colonel, the senior officer to survive. Apparently the Butcher was to rendezvous with some of his army supporters and make his way into the city as dawn broke.

Durran issued fresh orders which Fatima relayed. 'The Commander is leaving only a few men here but now we, the main party, are going to Pul-i-Charkhi. We have just learned my sister Zarina is there.'

'Your sister?' Wills was surprised.

'Yes, she has been working for us in Kabul for a long time. She used to be a member of the PDPA and later was recruited by KHAD. Then General Orlov, the head of the KGB, wanted her to...' Fatima stopped and Wills realised she was blushing.

'Wanted her to what?'

'Well ... wanted to sleep with her.'

'My God! Orlov made a pass at your sister? The sonofabitch!' Gradinsky was angry.

Fatima's cheeks were still bright red. 'You can imagine my sister Zarina's feelings. She hates this man, but she was ordered by the party, our party, to do whatever he wanted. So, when she was sent to the Panjsher as part of an assassination plot against Durran she was able to warn us. We think that Orlov suspected her of betraying him, and when she tried to escape he must have hunted her down and had her arrested.'

'Pul-i-Charkhi, isn't that the jail?' Wills asked.

'Yes, the big jail where they keep all the political prisoners.' Fatima shivered, although not from the cold. 'It's a terrible place. Many, many of our people have been tortured and killed there. Hundreds. Thousands. It is impossible to say how many. But we know that many of our best and bravest mujahideen have died there in agony. So we go now to take the prison and free the prisoners. I hope to God Zarina is still alive...' Her voice broke momentarily and there were tears in her eyes.

Pul-i-Charkhi has the reputation of being the grimmest prison in Afghanistan, a country not noted for the leniency of its penal code. When the Communists took power by a *coup d'état* in 1978, they rounded up their opponents by the hundred and consigned them without trial to Pul-i-Charkhi. Some languished there for years, but many more were summarily executed. The then governor of the prison said later that some 20,000 prisoners had been executed in the first few months of the reign of terror that followed the coup. The figure has never been disputed. Certainly, many who went into Pul-i-Charkhi never came out alive, and those who were lucky enough to survive were usually so deeply scarred by their experience that they never fully recovered. Even if they had not been tortured themselves — and those who had not were in the minority — they had all heard the cries of those who had been beaten until they vomited blood, whose fingernails had been ripped out, bare flesh burned with cigarettes and genitals racked by electric shocks. They had all seen prisoners so broken in body and spirit that they had actually prayed for death as a blessed release.

Surrounded by watch-towers and barbed wire, the prison lies on the outskirts of the city, the iron mountains in the background making it look all the harsher and more desolate. As they drove towards it, Wills was reminded of the line in Dante's *Inferno*: 'All hope abandon, ye who enter here,' and was thankful that he was not arriving at the place as a prisoner.

They were in the APC immediately behind the T62, with a T52 following them. Durran swept right up to the main gate and aimed his tank straight at it. The guards, who had been expecting the convoy to stop, realised what was happening at the very last moment and managed to jump out of the way just before the T62 smashed down the heavy gates. At the same time, a nearby machinegun post was rash enough to open fire. One tank round at virtually point-blank range left nothing recognisable of the DShK or its crew. The rest of the guards on the main gate came out with their hands up, white-faced. One or two were very young, their shaven heads making them look even more vulnerable. Durran sent a sergeant off with a message to the prison governor to present himself at once. He came quickly, looking as if he had just got out of bed, buttoning his tunic as he ran. Durran shouted at him and the governor, fat, unshaven and unsavoury-looking, stood trembling by the side of the tank. Fatima leaned over and whispered. 'He is telling him he wants all the prisoners released but first he wants to see the women's block... Yes, now he asks about my sister.'

The governor stammered, finally pointing to a prison block off to one side. Told to take them there, he was made to walk in front of the tank. Sweating despite the cold, the man hurried along the dusty road, the tank growling at his heels like some huge, bad-tempered Kuchi mastiff. A startled guard appeared at the entrance to the women's block but, after a sharp order from his superior, unlocked the outer gate. One of Durran's mujahideen quickly disarmed the guard and pushed the governor inside, a gun at his back, telling him to lead the way to the cells. The next guard raised his rifle nervously when he heard the mujahideen approaching but quickly lowered it again when he saw the strength of the opposition.

The governor took the master key from the guard and walked down the line of cells. Distraught faces with unkempt hair appeared at the small, barred cell windows and someone began to shout. Wills could make out the word, 'mujahideen', repeated several times and then more voices joined in what sounded like a wild victory chant. Soon, the whole cell block was reverberating with the singing.

The governor stopped outside the door of the last cell on the right and started to fumble with the key, his hands shaking so much he was unable to open the door. Impatiently, Azim snatched the key from him, turned it in the lock, flung the door open and Wills found himself staring at one of the most beautiful but ravaged faces he had ever seen. It was Zarina. When Fatima called her name, she threw herself forward, clutching her sister as if terrified to let her go, the tears streaming down her face.

By now the noise was deafening: all the mujahideen shouting at once, the women in the other cells hammering on their doors with their tin plates or spoons and chanting in unison.

'God, stinks to high heaven, this place. Worse than a soldiers' latrine. Let's get some fresh air.' Gradinsky pushed his way through the crush, Wills close behind him.

Azim had his rifle at the governor's back and was forcing him to open the cells, one after the other. Sweat stained the man's shirt and was dripping on to his hands as he fumbled with the master key. As he unlocked one door, the prisoner, a huge woman with a mass of dark curly hair, sprang at him with a scream, clawing his face. The governor tried to duck away, but slipped and fell to the ground with the woman on top of him, pushing and shouting abuse at the top of her voice. It took Azim and two mujahideen to prise her loose and pull her off. The governor's face was bleeding from the deep scratches the woman's nails had inflicted and his uniform was ripped and dirty. As Azim led him away, the mujahideen mocked him, hitting him with their rifle butts, while one of them grabbed the key and took over the job of releasing the rest of the women. The sound of their singing had spread to other parts of the prison and soon all the inmates of Pul-i-Charkhi were banging their doors and shouting.

Leaving a detachment of mujahideen to oversee the release of the rest of the prisoners, Durran climbed up into his T62 and signalled to the rest of them to follow. Fatima appeared, her arm round Zarina, who was so pale and shocked she looked like a ghost. Gradinsky made room in the APC and tapped the space beside him. As Zarina sat down, the APC lurched forward and threw her against Gradinsky. For a moment, the slight weight of this beautiful woman against him rendered him speechless. Then, with a smile at Wills, he said, 'Zarina has just given up the dubious honour of being the most beautiful political prisoner in the world.'

'And has the misfortune instead to find herself sitting next to you.'

As Gradinsky opened his mouth to retaliate with a choice insult, there was a shattering explosion against the side of APC and they veered off the road out of control. Wills was thrown violently sideways as the vehicle plunged and bucked like a small boat, ending up on the floor as they seemed to mount a bank and turned over with a hideous sound of tearing metal. Smoke began to fill the vehicle and Wills, conscious that they must get out before it blew up, struggled to get upright. He could hear Gradinsky swearing.

'Anatoly, if you can swear, you must be all right, eh?'

'Sonofabitch, it feels as if I've broken my arm. Hey, Fatima, you OK?'

'Yes, I am fine but I think Zarina is hurt, or maybe she got knocked out. Can you get the door open?'

'I'm trying to.' Wills was struggling with the heavy metal door, finally got it open and fresh air flowed into the smoke-filled interior. Coughing, their eyes streaming, Wills and Gradinsky dragged Fatima and a stunned Zarina from the APC. One of the big rubber tyres had caught fire and was burning furiously. It took Wills a few seconds to realise that they were in the middle of a battle. The T62 was thirty yards away, its big gun blasting furiously at several smaller tanks drawn up at a crossroads several hundred yards away. Azim came running up and spoke urgently to Fatima.

'Commander Durran wants you to get into his tank. We have been ambushed by the Butcher. Those are his tanks you can see on the road. I will look after your sister.' As if to emphasise the point, a couple of rounds went skimming over their heads and exploded among some houses behind them.

The T62 was so heavily armoured in comparison to the Butcher's old T52s, and its gun so powerful, that Durran could afford to stand his ground and shoot it out. While he kept the enemy busy, he had sent his own T52s to outflank them and take them from the rear, and suddenly the mujahideen tanks broke cover and engaged the Butcher's force at close range. Durran moved forward, firing as he went.

One tank at the rear of the formation was flying a pennant. Assuming it must be the Butcher's, Durran ordered his gunner to ignore all the other tanks and concentrate solely on this one. As the gap narrowed, the tension inside the T62 became almost unbearable. One round struck their hull with a deafening report and for a moment they zigzagged wildly.

239

Gradinsky spoke urgently to Fatima. 'Tell the Commander I can operate this gun. I can shoot that bastard right out of the ground. Want me to try?'

The first two rounds went wide, the first to the left, the second low and to the right, kicking up a spout of earth. The third landed high on the turret but the fourth hit what Gradinsky called 'the sweet spot', exactly where the hull and the turret joined. The fireball was instantaneous, leaping a hundred feet in the air.

Durran drove towards the burning tank at full speed but before they could reach it, two figures clambered out of the turret, slithered through the flames to the ground and disappeared down an alleyway.

Gradinsky and Wills clambered out through the turret of the T62 and started after them, Gradinsky slightly ahead.

'Do you think one of them's the Butcher?' Wills panted, at Gradinsky's shoulder. 'With a bodyguard?'

Gradinsky made as if to fire from the hip but the two Afghans changed direction, running towards a house surrounded by a high wall. Gradinsky and Wills were only thirty yards behind now, gaining steadily when the Afghans disappeared behind the curve of the wall.

'Careful...' Wills shouted, two or three yards behind. His words were drowned by a burst of automatic fire.

The impact stopped Gradinsky in mid-stride, punching a cry of pain from his chest and dropping him like a straw dummy.

Wills dived forward, getting off a first burst as he hit the ground. He caught one of the men with the second burst, but the other kept running and had disappeared round the bend of the wall by the time Wills was on his feet. He took a couple of steps in pursuit but stopped when he heard Gradinsky call out.

The Russian lay on his back, eyes closed, his face white, chest heaving painfully. Wills put down his submachinegun and dropped to his knees beside him.

Gradinsky's breath came in gasps. A fine froth of white spittle, flecked with blood, covered his lips and occasionally, a bubble of saliva ballooned from the corner of his mouth.

The burst of gunfire had caught him on the right side and seemed to have punctured a lung. Wills pulled Gradinsky's shirt up as gently as possible to reveal two entry wounds. They were quite small, but the exit wounds, he knew, would be much bigger, and he could see blood seeping into the ground beneath Gradinsky. Without immediate medical attention, the Russian would die from loss of blood. Gradinsky half raised his head to speak, his lips trying desperately to frame the words.

'Did you get the Butcher?'

Wills shook his head. 'One of them got away. But I fixed the other, the one who shot you.'

'Well done. I hope you get the other bastard, too.' Gradinsky's blue eyes glazed over. Wills felt his pulse; it was very weak. A few seconds later, Gradinsky rallied again. He was coughing and Wills had to bend close to hear the words.

'You know, Mike, it's been fun ... especially the tunnel. I'm just sorry we won't be able to set up in business together. Salang Partners Inc... I would have liked that.' His lips managed the shadow of a smile.

Wills heard the sound of running feet and looked up to see Durran, Fatima and several mujahideen. With only a glance at the body of the dead Afghan, Durran squatted down beside Gradinsky, taking one of the Russian's hands in both of his. After a few seconds, he spoke in a low voice to Fatima.

'He asks how it happened.'

Wills told her. 'He has two bullets in his chest and as you can see he's coughing up blood. Unless we can get him to a doctor soon, he'll bleed to death.'

Immediately Fatima had translated, Durran stood up and shouted orders. One of the personnel carriers arrived with a roar and Gradinsky was hoisted up, grimacing with pain and then, someone having spread a *pattu* for him to lie on, lowered on to the cold steel of the hull. The placing of the *pattu* under Gradinsky was more of a gesture than anything else, Wills knew, but he found it unexpectedly moving.

Gradinsky started to cough again as the APC moved off and Wills ran beside it for twenty or thirty yards, his arm outstretched, his hand on the Russian's for a few last seconds. As the APC gathered speed, he dropped back and watched it and Gradinsky's blond head disappear in a cloud of dust. He knew then that he would not see the

Russian alive again and the knowledge caused him a sudden surge of grief. He knew now that he was losing a friend.

Eyes on the ground, he walked back grimly to find the others crowding round the body of the dead Afghan. Durran looked up as Wills approached and said something to Fatima.

'Commander Durran says you have rid us of our greatest enemy, after the Russians. The Butcher was a murderer. He had many people killed because they dared to oppose him. Now he, the assassin, has been cut down himself.'

'Is that the Butcher?' Wills asked slowly.

Durran gave a sharp order and one of the mujahideen dragged the body forward, grasping it by the beard and pulling the head up to provide a better view. Durran spoke animatedly, pointing at the dead man's face. Fatima translated, her voice rising with excitement.

'It is the Butcher. Commander Durran says he knew him well. They were students in Kabul together. He could never be mistaken. This is the man we called the Butcher. You killed the right one. The one who ran away is not important.'

Wills found himself staring at the pale, aquiline features and bushy beard that had become familiar from a thousand political posters. 'Of course, you're right. I didn't recognise him without his turban.'

Durran walked towards his tank, and Wills and Fatima followed in silence.

As they reached it a message came over the T62's radio.

Fatima turned to Wills. 'General Mohammed and some of the elders of the city are requesting an urgent meeting at the General's headquarters. We go there now.'

Twenty-two

Wills recognised the entrance to the barracks where they had met the General in the dark such a short time ago. Now, in daylight, everything looked much less forbidding. This time they were ushered in through the main gate and waved up to the entrance. A young officer threw a smart salute and led them up the stairs to a big office. Inside, they found General Mohammed and his two colleagues who had visited Durran in the Bala Koh. Also seated round the big room were a dozen civilians of various ages, all of whom, Fatima explained, were members of the mujahideen underground resistance council.

The General got to his feet as soon as Durran appeared, embracing him warmly. Then Durran circled the room, greeting each member of the council in turn.

When everybody had sat down and been served with tea, the General started to speak. Fatima sat next to Wills and gave him a running translation. They were so close he could smell the fresh earthiness of her body, and for a moment he found it hard to concentrate on what she was saying.

'First of all, we congratulate you on liberating Pul-i-Charkhi and all the prisoners. Also for destroying the Butcher and his Kabul supporters. But we have some very serious news. Early this morning, when we were at the airport, we received a message from Tashkent, from Soviet military headquarters.'

The General paused and looked round the room. Wills examined the faces. One or two of the council members were greybeards, and a couple were young, but most were middle-aged, merchants possibly, one or two professional people, perhaps, but mostly men of the people, he guessed.

Whoever they were, they looked the part: tough, resourceful, self-confident.

'The message said that if we tried now to overthrow the government and, in particular, if we continued to occupy the airport, the Soviet Union would feel justified in protecting its ally, namely the friendly government of the Republic of Afghanistan, by intervening on its behalf.'

'How?' Durran interrupted.

'By bombing the mujahideen forces in Kabul until they cease their attacks.'

There was silence for a moment as Durran and his party digested this piece of news. Then one of the members of the resistance council spoke for the first time.

Fatima leaned towards Wills. 'This man is the leader of the council. He was in Pul-i-Charkhi for a long time and they say he was tortured very badly.' Certainly, Wills thought, the man looked as if he had suffered, but he still radiated a spirit of energetic defiance. Fatima whispered the translation in Wills's ear.

'Commander Durran, we know you well, many of us personally and all of us by reputation. We admire your great achievements in the *jehad*. We understand why you want to liberate our city of Kabul. We want to do exactly the same. We invited you to come here. We, too, want the capital of Afghanistan to be a free and independent city again, without the alien and barbaric influence of the Soviets and their Afghan puppets.' He paused to let his words sink in. 'But, honoured Commander, knowing what the effect of indiscriminate Soviet bombing would be on the two and half million people of Kabul, many of them already refugees, we must reluctantly ask you to abandon your present plans to capture the city and withdraw your mujahideen for the time being, until this immediate threat has passed.'

Silence fell. After a pause Durran cleared his throat and started to talk quietly but with great urgency.

'He says we all know what the Russians mean when they say they will bomb the mujahideen forces.' Fatima translated. 'They mean that if we take the city, they will retaliate by bombing everything in the city; mujahideen, civilians, men, women and children, everything, just as they have done in Herat and Kandahar and a hundred other places.

244

They know that they will kill thousands of civilians too, but they don't care. They will say it was the fault of the mujahideen, and they will hope that the population, the civilian population, will turn against us and curse us and the day we came here and brought this destruction on them.' Durran paused and glanced round the room. They were all hanging on his words.

'So, my friends, I agree. I say to you that we should not fall into this trap. We should not give the *Shurawi* the opportunity to destroy Kabul, an opportunity they would be only too happy to exploit. Let us avoid a showdown until you, the resistance council, decide the time is right. I, too, can do with more time to regroup and prepare. The winter, as you know, has been exceptionally severe. There is still deep snow in the Salang and the Panjsher and our supply columns are having difficulty bringing in arms and ammunition. The extra time will be well spent.' He glanced round the room, catching each man's eye in turn.

'And when you need us, we are ready.'

There was a low murmur of approval as the men around the room rose to their feet.

The meeting was over.

Twenty-three

They left early the next morning, driving past the same checkpoint they had arrived by. Wills was still not sure if the men on the barrier were Durran's mujahideen or troops loyal to the general. The sky was leaden, presaging more snow, and there was a sense of anti-climax, of being somehow cheated of a great adventure.

They drove in silence, in the same three jeeps that had brought them to Kabul. Durran with Zarina beside him was in front, then some of his mujahideen and finally Wills and Fatima. Gradinsky's presence seemed still to ride with them, Wills felt, his larger-than-life personality filling the jeep. In his imagination, Wills could hear Gradinsky's Americanisms and the sudden guffaws that accompanied them; see the big blond head and the vivid blue eyes. He blew his nose loudly.

'You are thinking of your friend?'

'Yes. I do think of him as a friend now.'

'So does Durran. Anatoly saved his life.'

'He may have saved mine too. He was in front, deliberately, I think, when we ran into the Butcher's ambush. He knew he was taking a risk.'

Fatima slipped her hand into Wills's. 'What will you do now? Go back to England?'

Wills took his time replying. 'No, I have no plans to go back to England. There is nothing for me there. I would rather stay here, if I'm allowed to.'

Fatima squeezed his hand. 'I will ask Durran, but I know what he will say. You can stay as long as you like. There is still a war to be fought. Now, you can stay in our village until spring comes. It is very beautiful up in the mountains.

Outside, it will be very cold and there will be a lot of snow. But inside we have big wood fires and plenty of fox-skins on the beds to keep us warm.' She moved imperceptibly against him.

'I didn't think you had beds in Afghanistan. I thought everybody slept on the floor.'

She knew he was teasing her. 'Only in the ordinary village houses. We have beds in our house, but you can sleep on the floor if you want to.'

Wills turned impulsively and kissed her on the lips.

'Not here, the driver will see.'

Wills glanced at the driver's rear mirror; it was broken.

They reached the turnoff to the Panjsher Valley and turned east, leaving Kabul and the Salang behind them. Ahead there were patches of blue and the sun played fitfully on the tops of the snow-covered mountains. It was a scene of breathtaking beauty, the great wall of the Hindu Kush towering up before them in awesome splendour. The mouth of the valley narrowed to a gorge, the river foaming between the huge granite boulders in a green and white cascade. The road ran dizzily between the cliff and the river, its steady roar loud in their ears. Then they were through the gorge, the valley widening in front of them, the river running sweetly now over banks of shingle between small stands of willows.

Soon, in a few weeks, the trees would be putting on their first, delicate leaves and the whole valley would turn palest green. The snow would retreat to the high peaks and the sky would turn a pure, cerulean blue. Spring could not be far away.